Women of the Third Reich

Dedicated to the memory of Lesley Adshead who died, aged sixteen, on 9 November 1984.

Women of the Third Reich

From Camp Guards to Combatants

Tim Heath

PEN & SWORD
HISTORY

AN IMPRINT OF PEN & SWORD BOOKS LTD.
YORKSHIRE – PHILADELPHIA

First published in Great Britain in 2019 by
Pen and Sword History
An imprint of
Pen & Sword Books Ltd
Yorkshire - Philadelphia

Hardback ISBN: 9781526739452

A CIP catalogue record for this book is
available from the British Library.

Typeset in 11.5/14 Ehrhardt by Vman Infotech Pvt. Ltd.

Printed and bound in the UK by TJ International Ltd.

Pen & Sword Books Ltd incorporates the Imprints of Pen & Sword Books
Archaeology, Atlas, Aviation, Battleground, Discovery, Family History, History,
Maritime, Military, Naval, Politics, Railways, Select, Transport, True Crime,
Fiction, Frontline Books, Leo Cooper, Praetorian Press, Seaforth Publishing,
Wharncliffe and White Owl.

For a complete list of Pen & Sword titles please contact

PEN & SWORD BOOKS LIMITED
47 Church Street, Barnsley, South Yorkshire, S70 2AS, England
E-mail: enquiries@pen-and-sword.co.uk
Website: www.pen-and-sword.co.uk

or

PEN AND SWORD BOOKS
1950 Lawrence Rd, Havertown, PA 19083, USA
E-mail: Uspen-and-sword@casematepublishers.com
Website: www.penandswordbooks.com

Contents

Introduction		vii
Chapter One	Dismembering Innocence	1
Chapter Two	Administrating Evil	13
Chapter Three	From the Beggar's Paw	33
Chapter Four	The Little Aryan	45
Chapter Five	My Infatuation	58
Chapter Six	Salon Kitty	71
Chapter Seven	A French Adventure	79
Chapter Eight	Keeper of Beasts	95
Chapter Nine	The Devil's Daughter	109
Chapter Ten	When Our City Burned	115
Chapter Eleven	Rotes Kreuz	130
Chapter Twelve	There be Monsters	144
Chapter Thirteen	Surviving our Youth	156
Chapter Fourteen	Shoot Straight	171
Chapter Fifteen	Maidens of Iron	184
Chapter Sixteen	Say Hello to God	199
Chapter Seventeen	Victory, War is Over	209
Chapter Eighteen	Erich	224
Chapter Nineteen	In the Absence of Men	231
The Future		239
Afterword		249
Further Reading		251
Acknowledgements		253

Violence is a discipline that requires as much effort, if not more, as the execution of peace.

Tim Heath

Introduction

Adolf Hitler possessed an intuitive sense of destiny as his aspirations to become an artist evaporated in the wake of the social and political chaos of the First World War. The collective feeling of betrayal spread like a disease through the social fabric of Weimar Germany. Its people were disillusioned, maddened by hunger and unemployment, and desperate for some miracle to lead them from the nightmare that resulted from defeat in the First World War. And so the German people embraced the National Socialists and their self-proclaimed messiah. Poisoned with Hitler's megalomania, German society sought to rid itself of the outdated values of its defeatist past. By 1939, however, Nazi Germany was ill prepared for a protracted war within Europe and beyond. She was lesser still prepared for a war that would soon have to be fought on two fronts.

How did the supposedly gentle and submissive *haus frauen* [housewives], bearers of children and guardians of the home become embroiled in the madness and horror of The Third Reich? How did their role within its administration, its concentration camps, its Luftwaffe flak arm, its fire service and militia units evolve in the way that it did? Why did they prove so vital to a system that expressed so much negativity towards womanhood?

This book explores the activities of young women who participated in the running of the most evil regime the world had yet known. Every testimony is unique, each a victim of circumstance entwined within the thorns of an ideological obligation: from those whose fingers issued typewritten dictates from above to those who operated telephones, radar systems, and fought fires as their cities burned around them; those who drove concentration camp inmates like cattle to their deaths, those who fired anti-aircraft guns at Allied aircraft and, ultimately, those who joined the militias when faced with the impending destruction of what should have been a one-thousand-year Reich.

For the many historians who have asked the question 'why' the answers may well be discovered within the pages of this unique work. *Women of the Third Reich: From Camp Guards to Combatants* provides an intriguing, sometimes humorous, but often dark, brutal, shocking and unrelenting narrative into the murky hell of the human consciousness. But while the author provides an accompanying narrative throughout, this is their Pandora's Box, written in their own words.

Chapter One

Dismembering Innocence

By 1939, membership of the Hitler Youth for both boys and girls was unavoidable. It was expected that all young Germans should join their respective organisation. Apart from the few sweeteners that the Nazis threw in to make Hitler Youth membership more appealing, it was merely an extension by which young people could be indoctrinated into Nazi ideology, its culture, expectations and principles. Girls and boys who excelled in the political ideology, sports, fitness and all of the basic practical aspects were rewarded handsomely. Certificates and badges were awarded for all manner of proficiencies within the organisation, and any boy or girl showing particular excellence in knowledge and leadership could rise through the ranks to become a troop leader within the Hitler Youth.

Ursula Betmann had joined the *Bund Deutscher Madel* [League of German Maidens] before it had become compulsory for girls to do so. She recalls:

> I was a fifteen year-old totally swept away by the political happenings in Germany just prior to the Second World War. I had girlfriends whose parents were reluctant for their girls to become involved. They had to pay subscriptions, even bribes, to ensure their girls did not have to join. Of course, anyone who did not join was considered 'unpatriotic' by others within the community. I had no such problems as my parents were hardline supporters of National Socialism. My parents paid for my uniform and I recall the first time I ever put it on. It was an amazing feeling and my parents looked at me full of pride. The BDM meetings held twice weekly were no holiday camp. The theory work was exhaustive and we could be asked any number of things about Hitler, his parents, and the Nazi Party.

If we could not give a clear answer we would be shouted at and berated for not working hard enough. We had to know many political things such as who was in charge of which ministry within the Reich, those who were killed in the Beer Hall Putsch, Hitler's parents' names and birthdates. Yes, there was lots we were expected to learn.

We learned much in daily schooling and after school we were given various books to study. Most important of all was Adolf Hitler's *Mein Kampf* ['My Struggle']. This had to be studied religiously. Now, they could ask you absolutely anything from that book and they would expect you to answer coherently. I read *Mein Kamp* two, three, four times over. I understood it clearly and, yes, I believed in everything that it presented to the reader; particularly us as young Germans of the new generation. I could answer most questions that I was asked, which impressed our leader tremendously. I was also very good at sports: running, high jump, ball throwing and swimming. I gained many certificates for sporting achievement. In fact, I gained many of the awards in rapid succession. I was part of a gymnastics team that would compete all over the country and we even competed in Japan, winning many classes there. We were superbly fit all of the time as keeping us active and well fed became a national priority. Only when the Second World War broke out did we become second to the soldiers nutrition-wise. On the BDM camps held throughout the summertime I would always be up first, asking the leader if there were any tasks she wanted me to do. Normally I would help rouse the other girls from their tents, make sure they were ready to start the day.

I worked very hard in all aspects of our BDM troop and, at the age of sixteen, I was given charge of a small group of our girls. I would be responsible for their discipline, appearance, conduct, safety, etc. on the camp. It was the precursor to bigger things in a way. Was I a bully? No, I don't think I was, but I was very harsh. I expected much from our girls and wanted them to give as much effort in everything they did, as I had done over the years. You only gained respect as a leader if you were feared; if people did not fear you they generally would not respect you. That is something I learned from my parents from a very young age. It was an ethos I personally believed in and took with me into my BDM leader role. We couldn't have weak girls in our troop. Our girls had to be the best, especially in the inter-organisational competitions held throughout Germany. We wanted to beat the other BDM troops and the only way we could do that was by persistent hard work coupled with discipline.

I was given a further promotion a few months later and, when I was seventeen, I was given promotion to BDM leader of our troop. Our senior at that point had left to complete service within the Labour Front so I effectively stepped into her role and took over. I enjoyed this role very much as it was, in essence, very militaristic. The girls had to be up early, wash, make breakfast, tidy up, dress into sports attire, complete exercise routines, wash again, change into uniform then march into the woods. When we returned from our march I insisted boots were polished and stowed away properly. Tents were checked to ensure they were tidy. A fire would be made and a meal prepared. Afterwards we would gather round the fire to discuss political theory and current events. There would be questions and answers and I expected my girls to answer me correctly when I asked them a question. Anyone who couldn't answer me would be punished with extra-hard cleaning duties. One of my punishments would be that a girl would have to polish the boots of all the other girls and clean the undersides of the boots too. I would also make them stand to attention if they displeased me. The discipline instilled in me I was now instilling in them.

I also lectured them on the greatness of our German race and Adolf Hitler. To me he was the most important political leader in our entire history. I made sure all my girls understood that, and followed the principles of National Socialism. Teaching racial theory to the girls on the camps was simple. I told them you should have no compassion at all for the enemies of our race. I also told them Jews had no place in Germany. Even a

German Jew is a bad thing for our future. If they have to be eliminated by force then so be it, was what I would say. For my theory to hit home in their minds I had to use fear yet again. The threat of being overtaken by a population who wished nothing but our own destruction was usually enough. Although my style of leadership was harsh, as it was meant to be, I also understood the emotional fragility of young girls. I had to maintain a careful balance, so after the serious stuff we would have lighter moments where we could share jokes and tell each other stories. I felt it important that I should be approachable to my girls in case they had any problems either at home or within the BDM itself.

We were a kind of sisterhood and we had a common bond of being females in the Third Reich where we had clear roles to fulfil. I would discuss children with them and this was always a difficult task. Even I as a BDM leader could not put explicit images in their minds, if you understand me. I had to use excerpts from the biology book supplied to our schools to explain reproduction. The childcare aspects were much easier to explain. As it stood at the time the males knew exactly how to make a girl pregnant and it was their job to deal with that business. The girl was merely the follower, doing as she was told. You were expected to find a man, marry and become a housewife after completing your compulsory labour service. At that point in your life as a girl you would be at optimum fitness and more than ready for reproduction. I myself had mixed feeling about settling down. I loved being a leader and retreating to the role of a submissive *haus frau* really did not appeal to me at all. The loss of that power would feel somewhat demeaning to me. That's how I felt at the time, but there was pressure placed even upon me to do my part of producing children for the future Reich.

I continued in my post as a BDM leader for as long as I could, yet other girls were showing great potential and had to have their chance. When I stood down I went and completed my labour service and came back knowing I would have to think about settling down and becoming a housewife. There were many local dances and pageants where we mixed with the young men. One caught my eye and he liked me and so we began talking. Typically, he asked me to tea and things like that. We went on picnics and walked in the countryside; all the normal things a courting couple would do really. I had never been kissed properly before this boy. He was obviously more experienced than I was and had probably had a few girlfriends before me. I didn't really care; I liked him and felt duty-bound to at least try.

Encouraged by our parents, we married. I was twenty years of age at the time and he was twenty-three. I was not nervous during the small wedding service attended by both families, just the thought of having to have sex with him later on. We drank lots of wine during the evening and then retired to bed late. When we entered our apartment rooms I wanted to sleep separately as that was still something which was traditionally acceptable to some couples. He did not really give me a straight answer as such so I went to one of the two single rooms, undressed and put on a night gown as he drank some more in the other room. Then he came in and argued that, as his wife, I should obey him and sleep beside him. I tried to reason with him, telling him I just felt nervous about having sex and needed a little time to get used to this idea. His whole attitude now was that I was his property and he could do what he wanted with me. He threw down his glass, which smashed on the floor. He grabbed my wrist and pulled me into the bedroom. I was thrown down on the bed and the door was slammed shut behind me. I found myself struggling on the bed with him. He would not stop. As much as I begged him to stop, he would not get off me. I got to the point where I was so exhausted he could do as he pleased with me. That's how my marriage was consummated. It was painful and not the most pleasant of experiences for a first time. Like most women back then, I got used to it and became more receptive. Yet I felt he was the one who gained the most pleasure from it. We had four children in all. My husband went to fight in the Second World War with the *Wehrmacht* [German army]. It was a fight he would not return home from. In a way

I was happy he was dead. It was not so much love but duty that drove me to marry. I would have my four children and I would bring them up with the values that I had espoused in the BDM when I was a leader. Even after the war I still believed in National Socialism. The events that happened after the Second World War, in my opinion, proved the National Socialist ethos was a rightful one.

Another young girl who joined the ranks of her local BDM troop was Trudi Lehrer. Trudi was born and raised in the German town of Heidelberg. She responded well to her National Socialist teachings but had known little else. She, like many who entered the BDM, dreamed of becoming a leader. She did not have the typical appearance of a BDM girl as portrayed by the propaganda posters of the time. Her hair was jet black and her skin rather tanned when compared to the blonde Aryan models which graced almost every BDM propaganda poster in Germany. She was an attractive looking girl with brown eyes, described by many who knew her as 'beautifully warm'.

National Socialism was like a fire burning out of control within me. I had been raised by my parents as a Nazi child and I grew up as a Nazi adult. Of course there was the German girls' league which I wanted to join very much. I loved the look of the uniforms and the fact of what they did. I thought it was great, I really did, and I aspired to do as well as I could once I'd joined up. I was always very good physically so sports of most kinds were something I enjoyed very much. Running was my favourite sport, and the javelin. Gymnastics was another form of physical activity we were very much involved with. Graceful movement, strength, beauty; all these things were what we represented.

To become a leader was an honour as it took a great deal of hard work and dedication to be considered for such a post. The responsibility which it gave an individual was of huge importance. As a leader, you were responsible for teaching Nazism to the girls. When I became a leader I was appointed to a *Jungmädelbund* troop and not a BDM one. This annoyed me a little at first as it felt like a kind of demotion rather than promotion. They were only very young most of them; ten to fourteen years on average. In my little troop most were aged ten and eleven and the oldest was in fact thirteen. In all they were very well disciplined and attentive. All the skills I had built up with the BDM I could now pass to these girls as their leader.

Political teaching was by far the hardest part of my task. Getting children to absorb politics is no easy thing. They can soon become bored, distracted and some start to fall asleep. This is where the respect part of your identity comes in. You have to be approachable to them but in order to instil the lessons regarding the filth of Jewry and pride in our Germanic racial heritage then they have to listen, absorb and understand you. Sometimes fear is the only method by which to obtain respect. If I had to show anger then I would show it. If I had to punish a girl in front of the others then I would do it. I did what I had to do. Awards, certificates and badges were just a few incentives for the young girls to work hard. Youngsters like to feel that they have accomplished something and receive a physical reward for it. Such diplomas were worthless really, but it gave them a feeling that they had achieved something. They were also something they could take home to their parents who would then be proud of them. Getting the youth of our country to do as we needed was much like training a dog to walk correctly on a leash. Reward them generously and they would get it right pretty quickly.

Cultivating hatred against Jews was not as difficult a process as many would think. We would tell them that Jews were the root of Germany's misfortunes. Most would accept that view as it was shared by many within our society. Did I personally care about these things and the violence we were perpetrating? No, at that time I did not care. We had our society to care for and that had to come before anything else. For a society to grow strong and become pure it has to relinquish those who are unfit to be a part of it. We were of the opinion that Jews were parasites. That they behaved like parasites in the way they invaded a host then bled that host dry. There was much hatred, and when Jews were sent to the concentration camps there were really no concerns. My parents often spoke of the camps and were of the opinion that we should build as many as possible with a view to destroying all of Germany's undesirable racial elements. Like a religion, it was accepted as the only way to deal with a particular problem.

For every young girl in the *Jungmädelbund* or *Bund Deutscher Mädel* who totally agreed with the political and social system being implemented in the new Germany there was, of course, a good proportion that did not. Thelma Ortge likened the *Jungmädelbund* and *Bund Deutscher Mädel* to a group of circus animals that had to be trained. She recalled:

I was fifteen in 1936 with Herr Hitler as the supreme leader of the German people. I noticed how quickly everything changed in our school. It was somewhat confusing, as the swastika flags were always previously a political emblem, yet all of a sudden it was our national emblem; our national flag. My parents were horrified as they were confident the Conservatives within the German government could contain the fascist Hitler. My parents absolutely despised the Nazis and all that they represented. At school they brought in new faces to teach the kids. The whole curriculum of education evolved according to the changes occurring within our society. Many of the old teachers who had been responsible for educating us were told to get out of our school. They were banned from teaching Hitler's generation and new teachers were brought in. Many of these new teachers were bastards, they were really not nice people. My parents sat me down and tried to discuss with me how I can avoid being indoctrinated. One evening my father sat me down and he said to me: 'What I am going to try to tell you is going to be the best advice I will ever give to you as your father. I know that you are in school and with the other children. Some of those children have Nazi-sympathising families. They will undoubtedly stand out from those coming from families who are not convinced supporters of this dreadful regime we are now under. My girl it is vital that you play the game, as we all must. But don't ever believe a word of what they tell you, or let them get inside you and destroy that beautiful mind of yours. Now, do you understand me? Be the actor, play along and do what you have to do and we will do the same. Maybe, if we are clever, we can all survive this.' That was quite intense coming from my father but I understood what he meant. He did not want them indoctrinating me or taking me away from them, like they would do with thousands of other young German children.

The 'taking away' referred to by Thelma was the way that the Hitler Youth organisations provided attractive perks to all those who joined. The young could be easily seduced by the pied piper of National Socialism. Many parents feared for their youngsters once they were in the Hitler Youth – which relished and encouraged violence – yet they knew resistance would bring them to the attention of the authorities, who would then ask questions such as 'why has your boy not enrolled into the Hitler Youth?', and 'why is your daughter not in the German maiden's league?' If a child was not encouraged to join either of these Nazi youth organizations, then cries of 'traitor' or 'non-conformist' were the usual response.

Thelma Ortge continues:

At school they all knew who was in the JM or BDM. Any girl who was not a member was asked why. I know one girl was interrogated one morning during class. That old Nazi teacher, he was a nasty, nasty bastard. He had a certain way of working on you to grind you down and to make you slip up, as they say. He would shout and ask you questions rapidly so that you had to answer him quickly. This one morning he picked on this girl and subjected her to a ten-minute tirade: 'Why are you not a *mädchen* [young member of BDM]? Do you not have any pride in being German? Do you not like National Socialism?' He just kept on and would shout, 'Well, answer me!' He broke her in the end, and she began to cry and said, 'My father told me to say nothing.' That was enough in his book to inform the local authority of possible non conformism within the community. Of course, the authorities did investigate and usually a threat of serious consequences was enough to bring people into line. I endeavoured to learn their poison and to play their game, but secretly I loathed them. I did join the BDM but never wore the distinctive uniform. My parents could have bought me the uniform but I would just say that we couldn't afford one. So I entered the BDM and felt just like an actor acting my part as a willing young Nazi girl.

Within the BDM troop there were, of course, the diehard Nazi girls who were infatuated with Hitler. One had a scrap book with pictures of Hitler that she had cut from newspapers. It was her pride and joy and she would say, 'Oh, how jealous I am of Fraulein Braun, how lucky she is.' It was all so delusional, a daydream. There were girls who were genuinely interested in the politics too. They were what today might be termed as 'nerdy types'. They could tell you anything about the National Socialist culture, and if we needed to learn, these girls would help you. There was one named Gabbi. Gabbi was kind of skinny and she sometimes wore glasses. I met her when I was twelve, when she first came to our school after moving from some town in the south of Germany. She would always be with her nose in a book and when you approached her she would look at you over the top of her glasses. She knew you needed help with something, so would say, 'Oh, what now?' I liked Gabbi a lot as she was like a mad professor. She was kind of crazy, but funny with it too. I liked spending time with her and was able to learn a lot from her too. My father warned me and said of my friendship with Gabbi, 'Don't be seduced by the devil.'

I did grow to like many of the girls and was sure some of them were not convinced young Nazis either, but felt they would stop short of actually admitting anything, even to close friends. It was sad really as what choices did we really have at that time? Gabriella 'Gabbi' Becker was a girl who would become more than just one of my closest friends. It was an unlikely friendship as Gabbi came from a well-to-do background while mine was very much a working-class one. She wanted me to come to tea at her home one afternoon, but I was worried what my parents might think. We were after all living a kind of charade but I liked Gabbi and wanted her as a friend. My parents agreed, after some discussion, that I should go and have tea with my friend. My father just reminded me to be careful. As it was, it was very innocent.

My father dropped me off at Gabbi's home. As we arrived Gabbi came out and she introduced herself to my father and shook his hand. She seemed so excited that I was there and took my hand and dragged me inside her house. I had visions of what her home might be like. I imagined a huge portrait of Hitler over a grand fireplace and stern Nazi parents. Of course, I could not have been more wrong. Gabbi's home was lovely and her parents seemed very nice. They shook my hand, introducing themselves to me. Gabbi took me up to her room and there she showed me her collection of books. Books were her biggest love in life and she had quite a selection ranging from fairy tales to science. Pride of place on her bookshelf was Adolf Hitler's *Mein Kampf*. I asked her what she thought about the book. She replied: 'What, *Mein Kampf*? Hmmm, well it is very political. It underlines the great struggle between the races. It underlines the Führer's political and social strategy to make Germany a great nation once again. But you should know all of this.' I smiled at her and she just said, 'Oh well, politics is a man's thing, is it not?' We sat and talked about things until her mother called us down for tea. The tea was just amazing, sandwiches and cakes all neatly arranged on the table, and Gabbi said, 'Help yourself to what you want.' It just seemed this was a million miles away from everything that was going on around us at school, in the German maidens' league and out on the streets.

After tea we went back up to Gabbi's room where we talked some more. I asked her what she was going to do when she left school. She said she wanted to go into chemistry, or maybe become a doctor. It was then she said to me, 'But our leaders feel that we, as girls, are only suitable for domestic purposes.

They feel we are less capable at some things than the men. I don't agree with that at all and hope that, with time, their attitude changes. I want a career before ever considering anything else.' Gabbi then asked me what I wanted to do when I was older. I told her that I wasn't sure. Maybe get married, have kids and settle down like everyone else. She laughed at me and I asked her, 'Why are you laughing? What is funny?', to which she replied: 'We are funny. Really, we have very few choices, do we, yet we work hard at representing the Führer's Germany. When we are all old, fat and useless maybe they will leave us alone. But it is our duty and we should carry out the will of our Führer.' At that point my father called to collect me to take me home. Gabbi said she would see me at school the next day and we hugged and I waved to her as we left.

In Thelma's father's eyes her new friend, Gabbi Becker, would be no more than a wolf that would have to be petted very carefully. Yet Gabbi Becker would figure significantly in Thelma's life in unexpected ways.

Chapter Two

Administrating Evil

Adolf Hitler's Third Reich was powered by an immensely confusing administrative structure. Many of the administrative branches within the Third Reich operated independently rather than as a single cohesive body. When one studies the plethora of ministries responsible for the day-to-day running of Nazi Germany, it leaves one wondering how it was able to function for as long as it did. Hitler actively encouraged this developing bureaucratic nightmare within his own administrative structure. Each office became so preoccupied with vying for individual attention that, often, the relaying of crucial military information became lost amongst irrelevant party matters and in the confusion that ensued. This would soon nullify the Third Reich's ability to communicate and execute the war it had started in any effective capacity. The Nazi Party became a series of competing interests which did nothing to help Germany's fortunes throughout the Second World War. With no centralised administrative authority the heads of the many different offices took it upon themselves to bypass others. The resulting infighting fostered distrust, hatred and competition within the Third Reich. It allowed unscrupulous and ambitious figures within Hitler's inner circle to ensure the implementation of more radical and extreme elements of Nazi ideology to flourish. It was hardly the efficient dutiful government that the Nazis portrayed to the people of Germany.

There were around fifteen different ministries within the Third Reich, combined with eight Reich Offices. The competition that such a system encouraged favoured the ruthless. Leading players within the Third Reich, such as Hitler's secretary Martin Bormann, would thrive in this chaos. Each individual had his own personal agenda, rendering mutual cooperation impossible. Changes were implemented within the employment structure to purposely exclude women from many areas of working life. Women were encouraged to stay in the home, freeing up jobs for men who had been previously unemployed. This policy worked wonders in dramatically reducing the unemployment figures, yet it soon occurred to many German women that the changes were discriminatory. Men dictated policy in Hitler's Third Reich while the secretarial posts within the ministries, offices and sub-offices were largely filled by women, and many of those young women who worked within the Nazi administrative system would soon find it an unforgiving environment.

Bertha Wuremfjeld was born in Berlin to hardline Nazi parents. Her upbringing is something she looks back on with some disdain:

> I am very sad to have to say that my father in particular was not a pleasant man. He ruled me and my mother with his iron hand. He was a Nazi through and through, and my mother too. I always felt that my mother just had to comply with his wishes. My father prided himself on being a thoroughbred of the Reich. As a result, my childhood was a heavily politicised one, devoid of love in its normal context.
>
> My parents considered themselves very religious and we had to attend local church every Sunday morning and evening without fail. Even if it was pouring with rain or we were unwell, we were still dragged along to that wretched church. Complying with a certain set of rules was laid out to me from earliest childhood growing up in 1930s Germany. If I did poorly at school, or below what my parents expected of me, I was beaten for it. My father would fly into a rage if he felt I was not doing well enough in my studies. He often used his leather belt to hit me across the backside. The pain he inflicted was horrendous at times. If I started to cry he would then shout, 'You dare cry, my child! Defy the pain and take your punishment!' The same would happen if I did not do exactly as instructed within the home.
>
> School was horrible back in those days too. As a Nazi child, so much expectation was placed upon us. Yet, as girls, we were told the boys and the men were the better half of our society. We were told that we should feed them and look after them so they would grow fit to go out and conquer the world. If you did

not do well at school they would beat you for it. Pain was a good incentive by which to get things right. They were very clever in their methods. Individual thinking was discouraged within the education system. They wanted group thinkers who all believed in one ethos, one goal. We had to be part of the single German weapon. We quickly became a weaponised society, even as young people. Viciousness, cruelty, ruthlessness were all attributes that had to be encouraged and nurtured within us. Even as infants, the influence of Nazism was introduced to us via the *Jungvolk* movement. The *Jungvolk* was a kind of very junior version of the Hitler Youth. It ensured that the very young were embraced into the movement and knew nothing else.

My father ensured that I joined the League of German Girls as soon as I could be permitted. I knew about them and about their activities and was not really concerned too much. The *Jungmädelbund* was not too bad, yet all the political theory was still there. We had to be able to explain our Nazi ideology, and woe betide any girl who could not. They would tell you, 'You have no excuses. You have your *Mein Kampf*, the only theory you need to understand is within its covers.' So you learned to memorise everything through fear. Fear is a great motivator, isn't it? Joining the League of German Girls senior movement, the *Bund Deutscher Mädel*, aged fourteen, was merely a cross over, a form of continuity. The skills we were taught orientated us towards being mothers, carers and wives. So much was taught about childcare and babies, yet they never told you what fucking was all about. Sex was censored very heavily. Learning about human reproduction was taught via nature. They did all they could to remove the basic imagery of a couple fucking to make a baby. They told us that fucking for pleasure was lustful. Our minds must remain free of the poison of lust. Only Jews sought the pleasure of the flesh. They always told us things like that. The boys knew all about it though, and it was as if they were the only ones allowed that right. The girls were secretly the subject of much contempt: 'young and dumb' Gertrud Scholtz-Klink, head of the Nazi women's league, once said. She said this entirely off the record of course.

Within the BDM, I learned to do all the things expected of me and I learned other things too. I became very good at typing. In fact, I was so good my father actually bought me a typewriter and he would often get me to dictate letters for him. He would stand there telling me what to type and I would type the document up for him. I would have to type on headed paper with the Nazi eagle symbol on it. He would say to me before he started dictating, 'Don't you dare make a mess of this as this paper is expensive.' That's the only respect I had from my father, as a kind of skivvy for him. My father's opinion of women was contradictory. We should renounce luxury to serve in the home. He would say, 'The air you breathe should be your one and only luxury.' My father had been involved with the Nazi Party from its birth more or less. He had many political friends in Munich and had followed Hitler from his early days as a speaker. My father became a Brownshirt and had been involved in the intimidation of Jews. He used to make no secret about it and would tell us. When the Brownshirts were liquidated my father became involved in the military as an officer with an artillery regiment.

When I reached my eighteenth birthday I was called for service in the RAD [*Reichsarbeitsdiens*]. This was compulsory labour service usually involving a placement on a farm. I was one of over thirty girls sent to work on a farm. We had a senior who was in charge of us all. She was not too bad, but if she didn't like you I can imagine she could have made life very hard. To be honest, the labour service was not that bad. We helped around the farm and picked crops in the fields. We did not have to get up too early nor work too late in the day. We ate good food and were well looked after. I did not find myself missing home at all. It was great just to get away from father for a while. On weekends we could go into the local town to the cinema, if there was one there (which there was). We could also go to church if we wished, but I did not go. I was sick of church and only a few of the girls actually attended. The leader expressed concern at me not attending church as my father had instructed that I not miss church on Sundays. I was surprised when the leader said to me, 'Well, if you are like me the only god is the Führer anyway.' When I returned home, it was back to the usual routine. My father said to me one morning, after I helped mother, that he would get me a job soon. All he would need to do is ask a few of the right people, he told me. So I waited anxiously to discover what this job he had intended for me was.

It would not be long before Bertha discovered that her first ever job would be in the Reich Ministry of Public Enlightenment and Propaganda. The Third Reich was meticulous in its documentation of even the most trivial of matters though Nazi menfolk viewed themselves as far too important to be seen sitting behind typewriters, single fingers tapping their way through pages of memoranda. Besides running the risk of being labelled a '*Blonde Arsch*' (slang term for a homosexual), men would take all day at this task. Bertha Wuremfjeld's father got her a job as a secretary in the Reich ministry, and she recalled:

It was 1941 and I was twenty-one years of age and a little nervous, as many are with their first proper job. Once sat down with a typewriter in front of me, it was like being at home. I could also write in shorthand too, which was very useful. I would at times sit and observe my surroundings and the other secretaries. Men in military uniform would come and go with bundles of paperwork for the department head to sort through. The thing was, I was able to read everything that went through the office where I worked. Most of it was nothing of interest. I noticed the men looking at me. I was the youngest girl in our little office. The men in uniform would posture like peacocks. I would laugh to myself and think that however much the men proclaim to be better at running things than us women they are totally deluded. We women make the finest administrators as we leave things tidy and where we can find them the next day. Have you ever seen a man trying to use a typewriter? They simply don't use them as skilfully as we do. It is also very amusing to watch.

Before the outbreak of the Second World War, the general attitude was that women should remain at home. But when war broke out, and more and more men were required for more urgent military tasks, women were seen as a valued resource in the workforce. Sofia Weiss was another young girl starting her first paid secretarial position at the Reich Ministry. She was nineteen and recalled:

It's six thirty in the morning and mother calls from outside of my bedroom door. It is a typical February morning. The skies are barely light. In fact they are grey and leaden and heavy with rain. The rain lashes against the window as I get up and sit on the edge of my bed. I can see outside on the street. People running about like an ant colony; umbrellas clash, impatience builds. It's the kind of Monday morning that everyone hates, but it's worse for me today. I start my first proper job today. It feels like almost a lifetime ago when I entered into my compulsory Reich labour service. It was not as bad as I had expected. I knew many of the girls as we all went together from the same area. It's now early 1941 and still does not feel like we are really at war with the English. We are suffering bombings, but still I don't feel that they are really an enemy in the usual sense of the word. I still think that if the Churchill government is overthrown then England would make peace with Germany and end the war. I don't think America would see things the same way though.

As these thoughts go through my head my mother reminds me again, I must get up, wash, get dressed, and be early for my first day at work. Mother makes us coffee. Father had already left for work at the postal offices. My little brother is still slumbering away. Lucky little bastard, I think to myself! But his time will come and what's the guess he wishes to become a soldier. Not just any soldier of course, one of the elite. All the boys want to be in the SS. On evenings out at the dances every boy you dance with tells you he has just passed his Waffen SS selection. They all naturally think this is the quickest way into a girls knickers; not so my friend! I dress, drink down the now-lukewarm coffee and I kiss my mother on the cheek, tell her I love her and will see her later. As I am grabbing my raincoat on the way up the hall she reminds me to make sure I come straight back home and not go wandering off anywhere. 'Me, wander off? Really, mother!' I say in reply to her.

The front door slams shut and I am soon in Berlin's busy metropolis. I know the city very well and I jump on a tram heading for the government district. The man opposite is reading a newspaper and smoking a cigar. As he draws heavily on what to me resembles a rolled up piece of shit, the end glows bright red. He flicks over a page and exhales the smoke. It is quite revolting to the point where I have to turn away. The tram stops and I jump off, noticing the man with the cigar jumps off too. The rain lashes against my face and I have no umbrella. Just a few hundred yards more and there it is. A huge building with two equally huge swastika flags draped either side of its entrance. A magnificent stone staircase leads up to the entrance.

I rather sheepishly peer through the door, like a naughty child about to receive a spanking for doing something wrong. A voice bellows out from behind a large desk in the reception, 'Can I help you, Frau?' I take out my papers from my coat pocket. I did not place them in my pockets with care. The rain has soaked through my coat and my papers are now very wet. The man scrutinises them and offers to help dry them by placing them near the large radiator in an office behind the reception area. Soldiers come and go and two or three look me up and down and smile. I know too well what they are thinking as I've seen it all before. I'm not the dumb nineteen-year-old girl they think I am. But I'm happy to let them think whatever it is they are thinking for the time being. Our generation has been blessed as the carrier of the new Germany. I am not stupid and I have been educated to a reasonable level for the most part. We are a National Socialist country now. We have a Führer and I am happy to be a part of this if it pays me a wage and keeps my parents happy. Maybe someday I can rent my own apartment in the city. The first step to freedom I know

begins here and whether or not I do a good job and keep my
bosses happy, whoever they are.

The man behind the reception, who has just put my papers
to dry near the heater, is now talking to someone on the
telephone. When he finishes his conversation he turns to me
and says, 'Friedrich will show the way.' This handsome young
man in a smart suit then offers to take me to the offices where
I will be working. We have to take a short journey in the lift.
I don't like lifts; I don't like any situation where I do not feel
that I am not totally in control. That slight wheezy sensations
as the lift pulls off upwards. The instinct to grab hold of
anything to steady oneself slightly embarrasses me. The fact
that I have grabbed hold of Friedrich's arm in this instance is
a double embarrassment of sorts. I quickly let go and smile as
if to say to him, 'I have no fear, I am fine'. He appears a good
sort of young man. There is none of that predictable drivel
or small talk you nearly always experience at the local dances.
The lift stops, the door opens and we are faced with a dark
corridor lined with cream-painted wooden doors. Friedrich
leads the way to number fourteen. He stops and says: 'Here
you are. This is the office of Herr Dahlgus, who you will be
working for. Please go inside and wait and he will be along in
a few moments.' I sit down on a sofa by the door and wait. My
senses are sharp and acute to the muffled sounds around me.
I can hear the full automatic sound of fingers against the metal
keys of typewriters followed by their characteristic click and
ding before the carriage is swung back to the start position.

I hear the lift doors open outside, then a cough followed
by a deep grunt. The office door opens and I stand up to
greet whoever is coming through it. It is none other than
the man with the cigar who I saw earlier on the tram. He is
short, bald and fat and stinks of cigars. When he smiles his
teeth are yellow like a rat. He introduces himself, 'Dahlgus
is the name, Gustav Dahlgus, and I am pleased to see you
got here on time.' He steps back, notices how damp I am and
helps me remove my coat and hangs it on one of two brass
hooks on the inner door. I am then shown to a small chair and

desk positioned to the side of his. There is a black typewriter at its centre and a pile of plain white paper neatly placed to the left of the machine. The paper is striking as it has as our eagle and swastika motif in its top centre. Dahlgus kindly but firmly informs me, 'Try not to make any errors and always ensure that you have a correction ribbon in your machine.' The little voice in my head says, 'Look, I know how to use a fucking typewriter, for God's sake. After all, isn't that what I'm here for?' I politely acknowledge his instructions and then he places a handful of handwritten dictates before me which all have to be typed up on the headed paper. He will sign them once the documents have been typed to his satisfaction. I run one through the typewriter as his heavy frame leans over me. I don't feel comfortable with him leaning over me like this but I continue as fast as my fingers will permit me to do so. Having typed his draft to his satisfaction he then reminds me I am privy to its contents and that these are highly confidential Reich matters. With a stern expression he informs me the contents are never to be discussed with anyone unless he has given express permission for me to do so.

The text had little impact upon me at first, but, as it became clear to me, I understood I was actually creating drafts which would be issued to the security forces in the city. The document was simply headed 'Acquisition of Jewish Property to The German Reich'. Did this worry me at that time? No, it didn't as to me it was just our government's policy. I didn't care about Jews at all; few Germans did at that time. The rule now was that Germany was for the pure Germans, not those of mixed race or blood lines. The Jews had not served us well either in the past. They were the executors of much misery. Few people really know about that. That's all I can say on that matter. I was born a National Socialist and I shall die a National Socialist.

She continued:

Herr Dahlgus is merely the executor of orders from higher beings. Apparently Propaganda Minister Goebbels is a regular visitor to these offices, along with Speer, Bormann and others that I have seen in the press but not had the pleasure of meeting as yet. I wonder what they are like. I have heard Goebbels is a letch with an eye for the ladies, and Bormann too. Apparently they all have an eye for the ladies, so one might consider oneself in a very precarious position as a young female within this branch. What happens to those who spurn their advances? Those who refuse to fuck their way to the top. Are they just as suddenly relieved of their duties, rendered unemployed and cast out into the retail world, the operations of which are dictated by the daily bombing raids? Well, we will see what happens, won't we? Mother and father have told me they will not tolerate anyone trying to elevate my career prospects via the requisitioning of sexual favours. I told them, 'Mother, father, really I would not have any of that you know that.'

I would rather work in a pool with just females. It's easier that way as one's intentions cannot then be misconstrued, can they?

On meeting the legendary charmer Joseph Goebbels for the first time Sofia recalled:

He was nothing remarkable. In fact he was what you would call quite unattractive. I could not believe that this was the man with such a legendary reputation for womanising. What attracted women to this man? He came through the offices, visiting each one in turn. He would pop his head around the door, wishing those inside a 'good morning' or 'good afternoon'. When he came to our room he actually came inside, as mine was a face he had not seen before. What did he say to me you will ask? Well, merely just the exchanging of pleasantries really. He asked me how I was getting on, if I had any problems I needed help with, did I have to travel far? It was just ordinary conversation really, after which he shook my hand and went on his way. He was, I suppose, very charming and obviously a man of very high intellect. Maybe the women he screwed were turned on by this high intellect.

A few weeks later I saw a different side to Dr Goebbels. He came into the ministry in a rage. I heard him outside in the corridor, shouting about something that somebody had got wrong. He came along the corridor almost kicking doors open in his fury. At lunch I was sat with Kathi, another of the typists, and she said: 'It does not do to talk about anyone or anything in this place. Do not talk about it to anyone, and if you do hear anything, forget what you hear quickly.' Much of the propaganda work produced in the early days was anti-Jewish. We had no input into any of its content either visually or within the wording. We were shown various artwork as a matter of course with our work within the ministry. To me personally I felt the artwork was a good representation of the feeling in Germany at the time. It had to be if it was going to have the desired effect upon German society.

Sofia had been employed in the ministry for around seven months when she fell foul of what she called 'the system'.

I worked well in every aspect and I did my job well. The thing I could not accept was Dahlgus's behaviour. I would be in the office working when he would come in. He had this horrible habit of leaning right over me while I was working. He leaned over me on the one occasion to the point where I could smell his breath and feel his breath against my ear. I just found this annoying and I asked him, 'Would you mind not doing that please?' He said nothing and moved away. Later on, I am just about to leave the office to go home when I am given a sealed envelope. I tear open the envelope, puzzled as to what it contained. It is blunt and wounding: 'Your services within the office are no longer required'. I am seething with anger, but I know arguing my case will be hopeless. I screw the letter up in my fist and throw it behind the desk in temper. I snatch my coat and walk down the corridor and out of the building. I wait in the queue for the tram. All the time I am thinking, 'These fucking men, they are all pigs'.

The short journey home is enough to quell my temper. When I walk through the door of my home, mother and father are sat down with their meals. Mother fetches mine and places it down before me on the table. I sit and toy with the food like a child to the point where my mother asks me what is wrong. I then explain the events earlier in the day. Mother is understanding and concerned while father just sighs. He then says, 'Well, you will just have to find another job then, won't you.' Then he says, 'Are you sure it was not your fault? That was a good job I found for you.' His remarks just make me angry again but are typical of his generation. 'You young women are far too hot headed. You should marry and give us grandchildren!' he snaps from across the table. I stand up and, fighting to contain my anger, I say to him, 'I am not some stupid girl who is going to tolerate some man pawing me as I try to work. I do not intend sleeping my way to the top of any career.' Father throws down his newspaper demanding I not use 'that tone of voice' with him. Mother interrupts by saying, 'Shut up, the both of you!' There is an uneasy silence before I leave the kitchen. We are like two dogs squaring up to fight. One of us has to back off before there is trouble. It has to be me of course.

I leave and go up to my room. I take off my clothes, throwing them into the corner of my room like some petulant brat. For a minute I stand before the full length mirror; one of my few luxuries. I pose like a model would for a photograph then I climb into bed, but as hard as I try to sleep, I can't. I lie and stare at the ceiling, and when I do fall asleep it's broken. I experience random dreams. Then the air raid siren sounds. I mutter 'Oh, fucking hell this is just wonderful' under my breath as I jump from the warmth of my bed, throw on my nightgown and head downstairs. We don't have an air raid shelter in the narrow area that forms our back garden so we use the pantry room under the stairs. There is just about enough room for us to squeeze inside and close the door. We hear a few booms in the distance but nothing else. A short while later an all-clear is sounded. We come out of the cupboard and I head back to my room. I peek out of the window but see nothing and then I jump back into bed and fall asleep. I am woken by my mother at 8am. I wait until father has gone then I come downstairs. Mother has made coffee and we sit and talk at the kitchen table. I tell mother I plan to go out to find myself some more work. I am not sure I wish to be a secretary for anyone again after what happened at the Reich ministry.

I meet up with Kathi on her lunch break and explain what happened. She is as angry as me about it but just tells me to be calm and try somewhere else. Kathi mentions there is a job in a food shop and that she knows the owner. I go to the shop, asking to speak with the owner. The pay is not very good but when I tell him I have experience with secretarial work he is excited. He tells me I could help his wife with paperwork and accounting for some extra money, if I am willing. I agree to start work the next morning and the owner will see how I get on. I return home a happier girl. The news delights my mother but father is not that enthused. Being in the military, he doesn't believe it patriotic enough for his daughter to be a shop worker. He continues to pressure me towards working for one of the other ministries. There are more ministries in Hitler's Germany than there are churches it seems. At this time I just want to be left alone.

The following weekend I meet up with girlfriends in Dahlem. It's beautiful and is a little quieter than Berlin central. We meet up at an inn we nickname 'The blind mice'. This is because it's mostly full of old men who sit squinting after they have drunk a few beers. We drink our wine and discuss things that have happened. A few soldiers wander into the inn. They look immaculate in their uniforms but we are not here for boys. Because we are now a little drunk they maybe think that they can get in our knickers. We decline their offer of drinks and leave the inn. Outside we link arms and make our way home. It's a long way on foot so we sing some patriotic songs we learned at school or with the BDM. We are stopped by a policeman who tells us off for disturbing the peace. He tells us 'Shut up and be quietly on your way.' We offer our apologies yet we can't help but giggle at him. One of the girls says 'fucking idiot' once out of earshot of the policeman. When I arrive on our street I notice there is a searchlight switched on. It sweeps the sky but there is no noise and no air raid warning so it must be a drill. I don't know. It has started to rain so maybe tonight it will be quiet. I walk in through the back door of our home. Mother is sat at the kitchen table, waiting for me. Father is out on duty at his barracks. Mother grumbles something then goes to bed. I drink a glass of water as my head is now throbbing from the wine. Then I make my way up the stairs. I hold on tightly to the rail as I negotiate the stairs. I don't bother to undress and fall into bed. I am fast asleep in seconds.

Hilde Ahrens was the daughter of a Munich couple. Her father worked in the postal service while her mother, a former maternity nurse, stayed at home. Munich had been the beating heart of National Socialism. Much of the history of the National Socialist German Workers' Party began there. Hilde grew up educated in the way of the Nazi Party, which both her parents fully supported. She was, as were many young people, expected to conform to the values taught to her by her parents. Having Nazi parents also meant following their political allegiances. Hilde recalls:

It was not difficult as I never knew anything else. I had grown up under Hitler, was schooled under Hitler and my parents loved Hitler. As a child I wanted to do something big; be a big part of our Reich. I wanted to play my part and leave my mark as they say. My education was very politicised and this continued in our home. There was just me and my younger brother and we were always eager to please our parents and do well. I did very well at school, due mainly to my knowledge of politics. Yet going through the Hitler Youth and then the Reich Labour Service was difficult. The impetus in these organisations was to orient the female youth towards childcare and wifehood. This was tough for me as I wanted neither as a young girl. I wanted to be adventurous and have a role to play, but I ended up working in the Brown House, as it was once known. This was the national headquarters of the Nazi Party in Munich. It was located on the Brienner Strasse, number forty-five. I would rather have been involved in teaching political and racial theory to our young children at the time but was always steered away from this whenever I tried to discuss it with the powers that be. I was told once, 'You will be settling down, marrying and having children soon. This is what the Führer expects of his women, not educational accolades; these are quite useless in the Führer's opinion.' It soon occurred to me that we as females were being pushed to the back in our society.

My secretarial position in the Munich headquarters was probably the closest I would ever come to glory at that particular time, in March of 1942. At the ministry I was involved in the preparation of all manner of documents. Soon I was also contributing to their content. The idea was let the men think they were the better thinkers, flatter them greatly, and they would subconsciously accept your ideas. More often than not many of my ideas were stolen by the men who would go to the higher officials and say it was their own idea. I knew that and had to accept it. My younger brother had just joined the Hitler Youth and he had aspirations of becoming a fighter pilot in the Luftwaffe. How I wish I could have those same aspirations, I often thought. The anger made me more politically aggressive. I needed someone to blame for what I felt was a hopeless situation. Rather than blame our leaders I blamed everyone other than them: the Jews, the foreigners, the Gypsies; it was their fault.

I had a boyfriend at the time. I was nineteen years of age. Marriage and motherhood were expected of all young women, but this was certainly not on my mind at that time though. My boyfriend suggested I apply for a post at one of the camps for political prisoners and enemies of the Reich. I did not think about it much at first. Then I thought 'yes, why not'. I would be given a uniform and power to exercise my beliefs rather than being stuck in an office. It would mean leaving home for long periods. I sat and thought, and the more I thought the more

I liked the whole idea. My boyfriend, who was due to leave for military service, told me where I must go to apply for a job in one of the camps. I knew about the camps and was aware of what they were. Though not everyone fully understood what they were for. They had been in existence since 1933. Regime opponents, homosexuals, lesbians, Jews, Slavs, Gypsies, Bolsheviks and common criminals all ended up in the camps.

The following week I gave up my job at the Munich ministry. I spent a few days visiting friends before the day came to pack my things. I caught the train to Dachau, where I had been offered a clerical position in the camp's medical section. I was very eager to start work as this was the very epicentre of our Germanic ideology. I viewed it as a kind of protector of our racial theories and hygiene. Dachau town was a beautiful location and the camp itself was quite extensive with many facilities. I had secured an apartment in the town, sharing with three other women. I arrived at the apartment on the Saturday morning and would start work on the Monday. I would have lots to learn but I could not wait. On the Monday morning we left our apartment for the main camp. We were all excited and felt finally we were involved in something that not many women at the time would have the opportunity to do. We relished the tasks which lay ahead.

What is apparent at this stage is that Hilde was fully aware of what purpose the concentration camps were serving. There was no ignorance in this case, as there was with a naïve few who would follow her into the concentration camp system. The question that many will be asking at this point is 'was she really aware of what she was getting herself into?' Hilde's story will continue in a later chapter.

Perhaps one of the most notable German females in the Nazi administration was Traudl Junge. Born Gertraud Humps, on 16 March 1920, in Munich, Traudl Junge served as Adolf Hitler's private secretary from December 1942 until April 1945. She was in the Führerbunker in Berlin when Hitler and Eva Braun took their own lives. The portraits she has painted of the Third Reich era, not only in her own published memoirs but the many interviews she has given since the war's end in

1945, have left many historians with conflicting opinions. I endeavoured to make contact with Traudl Junge in the summer of 1997. Having written a letter to the mayoral authority in Munich, asking whether they could forward my letter to Frau Junge or give me an address to write to, I was not optimistic of receiving any reply. However, a couple of weeks later I received a reply direct from Traudl Junge. The answers to many of the questions most people had asked her up to that point were more or less covered within the pages of her memoirs. I wanted to try to obtain something different, avoiding all the usual obvious questions she would have been asked over the years. Again, I put pen to paper and the following narrative is the result of my interviews with her.

> I was twenty-two years old when I first began working for him [Adolf Hitler]. Many of my female friends were so envious of me having managed to get this secretarial post. It was clear that somehow he liked me in a way different to the others. I could type and I had a sound knowledge and ability with shorthand writing too, something that served me very well. Did I sense any impending evil while in Hitler's presence? No, quite the opposite. You see, he was very much a charming, kind individual. He was very father-like, even somewhat protective. I felt protected whenever in his company. He did not approve of me smoking my cigarettes and I could never sit and work with him and smoke. This was something of a law whenever in his presence. It was not him being unkind or anything. He seemed to sense that smoking these cigarettes was detrimental to one's wellbeing. He would say to me, 'Frau Junge, you are poisoning your body with those things. If I were able I would eradicate the curse of tobacco!'
>
> Being in Hitler's company meant I witnessed many comings and goings. Goebbels, Bormann, Speer, Himmler and Von Ribbentrop: through my work for Hitler I associated with them all. People ask me 'were they beasts?' Von Ribbentrop was not liked amongst many of the Nazi Party leadership. People like Bormann and Himmler viewed him as a bit of an aristocrat, or toff as you call them. They were all of the opinion that a good Nazi came from humble roots. I recall some of the social

occasions we had. As part of Hitler's entourage I would always
be there. Himmler brought his daughter, Gudrun, with him
once. I can honestly say he was a doting father. He sat with
the little girl on his knee like any loving father. He had his
arms around her smiling and cuddling her. Gudrun was such
a beautiful little girl. She was one of the prettiest little girls
I had seen. She came and said hello to me. Yes, she was very
sweet indeed. The Goebbels children were also brought along.
They were all very lovely too and it saddens me greatly to think
that the poor Goebbels children would not live a very long life.
That they would die, along with National Socialism, in 1945.

I did not sense that I was around evil, but I was young and
maybe I had been a little naïve. I had my suspicions of what was
happening regarding the Jews in our country. Maybe I could
have tried hard and looked into all of the whispers which
surrounded the regime to seek the truth. I know now that
I could have done exactly that. I could have probably discovered
the truth that Jews were being exterminated in purpose-built
facilities. But I ask you this question, had I found out and stood
before Hitler and the others and shouted 'You criminals, what
are you doing? You are murdering Jews by the thousand and
I know you are doing this!' What would have become of me
had I done that? I think you understand quite well what such
an action would have meant for me personally. It would have
mattered little that Hitler was fond of me. Bad things would
have followed, of that I am sure. I recall von Ribbentrop once
joking to me, 'The Führer is very fond of you, Frau Junge, do
you realise?' Of course I knew he was fond of me as he gave
me gifts, but so did Eva Braun. I adored Eva and she adored
me back equally. I really thought a lot of her and remember
we would often talk privately to each other. I felt that she
was depressed on many occasions and she once confided to
me that she wished she could have her Führer all to herself
instead of having to share him with the German nation and
every female in it. She was really in emotional pain when she
said this. I did feel for her greatly but was warned not to get
too involved in matters that were none of my business.

I was told to do my job as I was told, be polite and friendly, and learn how to be discreet. Discretion often meant turning a blind eye to many things, especially the affairs that were very much going on at the time. Goebbels was always sneaking around with a new girl in tow. Bormann was much the same and had a predatory nature where naïve women were concerned. Others in the regime were all too aware of this. Without mentioning names, one said to me, 'Yes, Goebbels likes his women, but at least he seduces them in style, unlike Bormann who can't even be bothered to remove his shoes or boots!' This was a long-standing snipe behind Bormann's back. He was not popular as a man. In my duties I had my dealings with Bormann and I knew that he was a dark horse. He did not bother me in any way and I was courteous towards him in my duties. Rudolf Hess was another who was often subjected to ridicule in private. There were those in the Hitler circle who were convinced that Hess was a homosexual. I heard them arguing over the man they nicknamed 'Fraulein Anna'. One would say, 'I think he is a homosexual, look at him when he smiles.' Another would argue, 'No, that is quite stupid!'

There was so much hatred within it's hard to understand how the state functioned as it did for as long as it did. I am convinced all this infighting and competition from the men in Hitler's circle was highly detrimental and contributed to its downfall. Maybe Hitler should have employed women instead. We women got on very well for most of the time. One of the few women who didn't fit in with us was Gertrud Scholtz-Klink who was head of the German women's league. She wore funny clothes and was quite unfashionable. We did not view her as being in the same league as us. She was much like an ill-dressed old widow, as one of my friends once said. We could not have taken her along to one of our cocktail parties. Clearly she would have not fitted in at all.

Working in such high office in the Third Reich was very exciting and my pay was good and I had many perks which came with my job. Was I politically motivated? I would say that I wasn't. I had never been interested in the politics of National

Socialism, as we had been taught in the BDM. I understood its aim was to rebuild the German nation and regain our pride, and I was happy with that. I also have to say that I disliked Bolshevism and the thought of a world run by Bolsheviks horrified me as much as it did many others in Germany at that time. Anything that prevented us from becoming a victim again had to be a good thing. People expect me to ever present my conscience on a plate. I have said that for all the ills perpetrated under National Socialism and for my part I am truly sorry. I had no hate for anyone. I did not like Bolsheviks but that does not mean that I would have ordered them killed. Jews were presented as the enemy of the civilised nations; 'cockroaches' they used to say. I think I just blocked what I heard from out of my mind and got on with my job. I ignored the whispers and maybe I could have looked for the truth, but as I have already said, what would have happened to me had I challenged our system? Others did so and paid with their lives. I was too concerned with living to want to end up dead.

Chapter Three

From the Beggar's Paw

Although young women figured prominently in Hitler's Germany, their employment within the mechanisms of the Third Reich was carefully controlled. Having viewed his womenfolk primarily as bearers of children for the future Third Reich at the outbreak of the Second World War, this philosophy would of course continue. But the role of women and girls in Nazi Germany began to change following Hitler's disastrous invasion of Soviet Russia. As the Wehrmacht began to haemorrhage frontline soldiers, more men were required to give up their occupations on the home front and enlist for military service. Women were then called up to fill these posts and were actively encouraged to volunteer for work in the munitions and armaments factories. Under the sugar coating of providing a valuable Reich duty, many young women like Hellen Giehl – a twenty-year-old from Essen – answered the call. She recalls:

> I had been through all of the German youth organisations. I was still living at home with my mother and father in the city of Essen in 1943. It was not really broadcast that we were losing so many men in the Russian campaign. They did not want the public to know that our soldiers were being killed in their thousands and many more captured by our enemies. They kept all of that very quiet to avoid causing panic. There was just this change in the role of girls and women at the time. It was very subtle the way it was done. We went from health, beauty, husbandry and childcare to working in a factory, the postal service or signing up as an auxiliary in the military. I needed a decent job as my mother and father did not have much money so I went down to the Fried Krupp AG factory as they needed workers there. I didn't know a lot about what the factory did

other than it produced munitions and weapons of various kinds. I went down there and spoke with a clerk who gave me a form to fill in. I filled in the form there and then and was told to report for work the next day. It was as simple as that to get a job there at that time.

It was dangerous as the British and American air forces had attacked the Krupp works on many occasions and it remained a target until the end. My mother and father were a little worried about me being killed in the bombing. I had to reassure them that I would be safe as there was an air raid shelter there. I reported to the factory the next day at 6am and they put me on a line where I had to polish shell bodies. The shells were stacked on a conveyer belt and there was a gang of girls either side who had the task of polishing the grease, dirt and any other residues off the metal with a cloth. It was a dirty job and the factory was terribly noisy and the work was what you would call monotonous. There were slave labourers at the factory. Most of them were brought in from the east, places in Poland and Russia. I was told quite explicitly that I should not attempt to talk to any of these people, that I should not show any kindness towards them, smile or anything. These things were strictly forbidden and anyone disobeying the regulations in the plant was subject to dismissal. Anyone caught talking to or trying to talk to the slave labourers would face very severe punishment as it was classed as an offence against the Reich.

On my very first day in the factory there was an air raid alert. We were all instructed on what we had to do if the alert was given to evacuate the plant. We stopped what we were doing and quickly exited the plant, heading for the big air raid shelter which had been specially built for the workers. As we left I noticed the Polish workers continued on with their work. I asked one of the women, 'What about them?' to which she replied 'They will continue working. It matters not if they get killed as there are plenty more where they came from.' She then smiled and told me to hurry up unless I wanted to stay up here when the bombers came over. The air raid shelter was a solid structure and once the doors were slammed shut with everyone inside it was pretty quiet. Dull yellow lamps hung from the ceiling. These lamps gave out very little in the way of light but it was enough. I sat down and after some minutes I could feel myself drifting off to sleep. My dozing was interrupted by a deep rumbling sound. The rumbling sound was soon followed by the boom of the flak as it started to fire at aircraft high above in the skies over the city. The whole of the Ruhr was very heavily defended by flak and fighter aircraft. As the gunfire outside intensified, the light in the ceiling began to swing from side to side, much like the pendulum of a clock. A young girl sat next to me stared up at the ceiling and said 'It's ok, they are not that close today.'

Air attacks were nothing new to me as we had to contend with them at home too. Whenever the alert sounded we would leave the house and head down to the one of the big civilian shelters in the town. We used to get good advance warning, which gave us time to get to safety. Sat in the dimly lit shelter with the crescendo of noise above and the smell of sweat from all the bodies, all you could do was wait. An explosion shakes the ground, a little dust falls from the ceiling and the light flickers for a split second. Instinctively the girl sat next to me grabs hold of my hand. She squeezes it so tight I yelp in pain. She says 'sorry' and I reassure her it's ok as she releases her grip on my fingers. The rumbling sound continues for some time but the explosions of bombs sounds more distant now. The girl sat next to me asks me my name so I ask hers. Her name is Elsa and she explains she cycles to work each morning, a distance of two miles. She tells me, 'I will be glad when this fucking war is over and I can get a decent cup of coffee again.' We laugh and agree with one another how nice a real cup of coffee would be. The sound of the guns outside steadily decreases as the bombers have finished their work and are heading for home.

A short while later the siren sounds to announce the all clear. The door to the shelter is opened and we are momentarily blinded by the daylight. We are told that a bomb has struck the plant at the north end but damage is minimal. Repair teams are working away on the damaged area of the plant as we make our way back to work. When we arrive back inside, the Polish workers are still working away like nothing has happened. The conveyer belt is started up and we continue cleaning the shell bodies. We don't stop for any lunch as the time spent in the shelter has to be made up. By 4pm I am ready to go home but I'm asked if I will stay longer. I don't leave the factory until six in the evening. By the time I get home I wash and eat some food that mother has prepared then I go straight to bed. Before I fall asleep my mind replays the events of the day. I see the faces of the Polish workers. I can't seem to erase them from my mind. They will still be working as I enjoy the luxury of rest in a clean bed. I feel a degree of sadness for them, which is wrong I know. I am not supposed to feel any empathy towards these sub-humans, as my brother and father refer to them. No sooner do I fall into a deep sleep than my mother is waking me up. The air raid alert is sounding yet I never heard it until mother came in and woke me up. Clumsily I get out of bed, throw on some clothing and follow my parents down to the communal shelter. Once inside, the routine is the same. I find somewhere to either sit or lie down and I fall back to sleep. Then I'm woken again when it's safe and we can head back home. By morning I'm shattered and feel like I've been out drinking all night. It's hard to focus on work when all I want to do is sleep.

The next day I am put on a small machine opposite one of the Polish workers. I stare across at her but she doesn't look at me. In the end she lifts her head and our eyes meet. Her wretched state makes me feel so much guilt. I look around to see if anyone is looking and I don't know why, but I just smile at her. She looks nervously around, acknowledges and smiles back. I have not been here a week yet but I have already broken a serious rule, I think to myself. The Polish woman looks so sad and her physical state very poor. I ask myself has she had anything to eat or drink today. As much as I fight the feelings of pity growing within me, I just can't. When we stop for our short lunch break the Polish girl continues her work. There are foremen, as you call them, who walk about the factory floor observing the Poles. The foremen watch them as eagles would watch their prey. I have a few sandwiches wrapped in my little bundle. I eat two of the sandwiches and there are now two left to last me the day. I sit and think as I eat the sandwiches. The coarse bread is not the nicest but it's better than nothing. Soon we have to go back onto the line to continue working but I have put the sandwiches into the large pocket of my work trousers.

A few hours later there is an air raid alert, but just as we are all walking off to the shelter we are called back. It was a false alarm; the bombers veered away to the south of Essen. We trudge back and begin work again. Just before dark the air raid alert sounds again and we are told the bombers are some thirty minutes away from arrival. As we head for the shelter again the flak guns are already firing away some miles from where we are. The guns are arranged in belts around the Ruhr district. Fighters are also alerted and get airborne to take on the oncoming threat. Again the bombs fall around us and it is surprising how many fail to score a hit on the factories and plants. All we can do is sit and wait it out. The few men who are with us curse as usual. One says, 'I wish those planes would just fuck off!' Another man remarks that the flak will destroy many of them. The guns are pretty big: 8.8cm, 10cm and heavy 12.8cm. They fill the sky above with high explosives. To try and fly through this is said to be suicide. I know I would not want to be up there with all that danger. As the bombers pass out of our sector the guns of the next one are ready and waiting for them.

When the all clear sounds we emerge and as we come out the searchlights still comb the early evening sky. I walk fast as I want to get back into the factory before the others get there. I get to my machine and reach into my pocket. I quickly look around and throw the bundle of sandwiches over to the Polish girl. She looks up and I gesture for her to grab the bundle which is now lying on the floor by her machine. I smile then start up my machine and continue my work. The Polish girl drops a tool onto the floor. As she kneels down to get the dropped tool she grabs the bundle I have given to her and puts it down her jacket. An hour later I am relieved as my shift has ended. I look over to the Polish girl and I smile at her.

That evening at home I save some food from my meal so that I can try and pass a little more to the Polish girl worker the next day. I do not know who she is, what her name is or where she is from but she is on my mind all of the time now. I am torn by the guilt of perhaps being a traitor to my own country and feeling so sad for this poor, wretched slave girl. The next day at the plant I try to be first in before the other women. I start up the machine and then look over and the Polish girl is there. I have to be careful as I don't wish to put her in any danger, but I want to pass her the extra food, which includes a piece of my mother's own fruitcake. I figure out how I am going to get the food to her without it being obvious what I am doing. I look around to see where the foremen are and then look around to see if all the other women are busy working. I throw one of my machine tools onto the floor. No one hears the noise it makes over the sound of machines. I throw my hands up in the air and say 'Oh, fucking hell! Fucking machine! For God's sake!' One of the foremen comes over and asks if I have a problem. I explain I'm fine and that I have just dropped a tool. He walks off, smiling, and I take my opportunity to pass the bundle of food to the Polish girl. I kneel down on the floor, pretending to reach under the table. I can see the Polish girl's shoes and I take the bundle from my pocket and gently throw it towards her feet. I watch as she nudges the bundle under her machine and out of sight. She can then pick it up and put it in her pocket when it is safe to do so. I look across at her after a few minutes and she looks back and, although I cannot hear her voice, from the way her lips move I can see she is saying 'danke'. This means 'thanks' in Deutsche. I hope the few items of food make her feel better and help her stay a little healthier.

As time went by I learned that the Polish girl's name was Leena or Lena and she was just nineteen years old. She had lived in Warsaw and had been sent to forced labour in our country along with her parents, brothers and sisters. She said that she had worked in a factory prior to our forces invading and so she was sent to work here as she knew how to operate these machines. I continued to bring extra food whenever I could, although it was never always so easy to get the food to the girl. Some days I would try all day long but could not due to too many people being around and foremen paying extra attention and things. I know I was risking a hell of a lot, but when I came to Krupps and I saw this I understood, despite all the political rhetoric, that what we were doing was somehow evil and that it was wrong. I continued to help the girl for almost a year. Then one morning I went into the factory as normal and the girl was not there. She had been replaced by an elderly man. I did try and look out for her but could not see her, even after almost a week. Asking questions would have aroused suspicion so finding out where the girl had gone was not easy at all. In order to find out I said to one of the foremen one morning 'Who is that old man over there? Where's the girl gone?' The foreman replied that she had been sent out to one of the sub-units to replace a number of labourers who had died as a result of a bombing attack earlier that week. I knew the chances of me being able to help her were now almost non-existent.

I never saw her again but I have never forgotten her either. I did some research after the war and, from what I could find, I believe that the girl did survive and was able to return home. I recall a number of years after the war I received a letter. I wondered who this letter could be from as I did not recognise the surname or anything. I was thrilled to discover after reading it that it was the Polish girl I had helped at the factory. She had somehow managed to track me down in Essen as remembered my name. It was some months before we finally had a meeting. We greeted each other like long-lost sisters. She just wanted to say thanks for what I had done and for not hating, like many Germans did. She then gave me a gold locket with a small photograph of her baby son inside it. She held my hands and said 'If it were not for you I may have lost the will, and I may not have made it to be here today and have my son.' She put the locket around my neck and I have never taken it off since. I never told my parents of this as they would have gone mad and my brother would have disowned me. They would always be Nazis. Even when we lost the war they didn't change. I just did not tell them about it as I felt that was the best way. After the war I just wanted to get on and restart my life.

Another young German woman, Danielle Heimer, was a twenty-three-old who worked in the Krupp factory in Essen, and spoke of her experiences.

It was shit, a horrible place to work really. The dirt and grease got right into your skin and hair. The air was putrid and unhealthy in there too. I was always getting these really bad sore throats during my time working there. My doctor said it was probably due to the dust, fumes and general bad air quality in the plant. He told me I shouldn't complain as I was carrying out a valuable duty to my country. There were many workers in the plant, including slave workers from the east. I recall that these people lived in barracks that were surrounded with barbed wire and heavily guarded. I personally did not encounter the slave workers very much though I did see them around the plant from time to time during the course of my work. I was trained to operate a thread machine that put threads into screw bolts for artillery guns. The good thing was you could sit down to do this work. The oil that was used to cool the metal as you drilled got everywhere. It got in your face, eyes, mouth and hair. I covered my hair with a scarf but it still became contaminated with the oil. My hair would come out in clumps but if you said anything they would just tell you to shut up, stop moaning and get on with your work. I would be there on long shifts threading bolt after bolt and filling up metal trays with these bolts. The machine had a counter on it and at the end of the shift you had to fill in a form with the reading on the machine so they knew how many bolts you had threaded. Once you had filled in the form you reset the counter to zero. If they felt you had not done enough they would come and shout at you. The problem was when I first started I had a habit of breaking the thread tools. If you tried to go too fast and drive them through too quickly they would snap in half. You would have to call one of the bosses who would then replace the broken thread tool. He would then stand there and berate you. 'You stupid woman, you must concentrate. If you break anymore we will deduct it from your salary,' they would say. One said to me once, 'It's a pity we have to let women do these jobs. Men are so much better at these jobs than you women!'

Bullying was a problem and not just amongst the bosses at the plant. The women could be pretty nasty too. I did not know any of the women I had to work with; most were older than me. We worked in a kind of chain where production relied on everyone working steadily and not fucking anything up, so tension was never far away. If you messed up, it affected them too you see. Some of these women were proper old Nazis. They had husbands and sons away fighting in the war. Some of them held us girls in contempt. Their view was we should be at home having children and not be here getting in their way and slowing them down. That said, some were very nice and would help you and tell you to 'ignore those bitches over there'.

The air attacks disrupted production but the repair teams soon got things up and running again. I remember a bomb coming through the roof once and it had failed to explode. The bomb had to be defused then taken away. As it came through the roof it smashed into one of the lathes. The damaged lathe was repaired but the hole in the roof remained for a day or so. It rained and water began to pour through the hole made by the bomb. They just cut out a huge sheet of corrugated metal and covered the hole until a proper repair was carried out.

I saw women who became so tired they lost concentration and suffered accidents. The worst accident I witnessed was a young woman working on a lathe. A piece of clothing caught on the wheel. It pulled her into the turning wheel and her head was almost torn from her shoulders. It was a horrible sight. The woman's body was removed then the machine was hosed down with water before going straight back into use again as if nothing had happened. All that mattered were the production figures so Mr Albert Speer, or whoever, could boast that he had exceeded production from the previous month.

Albert Speer was Hitler's architect who, for most of the Second World War, was Reich Minister of Armaments and War Production in Nazi Germany. Danielle Heimer continues:

Speer was aware of the general conditions in the factories and the fact that slave labourers were beaten and abused during the course of their work. Speer had visited the Krupp works on a few occasions as Krupp was one of Germany's best producers of weapons and military hardware. Yes, I saw him at Krupps on a few occasions. He would be dressed in a fine suit with his hangers-on smiling at us and offering his congratulations. He would come and shake hands with some of us. I offered to shake his hand once but he recoiled in horror at the sight of my dirty, oily hands. Instead he smiled and raised his hand almost like a salute. He seemed almost embarrassed to be amongst us. Some of the girls really liked it when Speer came round. He was an attractive man but not taken to pulling out factory girls and taking them for dinner and to bed, like most of our leaders at the time. If he did then I never heard of it [she laughs].

Regarding the slave workers, as I have said I did not really have dealings with them. I did witness one of them being beaten outside once. I do not know what the man had done, but he was given a real thrashing. They beat him over the head and body with sticks then they kicked him in the ribs and stomach. The beating didn't stop there though. He was ordered to his feet then punched full force in the head. I watched by a doorway for some minutes as this continued. The man was punched a final time in the head after being dragged to his feet and I think he was knocked unconscious. I was pulled back into the workplace by one of the women who saw me watching what was going on. She scolded me and told me off, shouting 'You don't look at these things when they happen, do you understand? You walk away. You see nothing and you say nothing!'

Near the war's end we looked much like the slave workers. We were hungry, we had lice in our hair, boils on our skin, nothing on our feet and rags on our bodies. What was it all for, I asked myself. I had wanted a better Germany and I guess we believed Hitler would deliver. My parents and extended family were excited when Hitler came to power. We felt he was a light in the darkness and a strong, resilient leader. Of course he was a strong, hard leader, but he wanted war. We understood that we had a leader who would probably end up waging war with the rest of the world. What we failed to understand were the consequences of us losing such a war. We never felt we would lose in the way we did. When all the lies and propaganda were thrown aside, and it dawned on us that we were going to lose the war, the mood of the people changed. What makes me angry when I look back now is the fact we were all betrayed and lied to. We did not have anywhere near enough soldiers to defend our territory from either the Russians or western allies. Their boots were filled with any able-bodied civilian. Our leaders sacrificed us when there were no more soldiers.

On 11 April 1945, Essen fell to the US Ninth Army, along with Bochum and Goslar. Danielle Heimer recalls:

When the fighting finally ended we came out of our basement with a white flag on a stick. Our home, like many others, was nothing more than an empty shell. My father stuck the stick in the ground on the top of a pile of rubble and both he and mother then sat with their heads in their hands. There was nothing but destruction all around. Buildings burned and smoke rose up into the sky. People wandered about in a daze and there was no food or water. Resistance against the Americans was foolish. During the fighting I heard that the Hitler Youth had been active, causing the Americans some casualties. I had caught glimpses of boys and the odd girl with *Panzerfaust* [anti-tank] weapons being called by soldiers to where they were needed. Was I a coward for not joining them? Only God can be my judge on that question. I just thought at the time 'what is the point now it's all over for us'. My mother and father would have killed me themselves had I tried to join in the fighting. We stayed out of the way and waited for the battle to end. After it ended there were many Germans who could not look one another in the eyes. But Essen was our home and we all had to rebuild it and live together in it. The one thing that really occurred to me afterwards, in the wake of the revelations of the Nazi atrocities, was that we were going to be in serious trouble this time. With Russia occupying half of our country, were we going to be enslaved and starved to death ourselves. We were going to have to live from what we used to say was 'the beggar's paw'.

Chapter Four

The Little Aryan

In 1939, BDM *Reichsreferentin* [Deputy Leader] Jutta Rüdiger examined the feasibility of creating a *Bund Deutscher Mädel* [League of German Maidens] version of the male Hitler Youth *Streifendienst* or SRD as it was known. The SRD was basically an internal police/ security organisation within the Hitler Youth and liaised closely with the SS and Gestapo authorities. Membership of the SRD was often a precursor to enrolment within the ranks of the SS or Gestapo and SRD members were often highly respected due to the immense personal power that membership endowed them with. There were many sinister elements surrounding the SRD. Their primary role was not only general policing duties within the Hitler Youth but also rooting out and informing on all aspects of non-conformism. Typically, an SRD member would be tasked with ensuring correct discipline was maintained and that Hitler Youth boys complied with the rules of the organisation such as following the correct dress code. Many boys aspired to become members of the SRD but the criteria were very strict. Only the most physically and politically dedicated individual stood a chance of joining what was viewed as an elite within the Hitler Youth.

Jutta Rüdiger proposed the formation of a female version of the SRD, which would play the same role and follow the same principles. However, there appeared to be some immediate opposition to her idea. There were many within the Nazi hierarchy at the time who felt that such an idea was in contravention of the principles of the BDM. At this time the war was in its infancy and the Nazis felt that the girls of the BDM were best employed in a domestic role. But though Rüdiger's proposal was rejected, some of her ideas were put to use, particularly later in the war. Though never officially SRD members, some girls were selected to assist the SRD in certain aspects of their operations. These girls were never issued documentation or membership cards and by all intents and purposes were just ordinary members of the BDM.

Kathi Emler, from Spandau, can personally testify that certain students in the BDM were actively sought out to assist with the Hitler Youth SRD. Kathi came from a large family with two sisters and three brothers. Her parents were devoted National Socialists and ensured that their children followed every principle by the book. She recalled:

My family were natural National Socialists as my parents had followed the organisation from the very beginning. In our home there were very strict rules, which we had to observe at all times. As soon as we were old enough, we all joined the Hitler Youth. I loved the BDM and its competitive elements and enjoyed the sporting tournaments we engaged in. The gymnastics and everything else, including the camping holidays, were wonderful. I loved it all. The politics came naturally to me, just like a child learning to ride a bicycle. I embraced and absorbed the Nazi culture and wanted to serve my society to ensure the greatness of Germany. None of us wanted to return to the old Germany. We despised the old Germany because, in our view, it was diseased, with weak political leadership. Germany of the post-1918 period was not for the German people. We had been taken over by people who did not even belong in our country and were not German born. Jews had all the money and controlled big business and we were taught that they had caused many of our problems after 1918. I accepted what was an apprenticeship of hate in many ways, but at that time in my life it was a personal destiny I had to follow. My brothers all went into the army and between them fought on almost every front during the Second World War.

In the BDM I did as much as I could in every duty. I helped the other girls with everything I could and helped our leader too. I also became a leader after putting in so much hard work. The BDM leadership rewarded those who made every effort to succeed, not only with awards and certificates, but various promotions too. I recall one day I had been called to a meeting with eight or nine other girls. We were asked to take a seat at a desk in what looked like a school classroom. We were each given a paper with questions, which we filled in and handed back as soon as we had completed them. It was noted how quickly each of us had taken to fill in the questionnaire and a time was written down on each paper. The person doing the test was a man named Walter Hornig, who I thought looked to be in his fifties. Then he asked us a very simple question. He said, 'What would you do if you discovered that your dearest father, mother, brother or sister had assisted a Jew, or maybe a political adversary, to elude our authority's attention?' There was a deathly silence, which was broken by me as I thrust my hand in the air. Herr Hornig asked me to stand and explain my answer. I told him, 'I would report them to the nearest government authority.' He asked me to sit down and then addressed the others: 'None of you raised your hand to answer as eagerly as this girl has.' He then asked the others to leave the room and took down my personal details, including my full name and address. I was then asked how I felt helping with security and if I would be interested in doing so. I replied that I would like to do this work. He told me, 'This will be all for now. You will be contacted to report for a medical in a couple of weeks' time when you will be assessed.' He smiled at me and thanked me, telling me I could go home. When I got home I told my father all about it. I was told to keep it secret from my sisters at that point. Both my father and mother seemed elated.

A week later I received a letter asking me to attend a medical examination at a surgery in Spandau. I was eighteen at the time and due to start Reich Labour Service soon. In fact, I was waiting for my documents to be issued instructing me where I would be going. The medical examination was quite thorough but I felt fine about it as the doctors examining me were all females. They took my height and chest measurements and weighed me, then I was asked to remove my clothes, which I did. They examined me all over and looked into my mouth and eyes. Each part of the examination was followed by notes being written down. They checked my medical records and my school and BDM records. It was a very thorough examination in many aspects. Afterwards I got dressed and was told, 'That is all, thank you. You may go home now.' I walked home with my mother and we stopped off to collect two of my sisters from school.

Around a week later I was informed that I was required to assist the SRD with what they called 'certain special duties', though I would not be a member of the SRD as such. I would carry out the tasks asked of me and then report directly to the Hitler Youth SRD. I was basically recruited as a kind of spy, operating within our local community and reporting on anything I felt suspicious. I was told to go into beer houses and cafés and just sit and listen and make idle conversation with the locals. I should get to know as many people as possible, especially men, and find out what they were thinking. To me, this was a very exciting thing. I was given money so I did not have to pay for any drinks or food while doing my work. I found it easy to strike up conversations with people. I would get to know them a little first and then ask them questions later, but not in a way that might arouse their suspicions. It was easy with the men. Men are men, and most think only with their dicks [she laughs]. If they think they can get you into bed they are stupid enough to open up and tell you anything. That's what I discovered so it wasn't difficult to find out things. I never once slept with anyone, of course, but used the promise of letting them take me to bed later to get them to maybe relax enough to let their guard down. One revealed that he and his family hated Hitler and that Hitler would be the destruction of Germany. Such a statement was enough for me and I would finish my drink, make my excuses, then leave. I would then make a report by phone and the SRD would process things and take over. They would watch an individual or maybe get him or her in for questioning. Any denial was met with the statement that they had made to me.

Women could be trapped in much the same way as the men. One of my tasks was to try and seek out lesbian women. To be honest, I only ever encountered two and one was far more rampant than any man I had ever met. In fact she was like a wild animal. She wanted to have sex with me in the bathroom of the café, which I declined, I have to tell you. As instructed, I reported these things to the SRD authority, but I have no idea what happened afterwards.

I did this work for at least a full twelve months before I was called in to the local authority office. I was then told I would stand down as other girls would be taking my place. They said there was a danger my face might become too familiar so a change was needed. I remember this rather short, blonde girl with pigtails and big, blue eyes. I remember thinking, 'Those men or women won't be able to resist you. God help them.' She was seventeen at that time and, like me, she had a strict National Socialist upbringing. I gave her the nickname 'Der Kleine Arier'; 'The Little Aryan' in English. Her name was Adelheid, which also means 'sweet' or 'noble' in the German language. We became very close friends and, contrary to the rules, we often discussed our exploits with one another; in private, of course.

I have to admit that young girl was ruthless in her pursuit of her duties. Adelheid went much further with things than I would ever have dared. In our private discussions she revealed that she had helped secure the arrest of a local shop owner who, she had discovered, was sympathetic towards Jews. She learned this information after starting a relationship with the shop owner's son. She had been instructed to find out if the authority's suspicions had any substance. Such things became commonplace in Germany through that time. We were of the opinion that such duties were necessary for Germany to win the war against our ideological enemies. The 'Little Aryan' set about her task very well. She went into the shop to buy some goods, and did this over a period of time before striking up a conversation with the shop owner's son. It was more or less inevitable that he would be interested in meeting her at some point to take her for coffee or dancing. It amazed me how easy it all was. Did these men not think about such things? I don't think they did. The boy asked her all the usual things and then she hit the jackpot when he asked to take her out to a dance. She obliged and the trap was set. How long it took to find out information was entirely down to how persuasive the 'Little Aryan' could be.

I asked what happened and she told me: 'Really, it was not that difficult. I went to the dance with him and afterwards he took me back to an apartment that belonged to his father. We would just talk over coffee. I would play the perfect girl, sweet and innocent, and let him think of me as vulnerable. I would steadily get him to open up by saying that I felt things were going the wrong way in Germany and that the Nazis were going to end up killing us all. He would be shocked and say "What! You are anti-regime?" He would behave like a child in a sweet shop. Even so, it took a long time for him to reveal that his family had assisted Jews in evading detection by the authorities. Over a period of a few months I was able to implicate a few people, including a doctor. I had a great memory and could remember the names I was told, and once home I would write the information down. I would have to report my progress to the SRD and I would tell them "I am doing very well and the rat is in the barrel". The information was of such importance that I slept with him several times. He would insist I put make up on and then dress up for him. He used to like me to wear one of his white shirts and nothing else. I was always told to do what I had to do if the information could prove valuable. Letting him make love to me was a relatively small price to have to pay to get what I needed from him. I just lay there, closed my eyes and pretended to enjoy it. He certainly enjoyed himself, as he never lasted long. It was during his post-coital bliss that he would be more likely to reveal something. There were times he wanted to make love again and I had to beg him to get off me as I had to go to work. I got dressed, we kissed, then I told him I would see him tomorrow. One morning I was able to hand over an extensive list of names and information to the SRD, who then informed the SS and Gestapo. They wasted no time in arresting them. That was it. That job was now done. They told me to lie low for a while and they would use me again.

After a couple of months or so the SRD contacted me again. They had a little job for me, they said. I was given details of where I had to go and was told to get a tram ticket to my destination, which was fifteen miles from where I lived. I arrived and was just told, "There are some females here acting strangely so see what you can find out." There were suspicions that the girls in question were acting in an inappropriate manner. I did not exactly understand in what way but, after a little time, it became obvious. There were a couple of girls who, it was felt, were spending far too much time together. They were never seen with boys and they wanted me to find out if this was innocent or if the two were in some kind of relationship. Again, it was not that difficult to befriend subjects under suspicion. You just said the right things to them and saw what their reaction was. I told them I had left home and was new to the district. I needed advice on where I could go to stay as I had nowhere to stay or any money. They told me I could stay with them for a few nights until I had sorted myself out. They were curious, naturally, so I told them I had left home after falling out with my parents. I shared their apartment and had to sleep on their couch. They had separate rooms, which appeared quite normal. After three days they said, "Please stay with us a while longer as we like having you around", so I stayed longer.

One evening one of them came back to the apartment with alcohol. I told them I did not drink but they would have none of it. So I had one glass of wine, then another, and another. After that I was hopelessly drunk and fell onto the living room floor. I couldn't remember much apart from giggling like an idiot and I remember kissing them both. I recalled them both taking it in turns to perform oral sex on me. I woke early the next morning on the couch where I had fallen asleep as I felt sick and needed to go to the bathroom. I knocked the door of the one girl's bedroom but got no answer so I knocked again and opened the door and peered in. The girl was not in her bed so I went and knocked on the second girl's door. Again there was no answer so I opened the door and slowly peered around it. There they were, blissfully asleep and naked on top of the covers, entwined like lovers. It was obvious to me so I slowly closed the door, got myself dressed and left the apartment. I informed my authorities of what I had seen and it was up to them to pursue things. I then returned home.'

Although the honesty with which the 'Little Aryan' spoke of her work shocked even Kathi Emler, her response to the question of regret was somewhat cryptic. When I asked Kathi if she felt any regret for her or her friend Adelheid's conduct during the Second World War, she replied:

Both Adelheid and I were guilty of aiding and abetting the persecution of people in Nazi Germany. I understand that, but I cannot speak for Adelheid as I have not seen her for a great many years now. She moved away after the war and we did write to each other for some years but then our letter writing stopped. Do I feel remorse for everything I did? I have questioned my own conscience many times over the years. At the time I felt nothing other than what I was doing was the right thing. Adelheid would probably tell you the same if she were here now. What you construe as right or wrong in times of war has no relevance in times of peace, does it? We were locked in combat and the very survival of our race was dependent on everyone doing their part. Seeking out the traitors within our society was vital. They had to be eliminated. Our methods may not have appeared very fair but they were effective. You might ask, if I could go back and do it all again, would I? I am not sure what to say. We lost the war, didn't we. I could not go back again just to lose again. What sense would that make?

Ruth Gellert was sixteen years old in 1943 and had an older brother who served in the SRD after joining the Hitler Youth. In an interview she recalled:

Officially a girls' or BDM SRD never existed. It was something the supreme leader of the BDM, Fraulein Rüdiger, wanted to create. She felt we girls could have done as good a job as the boys, which is why she attempted to implement it. The thing was, after Rüdiger's plan had been examined they must have sat there scratching their heads. While never officially recognised or approved, BDM girls began to assist the Hitler Youth SRD. Some were given pretty menial tasks such as escorting other girls home after their BDM meetings, or delivering disciplinary notices. They could also be asked to remove girls from areas where they were not permitted to be. I know of girls who were given much more important tasks but these were strictly off the record; no documents were issued or anything and no lists of names. There was absolutely nothing to incriminate them in the years after the Second World War. I think Hitler was of the opinion that his women adored him so much that he could exploit their devotion in certain ways.

We have already discovered, contrary to what many historians believe, that there is a degree of truth in Ruth Gellert's hypothesis on the role of BDM girls assisting the SRD, however limited a role they may have performed.

Hitler became increasingly paranoid regarding the threat of assassination. In all there had been fourteen attempts at killing him. Four were carried out before the Nazis seized power in 1933. In one instance an assassin tried to kill Hitler with poison at the Hotel Kaiserhof in 1930. After 1933 there were ten more attempts made on the Führer's life, including one in Obersalzburg. The Obersalzburg assassin had been an unknown member of the SA, or Brownshirts, as they were known. Hitler was well aware of his own mortality, yet at the same time he was delusional enough to have believed that any attempt on his life would incur some form of divine intervention. To those who supported killing Hitler this was something that appeared to increase with every attempt made on his life. The paranoia and suspicion that began to consume Hitler appeared to permeate Nazi German society, which in turn began to prey upon itself. Any society which follows such a path will inevitably end up destroying itself.

Ruth Gellert continues:

I knew of girls and women who informed on their own parents and family members. This of course could only be achieved through skilful indoctrination. I myself went through the same indoctrination, but I remained in control of my common sense. I heard my father call Hitler a very offensive word on more than one occasion. I would never have told anyone or informed the authorities of what he said though. I would never have informed on any of my family or my friends either. Some of us had that ability to control our emotions regarding the Hitler government yet others just did not have it. All I can say is that they must have allowed themselves to be totally brainwashed and became consumed with hate. They could not see that they were being used. Some were unrepentant, even long after the war had ended. I knew of one girl who was responsible for having her parents imprisoned by the National Socialists. I remember seeing her after the war and we talked briefly. I asked her, 'Do you feel bad for what you did to your mother and father now the Nazis are no more?' She looked blankly at me, shook her head and said 'No, they were traitors.' I was told she still kept a photo of Hitler by her bedside and had a large framed portrait of him on her bedroom wall. She was still possessed by the Hitler allure. After the war it was considered an offence under the de-Nazification laws to have such things as portraits of Hitler in your possession. If you were caught you could face fines or even imprisonment. She didn't care at all. I found out that her parents' sisters and brothers disowned her after what she did. She died a couple of years ago having never repented. She went to the grave a Nazi, as they say. The SRD were most definitely active in encouraging females to co-operate and assist them in their various security and policing activities. They were an evil organisation which wielded far too much power.

Another interesting account was sent to me by Dagna Baier, which I felt should be included here. She recalled:

Police, security, they were everywhere in our National Socialist society. We knew that and we learned to live with it. I understood the fact that total control had to be administered over our society for it to develop the way our leaders wanted. The problem was they gave certain security and policing powers to individuals in the boys' Hitler Youth. This soon had an influence on the BDM, although the BDM never had its own internal SRD-type police and security force. Girls were used by the SRD for certain things. I was a member of the BDM when I was fourteen years old in 1944. We were living in Berlin but were forced to move into a special BDM camp, as they called it, outside the city in the safety of the countryside. We were told we would be much safer from the bombing raids there. The raids grew consistently heavier until it was soon impossible to live in any normal capacity in the city. The BDM camp was situated in thick forest and it was kind of exciting living there. Our freedom as individuals was still very much controlled. There were strict rules in place and the SRD were active in maintaining these rules. Our BDM leaders were always talking with the boys of the Hitler Youth SRD. Near to the end of the war, discipline seemed to break down. I knew of girls who started to sneak off at night to meet Hitler Youth boys who were placed in a camp near to ours. This was done on purpose. One young girl, with nothing but her nightdress, was stopped in the forest by one of our BDM leaders. That same BDM leader was one of the girls we saw talking to the SRD. She actually escorted the girl to the tent of the boy she was on her way to visit. The boy in question was of course a member of the SRD. The two of them went inside the tent and had their fun and the BDM leader escorted the girl back to our camp afterwards. That would have never happened in the earlier years. It would have been viewed as very serious misconduct. Everything was slowly breaking down and couples were sneaking off to have sex all over the place. The authorities encouraged it to a degree. One SRD member once said, 'I don't care anymore. Let them go and fuck. The Führer needs as many children as possible to be born National Socialists.' Promiscuity among German girls was a Reich offence and always discouraged, yet here we were near the end of the war and fourteen year-olds were being encouraged to go out and meet with the boys in the woods.

Most were so naïve they knew nothing until they ended up pregnant.

The Hitler Youth was, in effect, destroying itself at this point. Later it would also sacrifice itself in futile attempts at holding our enemies back. Boys and girls were sent to fight or defend towns, cities and villages. It was disgusting really how so many young lives were destroyed. Even as our enemies entered our cities, the SRD banded together in groups. Not just boys but girls too. They sought out people fleeing from the fighting and, with their puppet courts, they tried and executed people for cowardice and treason. They usually shot them with pistols. Some were then hung up from trees as a warning to others. The SRD members often encouraged the girls with them to take the fatal shot. It was if it were like a right of passage or something. The victim would be forced to kneel down, a pistol would be aimed at the back of their heads, and they would be shot without mercy while often pleading for their lives. I watched one girl pull the trigger. She held the pistol with both hands. I could see her hands and arms shaking with adrenaline as she squeezed the trigger. Afterwards they ran off to find another victim. I witnessed these horrors and they have stayed with me ever since. Talking about these things helps a little to come to terms with it all, but it never goes away. Once you have witnessed these events they haunt you.

When asked to summarise her past and her feelings in the present, Kathi Emler wrote a letter to me. Its contents paint a picture of fear and the retribution that may lie beyond her life. She wrote:

The memories of my youth remain as tainted waters. I used to have dreams that I would be swimming in these waters, tainted red with the blood of our own people. The problem was, the blood of traitors was the same colour as that of the innocent. In my dreams I would see the Little Aryan drowning. I would be swimming with all my strength towards her but could never reach her to save her. Did the 'Little Aryan' represent me trying to come to terms and rescue my own conscience?

Today, I say to myself, 'Little Aryan', you are so like me. Your hair is now greying and no longer blonde, your faultless skin withered like an animal's hide, your eyes are still blue yet they are blurred. They are like broken windows into another time where people suffered due to our actions. Do you sit and stare from an apartment window and reminisce while patiently waiting for death, as I sometimes do. What judgement awaits us in the hereafter? I am afraid, 'Little Aryan', I am so afraid.

Chapter Five

My Infatuation

Hitler's relationships, along with his personal views on women, are now well documented. Many have sought, over the years since 1945, to explore further the mind of one of the most evil men the world has known. In many aspects, Adolf Hitler was a psychologist's dream. Many have sought to understand the conscious and sub-conscious phenomenon that was Hitler. Yet even with all the psychological profiling which began with Britain's SOE [Special Operations Executive] in the Second World War, much myth, mystery and fascination surrounds the man. Much of the resulting data which emerged from the work carried out by Britain's SOE was of an empirical nature.

Hitler enjoyed the adoration of thousands of young German women in the Third Reich. He was also rumoured to have had relationships with some of the Third Reich's most beautiful and successful women. Many today will look at Hitler's image and ask 'how did a man like him create such a powerful allure over so many females?' The men of the Third Reich were seduced politically and economically. The promises of work, prosperity and a greater Germany appeared enough to secure the support of Germany's menfolk. Jews were, of course, made the scapegoat for many of Germany's ills and both men and women embraced this hatred of Jewry. Yet it soon became abundantly clear that without the overwhelming support of Germany's women Hitler could not have gained the level of power that he did. Many of the girls and women who supported Hitler would never meet the man, or even see him. To them, he appeared as a form of messiah. Hitler in turn encouraged the infatuation of his people, particularly his women.

Eva Braun had met Hitler when she was just seventeen years old. Thus she had been a romantic part of his life for many years before their relationship was officially revealed. The almost twenty-three-year age gap between the couple came as a shock to Eva's friends and family. Yet this proved to be no impediment to their relationship. Hitler understood that to maintain his appeal he would have to keep his women open to the belief that he was theirs and belonged to them exclusively. This was just very clever political marketing. Eva Braun was forced to exist in Hitler's shadow. She could never be seen walking arm in arm with him at official engagements or social functions. Though surrounded by wealth, Eva Braun lived a melancholy existence while her lover was fawned over by his people as he planned the destruction of millions. Despite suicide attempts triggered by her misery, Eva Braun was as helplessly transfixed by Hitler as were thousands of other young women. It was a kind of emotional spider's web that she could not escape.

It is true that many young German girls dreamed of being married to the Führer. Some became so obsessed with Hitler they refused to take a boyfriend or accept marriage proposals. Yet many of the women who worshipped him and lusted after him as young girls can find no explanation for their emotional behaviour today. Whenever Hitler approached large groups of German females, hysteria would break out. No politician of the modern world has ever have received the adoration that this man did during his brief and violent career.

The only way we can really explore Hitler's influence is to talk to the women who, as young girls, fell under his spell. Those women who are prepared to reveal their feelings from that time often do so through written narratives. Even today, many are too embarrassed to speak openly of their emotions in face-to-face interviews. This is perfectly understandable. Such a subject is highly personal. The following material is very intimate. Some may construe it as erotic, others pornographic. Yet to clearly understand the Hitler personality cult we have to pull back the curtains to reveal the deep desires that once lurked behind them.

Dana Hahn was fourteen in 1938 and recalls:

> Naturally my family were sympathisers of National Socialism. In our home Hitler was like a god. My parents and grandparents all adored him. His speeches were listened to on our radio. A few years before 1938 my father took me to a meeting where Hitler briefly addressed the crowds. I kept asking my father 'Who is that man? Who is he?' He kept saying 'Be quiet, Dana,

just listen'. The fury with which Hitler spoke was like being struck by a stone. He berated those he viewed as traitors to Germany and threatened to expel every Jew and traitor from our land. They were powerful sentiments and, as a youngster, they proved influential on my outlook.

With my parents' direction this was unavoidable. We had Hitler's picture on a wall in our small living room and in the hallway. I don't know what it was, but I just became so fascinated by the man. I was at a rally of the BDM as we were all in the girls' league. Hitler came among us and shook hands with us. He had a warm, friendly smile and gentle handshake. Baldur Von Schirach was at his side but I was not interested in him at all and I ignored him completely. It was not because I did not like him or anything, just that Hitler had me riveted. I could not take my eyes off him. This was the great man himself and I had just shaken his hand. I was enthralled and all the other girls were too. When I got home I ran up the stairs to my room and lay on my bed thinking about Hitler. I wanted a poster of him to put on my bedroom wall. My parents would not permit any wall hangings in my room other than a Hitler picture. I got a nice poster of Hitler through the BDM. I put it up on my wall where I could kiss it each night before I went to sleep, and each morning when I got up for school and things. I can't describe what I felt though. It was just some strange kind of magnetism. Here was a man old enough to be my father and I just wanted to get close to him again. I used to daydream how nice it would be to be with him or working with him. I think most of us felt the same way. I know some of my friends did as we talked about how we felt about Hitler privately amongst ourselves. Initially there was no sexual attraction or feelings, but over time this slowly changed.

Karin Metzl recalled:

The first time I saw him [Hitler] in Berlin I do not know what came over me. I was twenty-two years old at the time so was no baby. I pushed my way through the crowd and even knocked one girl over in the process. I recall the girl on the floor nursing a cut knee and cursing me with 'you stupid idiot'. I was just driven by some invisible force. I had to get to him and feel his hands around my hands. I had to look him in the eyes and, if nothing more, say hello to him. I had to have his acknowledgement in some personal sense. I pushed my way through the crowd. I was thinking of nothing or anyone else. When I got to the front of the crowd, I shouted as loud as I could over the top of the others who were also shouting for his attention. The soldiers were straining to stop us all from breaking out and rushing him. I shouted 'My Führer! My Führer' repeatedly. Hitler looked across and walked towards me. I thrust out my arm and shouted 'Heil Hitler'. Then I reached out to him with my arms fully stretched. The moment he took my hands in his and smiled at me time seemed to stop. It seemed in that instant there was no one else around me, just me and him. I held onto his hands tightly even though I knew he could not stand on the spot for too much longer. I felt if I let him go that would be it. I would lose him forever and never see him again like this. One of his entourage quickly but gently pulled my hands away from him, breaking the link I had with him. He did glance back at me and just smiled and I think he said 'Thank you'. As I watched him walk on I could see many girls who had already shaken his hand running off ahead to try and get another handshake with him. Thinking that was a great idea, I did the same and ran after them. We were all shouting 'Heil! Heil!' The noise was just deafening. We grouped together like a beehive, all waiting once again for him to come near and another chance to hold his hands. As he approached I could feel myself being pushed from behind as the crowd tried to surge forwards. The soldiers trying to hold us back looked at one another, totally bemused by the spectacle. Again we held out our hands and shouted as loud as we could. Again he looked, and I don't know if he recognised me, but he again took my hands, then quickly went on to the next girls. As he walked away and got into his open-top car the emotion of the moment became too much.

I covered my face with my hands and cried. I was not alone. Afterwards all the girls were crying and wailing.

I was totally in love with Hitler at that time. I had a boyfriend and I saw him a couple of days after. I felt nothing for him anymore though. In an instant I lost all interest in him. I tried hard to ignore it and not to be mean to him. As he made love to me all I could think about was Hitler. I closed my eyes and imagined it was Hitler making love to me rather than my boyfriend. I occasionally opened my eyes and glanced across the room at the picture I had hanging on my wall. It was a portrait of Hitler. Orgasms ripped through my body in a way they had never done so before. I dug my nails hard into his back and cried out loudly. He must have enjoyed it as he did the same. Afterwards, there was an awkward silence. I couldn't tell him how I felt at that moment. It would not have been fair. I decided once he'd gone I would write him a letter explaining it all and telling him we were over and that he should not come back.

The following text was a piece received from Ursula Krause-Schreiber, the daughter of a former BDM girl from Hamburg. She explained that it was discovered in a scrap book which belonged to her mother. The scrap book was filled with newspaper cuttings of Hitler, along with her mother's proficiency certificates. There were also numerous handwritten notes which her mother had included in the book. It appears her mother had penned numerous love letters to Hitler, none of which had been sent to their intended recipient. The existence of the book was known to Ursula, though her mother would never let her look through it. It was only after her mother's passing, in November 1997, that she was able to read through its contents. Discussing the book with me, Ursula said:

I was aware of this scrap book that my mother had kept hidden in her wardrobe with other personal letters and things, yet I was forbidden to read it. I used to ask her and she would flick through certain pages and just show me the certificates she had earned, which she had glued into the book's pages.

After that she would say 'That is it, no more', and she would put the book away. I never dared to go through her things while I was at home. To be honest, when she died that November in 1997 I expected to find the book gone. I had imagined she would have thrown it out or burned it. That is what I thought when I first read through it. It shocked me, as it would any child reading their mother's words like that. Some of the things she had written were very explicit. She would have been sixteen years old at that time and, of course, living at home. My grandparents died years ago and they never talked about the war so this book was the only real view of it I had.

Although unwilling to reveal her mother's name, or allow any photographs of her to be used, the following piece from the book written by her mother provides some insight into the infatuation some girls developed for Adolf Hitler.

I lie in my bed and stare at the ceiling. There is only the flicker of the candlelight which casts shadows around the room. These shadows are like dancers at some kind of pagan ball. A moth flutters in, carried by the warm breeze. The moth begins its orbit around the source of light. It is drawn ever closer to the flame, unaware of the danger. I watch, fascinated, as both moth and flame meet. Under the caress of the flame the creature shrivels and falls onto the bedside table. The wings of the creature burn like those of an enemy plane. The heat is somewhat stifling in this room. I kick off the covers in the hope that somehow I might feel cooler. I can't sleep. I am totally restless. On my wall hangs the Führer's picture. It is the only picture I will ever have in my room. I love our Führer. No other man could possibly hold my heart as dear as him. I look at the picture and wish I could live with our Führer. I know this can never be, but I dream about it all the same. The masculine features combined with my own thoughts arouse me. I try and close my eyes and sleep but the thoughts grow, along with the images within my mind. My hand moves down below and I pull up my nightgown.

I am exposed to the Führer. I imagine I am waiting for him.
My fingers run down my stomach to the insides of my thighs.
Just a few circular motions of my fingers and I am in heaven.
It feels so nice. I don't want this feeling to stop and it seems
to last for ages. A stifled moan is heard by my parents. I start
coughing and pretend my throat is dry. My father shouts
out for me to extinguish the candles and to go to sleep this
minute. I roll out of my bed blow out the candles and smile
to myself and shout out 'Yes, papa'. I climb back into my bed
roll onto my side and within minutes I am fast asleep. I am
happy and content. I wish my Führer a goodnight wherever
he is tonight and I pray for his safety, for now and the years to
come. In this darkness remain only the dark secret whispers
of my own thoughts. The reptilian intentions of all other men
mean nothing to me.

In another passage Ursula's mother wrote:

Today I walked into the town with Herr Wardorfer's son
Erich. It was very pleasant and I allowed him to hold my
hand on the way back. I think he thought I must like him
or something. We sat on the bridge for a few minutes and
watched the stream below. He threw sticks into the water
and we watched them disappear. It was then he took my hand
and attempted to kiss me on the mouth. He was visibly shocked
when I pulled away from him. 'What are you doing?' I asked
him. He just replied that he liked me and thought I liked him
too. I had to tell him, 'There is only one man I want to be
with'. He was becoming angry because I wouldn't tell him who
it was. He went through a list of all the local boys in our town
we knew. Eventually I told him I was in love with our Führer.
'What', he said, 'You're in love with the Führer? Are you out
of your mind?' He then went on to say, 'The Führer has a
woman. Do you not understand this? What's the matter with
you?' I did not reply and just sat watching the water. He then
said 'I am fucking over with this, goodbye.' He stormed off
and he did not call at our house again. Why is it such a problem

for these boys to understand that if one is in love then it can't be betrayed? The trust my Führer has in me to be totally loyal to him extends far beyond all my social duties and other considerations.

Vaida Raab, a former BDM girl I had the pleasure of talking to many times during the writing of *Hitler's Girls – Doves Amongst Eagles* recalls her feelings towards Adolf Hitler:

With me there was of course excitement every time Hitler's name was mentioned. It was not a sexual excitement though. Oh, God, no, it was never like that with me. It was more a pop star kind of excitement, if you understand. I felt excited to see Hitler because he was this famous figure of ours. He had made the German nation great and respected in the eyes of the world again. Well, he did this for a short period, didn't he? He was like a god to us. We had been raised and educated to believe in him in that way. Of course, I knew many girls who felt differently towards Hitler. Some of them used to say how they would give themselves to Hitler if he so desired them. Was it love or just juvenile infatuation? I don't know, but the way some of the girls spoke about Hitler they were genuinely besotted with him. I revered him more in the religious sense than any sexual or emotional sense. As god-like as the Führer was, his looks did not appeal to me, and he was very old [she laughs]. Of course, if I had told anyone that back in the day I would have been in serious trouble. I remember one of my friends in the BDM. We were both fourteen at the time. She developed an obsession for Hitler. At first it was *Mein Kampf*, the book Hitler had written. After she had read that book from cover to cover she went on to other things. She would start saving up the *Deutscher Beobachter* press cuttings and any other publication with Hitler's picture in it. Her father collected all the Hitler cigarette card photos and I remember this album with them all inside. It was a prized possession of hers and she adored it. She kept it under her pillows. I used to go round to her house and we would be up in her bedroom. She would be there, lying on her bed, wearing just her gym vest and shorts and she would be looking through her latest collection of Hitler cuttings. She would lie there, like some naïve Lolita, saying, 'Do you know, Vaida, I so love him, you know'. I would just say 'Oh, how sweet of you'. She was a lovely girl but I had the feeling she was kidding herself and maybe taking things a little too far.

Rochus Misch, who served in the *Führerbegleitkommando* [Führer Escort Command, or FBK] from 1940 to April 1945, gave some unique perspective to the subject of Third Reich 'groupies'. Rochus Misch had served as an *Oberscharführer* [Sergeant] in the 1st SS Panzer Division *Leibstandarte SS Adolf Hitler*. He was badly wounded during the first month of the fighting in the Polish campaign. Within the FBK he served as Hitler's bodyguard, courier and telephone operator. Rochus Misch was present in the Führerbunker when Adolf Hitler and Eva Braun committed suicide on 30 April 1945. While he was not in the room with them during the suicide, he was one of the first to see the bodies of Hitler and Braun. Rochus Misch gave many interviews over the years prior to his death on 5 September 2013 in Berlin. He was a man who never attempted to deny his past and would speak to you in a friendly and honest manner. When I asked him about the effect that Adolf Hitler had over so many women during the Third Reich he recalled:

Of course, I can only give an opinion from a male perspective. I was on the Führer's staff and even this carried with it a great amount of prestige. The people envied you for it and your glass was never empty of the best wines and champagne. You would have no end of offers from the ladies either. I was not stupid. I understood that many, if not all, of them were only trying to get close to you because you were on the Führer's staff. Maybe they felt that this would elevate their position over their peers and within our society. I knew officers who used their positions in Hitler's staff to get the girls. It was all too easy for them really. Once they had their fun they would go on to the next one, and so on. Many of the girls were just so young and naïve they could not see that they were being used.

Martin Bormann enjoyed the women that were attracted to him purely because he was the Führer's secretary. The women had sex with him knowing full well that he had a wife at home waiting for him, and children of course. This didn't seem to matter though. There were those who used their position within the administration solely for the purpose of procuring young women. Personally all that business was not for me. First and foremost, I was a soldier of the Waffen SS. I was, and still am, proud of that. I have no regrets about that whatsoever. Honesty and loyalty were my sworn attributes and I never once deviated from them. People ask 'why did women throw themselves at Hitler in the way they did?' Many were teenaged girls and you would think him more their father than lover. They did not see it that way though. The mind of a female, they used to say, was governed solely by their emotions. I don't know what it was, I really don't. Hitler was what I would describe as friendly and polite to me in the working relationship I had with him. I saw him angry on some occasions, but he never got angry with me, just those fools he had surrounding him [he laughs].

Martin Schneider, who also served in the FBK, recalled how many of the leading Nazis, including Goebbels, Bormann and Von Ribbentrop, scoffed at the droves of females expressing their love and adoration for Hitler.

These young girls and young women were ripe for being sexually exploited. People like Bormann and Goebbels were sexual predators. They were carrying on all the time with women on the side as you might say it. These men had utter contempt, not only for the girls and women they were having sex with, but their wives and children too. Hitler had to intervene on more than one occasion with Goebbels because of his sexual antics. Bormann was a little different. He was more discreet, and Hitler did not have to keep warning him about scandal like he did with Goebbels. In private these high ranking figures would often voice their contempt. When Goebbels was in private and drinking champagne his true personality often came through. He said once, 'Many a young girl pleasures herself over our Führer's image [...] If it brings them comfort, that overwhelming sense of belonging that all women crave, then leave them alone, let them do it. So long as they are doing this we understand we have their love, dedication and, most importantly, their loyalty.' One of the group then said to Goebbels. In fact, I think it was Wunsche, who said it jokingly, 'What if one of your girls was doing the same?' His mood changed, then the smile vanished. He sat there with a face like thunder yet said nothing. For a few seconds it was quiet then we were dismissed from the room. The doors slammed shut behind us and, as we walked down the long corridor, I could hear shouting [...] Someone had touched one of Goebbel's raw nerves. These things happened frequently in private. They were always squabbling over stupid things and people today wonder why we lost the war.

Former BDM girl Wiener Katte, from Aachen, gave her personal opinion on why Adolf Hitler seemed to captivate girls and women:

Hitler, in the physical sense, was not attractive. He was too old for one thing. If I had ever brought a man home five years older than me to meet my parents and brother they would have killed him [she laughs]. Hitler was twenty-two years older than Eva Braun when they first met. She was seventeen and he was forty. I could never have got away with that. I think what captivated most women was the sense of power that he had over the nation and them too. Maybe that excited them emotionally, though some were really attracted to him sexually and felt compelled to not take boyfriends. It was only when, through state influence, they were told that marriage and producing children was the best way a girl could express her love for Hitler that attitudes changed. Some of these girls were very deluded in dedicating themselves to Hitler in the wrong way. I knew one girl who swore she would remain celibate until Hitler himself took her virginity and innocence. It was quite crazy. I think the whole, thing the allure as you say, was based purely upon Hitler's power over his people. That was enough to captivate and secure the adoration of many German girls at the time. Others may tell you differently, I don't know, but this is just what I think.

Jochen Maier, who was a young private soldier, recalls:

During our military training at the barracks in Spandau some of the soldiers would bring girls into the barracks. I remember one, and you would not believe what I saw the one time. I came back after having some drinks with some of the boys from my regiment. I walked into our sleeping quarters and found another private having sex with a blonde, pigtailed girl. She looked way younger than he was. He was having sex with her from behind. She was kneeling down on all fours on his bunk. What shocked me most was that she was holding onto to this picture of Hitler. She was looking at this while he was having sex with her. After a minute they noticed my presence. The girl just looked across at me and giggled. He just carried on and gave me a look that said 'bet you wish you could have this'. I left and went back outside, where I stood and smoked a cigarette. When I returned a while later the girl had gone, but she had left the picture on the private's bed. After the Second World War I used to think 'what did these young girls see in a man like Hitler?' Maybe his intellect attracted them, I don't know. I just thought it was all very weird. Our girls were not promiscuous. We were young and healthy and enjoyed sex like everyone else. Why should we not have?

Ellie Kauffmann recalls:

My best friend had a sister. Whenever her older brother came home she would search through his jacket pockets for contraceptives. They were a brand called Vulkan or something. She used to say to me, quite brazenly and without any embarrassment, 'I like the feeling of being fucked, it is wonderful. I close my eyes and all I can think of is him.' I said to her, 'Who are you referring to?' She said to me, 'Oh, come on, Elizabeth, don't be so silly. Our Führer of course.' I was quite shocked, but she then went on to say, 'My boyfriend is just a boy, he's hardly a man.' She was of the opinion that any young girl who had not satisfied herself by fantasising over Hitler was not a true follower.

Chapter Six

Salon Kitty

Salon Kitty was the name of one of the Third Reich's lesser known institutions. Although operating primarily as a brothel, Salon Kitty was soon put to far more sinister uses by the SD [*Sicherheisdienst*], the intelligence agency of the SS and Nazi Party. Although brothels, and prostitution in general, were declared illegal in Hitler's Third Reich, it appears an exception to this rule was made for 'Pension Schmidt', as it was originally known. Pension Schmidt had been in existence throughout the 1930s and began to thrive as a business from around 1940. Its premises were at 11 Giesebrechtstrasse in Charlottenburg, a wealthy district of Berlin. It stood next door to the apartment of Ernst Kaltenbrunner, who was head of the Reich Security Service. The brothel was managed throughout its existence by its original proprietor, a woman named Katharina Zammit, who became known as Kitty Schmidt. Far from being sympathetic to National Socialism, Kitty had been transferring large sums of money into British banks prior to her attempt at leaving Germany. She did this by using those fleeing Germany as her couriers. Kitty made an attempt to leave Germany on 28 June 1939, but was arrested at the Dutch border by members of the Nazi intelligence agency. She was taken to Gestapo headquarters and, after some questioning, was presented with an ultimatum by Walter Schellenberg.

Schellenberg worked in the counter-intelligence department of the SD. He told Kitty she could either work for the Nazi intelligence-gathering agency or be sent to a concentration camp. Kitty was not happy with this arrangement but had little choice other than to comply. It was proposed by SS General Reinhard Heydrich that Pension Schmidt be used for intelligence and espionage purposes. Once this had been agreed between Heydrich and Schellenberg, the brothel was expanded and renovated to the highest standards. Schellenberg had covert listening devices fitted in each of the rooms: inside pictures, in bedside tables and vases, and in the headboards of the beds where conversation made during lovemaking could be clearly detected. The basement of number 10 Meinecke Strasse, just a short distance from the salon, served as the main intelligence gathering suite. Here a staff of five 'listeners' would record and log all of the conversations taking place in the bedrooms. In January 1941 it was decided that the whole monitoring operation be transferred to Gestapo headquarters in Prinz Abrechtstrasse.

Naturally, young women had to be specially selected to serve in this establishment. An advert was drafted which read 'Wanted – women and girls who are intelligent, multilingual, nationalistically minded and, furthermore, man crazy'. At the same time, Berlin's *Sittenpolizei* [vice squad] went out on the streets arresting dozens of local prostitutes, who were then taken back to the *Sittenpolizei* stations to undergo selection. The *Sittenpolizei* were under strict orders to select only the most beautiful and sexually attractive girls. After selection, they were interviewed to ascertain their suitability and then asked if they would be prepared to work for the intelligence services. Those who initially declined the offer were threatened with incarceration in a concentration camp. Evidence also suggests that young girls and women from outside Germany were sought out for service in Pension Schmidt. There were even girls from the East who were brought in for the gratification of the Nazi elite. Beautiful young women from the East with blonde-haired and blue-eyed Aryan appearance were deemed fit, provided they passed some basic tests. Refusal to comply would be met with death threats to the women and their families. The girls who were selected to work in the salon then underwent training to recognise military uniforms and insignia. They were also schooled in the techniques of gaining information through innocuous conversation. The girls and women were not told that the rooms were bugged so each girl had to make an individual report after each client had left the room.

Surprisingly, some of the women working at Pension Schmidt came from some of Berlin's wealthiest families; and most of them were married. Their motivation derived from providing a valuable service to the Reich while also having an opportunity to sleep with some of the most powerful men in its service. The salon was not only designed to attract the elite of German society. Soon it was graced with the presence of wealthy foreigners such as politicians, industrialists, high-ranking military officers and diplomats. The salon also had a number of hand-picked girls who were allowed to leave the premises and spend the night with various important figures.

Some of the Third Reich's most senior figures became frequent visitors. SS General Sepp Dietrich was one such client. Dietrich once requested twenty girls for an all-night sex party. He was unaware that his room was bugged but revealed nothing of interest to those listening in. Joseph Goebbels was another frequent visitor. Goebbels was known for enjoying lesbian displays even though such behaviour was, at the time, considered anti-social. Italian dictator Benito Mussolini's son-in-law, Galeazzo Ciano, visited the salon at regular intervals. Perhaps the most important Nazi visitor was Reinhard Heydrich. He presented an image of a supposedly happily married father of two young boys and a champion of Aryan philosophy. Whenever Heydrich visited the salon he insisted that all listening devices and their associated communication lines be disconnected. One of the Third Reich's most evil figures, and one of the main architects of the Holocaust, Heydrich was meticulous in covering his tracks.

To say that it was difficult obtaining first-hand information about Pension Schmidt and those who enjoyed its services, other than what is generally known, would be an understatement. After some three years of research into the women and girls procured for the salon, I was contacted by Rainier Poehl. Her great grandmother, Wilhelmina, was just twenty years old at the time. It appears she had drifted in and out of prostitution for some years, but Rainier could find no indication of when she became involved in this trade. It is known that Wilhelmina frequented the Kurfurstenstrasse, the infamous street that has been the haunt of Berlin's sex workers for over 130 years, and had been unfortunate enough to have been arrested outside a house near the street. Born in Berlin in October 1920, Wilhelmina was a captivating beauty and, although she spent the next two days in jail after her arrest, she was visited by a person whose identity remains unknown. It was after the visit of this unknown person that she was referred to Pension Schmidt. Rainier never discovered her great grandmother's past until she inherited a small diary which had belonged to her mother. Rainier told me:

> I think it's all very sad. I don't even think my mother was aware of the significance of this document. I don't believe in

all honesty that she could have ever read it. Had she done so, and discovered certain truths, she would have most certainly burned it to protect the family name. She was very much like that. Very much an old-fashioned woman, you could say. She would not have approved of this at all. She may have known, but if she did she never spoke of it once. I know my mother was largely brought up by an aunt and I sensed her childhood was not all happy. I sensed something, but could never figure out what it was. It was something we did not talk about.

Wilhelmina's diary was by no means extensive, but her writings record some of the activities of the clients she had been forced, under the threat of death, to entertain. She wrote:

Under duress we come to this place. Myself, two other women and another girl who says she is eighteen, but I don't believe her. She looks more like fifteen. It's a way out in some ways. We get good food, the best medical care, a roof over our heads and, quite often, as much champagne as we can drink. We are told we can either work for the Führer or get on a cattle truck to one of the camps. We all understand what that meant. Not one of us wishes to join the cattle trucks, so what choice is there really? They try and teach you to be the best seductress. Seduction is not something you teach a woman. A woman's seductive skills are in her instincts as a woman. There is no love in this trade and we women are all actresses here. They look after us well and we have many luxuries that many people don't have.

Only the very elite come here. It's an exclusive club. We are asked to talk to the clients and discover their opinions on current affairs, people and news. Any political opinions or words of discontent we have to write down, but only when the client has left the room. Any information we write down is collected afterwards. But where does this information go to? It doesn't bother me and is not my concern what happens to these fools. If they are so dumb that they cannot smell a rat, or that other motives exist within the walls of this place, then so be it.

Dietrich, the SS General, is one of the worst. He comes here and asks for me. He is fat, balding and old, and smells of bodily odour when he removes his fine white, silk shirt. He is fit for a man of his age and makes good use of the time he has with me. It is far from pleasurable. He enjoys the whole process; a striptease, a massage. He insists I use my mouth on him and then there is the act itself. He asks me to sit astride him as if I am riding a stallion. I feel his course grey chest hair against my nipples. I try hard to make this old man come quickly so it will all be over. His stamina is good. He rolls me over onto my back and I am just thinking 'In God's name, hurry up'. There is nothing I want more than to roll this fat, naked old walrus from off me. Should I ever dare, no doubt I would be taken away and a pistol put to my head. Men like Dietrich are all the same. Their lust for young women is an allure they can't fight. They paw and kiss your body then do what they want and you can't say no. Dietrich is a bore. He doesn't talk much, other than the most basic of pleasantries. He often brings good champagne, unlike the rat's piss the others sometimes drink. I don't mind as it helps nullify the whole experience. Many of us will be alcoholics before long. Alcohol is the only thing that kills the pain. I'm sure a man like Dietrich has opinions and dislikes but his loyalty is unquestionable. It's the only honourable thing you can say of an SS man like him.

Goebbels is another. One of the worst. A 'filthy dwarf' one girl once called him. She was taken out of the salon in just her underwear in quite a brutal fashion. We never saw or heard anything from her again. No one knows what happened to her, but it is obvious to many of us. They probably killed her. Goebbels is the creature we all dread. He cuts a poor physical specimen. Not content with his wife and children, he comes here regularly. He wants to go through every girl in the house, he says, laughing. Worst of all, he requests another girl to join me. He asks us to do what girls do to one another when they are consumed with passion. He sits in a chair, watching us kiss on the bed before him. He makes jokes that are not funny, yet we have to laugh all the same. It's like another day in the office for him. Then, of course, we have to entertain this plucked chicken of a man as he joins us on the bed. He has a deformed foot and, not surprisingly, he keeps this ugly feature covered. He keeps one sock on. We take it in turns to pleasure him, hoping he will come then not want to fuck us both. He stops us, of course, then makes love to both of us. When he finishes inside me, he just gets up and stands there, as if expecting us to applaud or bow to him. He then leaves, presumably to go back home to dear Magda and the children. Does she know of her imp of a husband's little games here with us? I can only imagine that she must and is happy with this arrangement. Does he share his perverted desires with her too? When he leaves we have nothing to write, other than the fact he has showered us with remarks upon our German beauty and what he did with us.

Martin Bormann is another regular guest. He enters the salon with the stealth of a weasel. He appears shy, uncomfortable and twitchy, as if ready to flee at the slightest sound. Bormann's behaviour is typical of any man who is cheating on his beloved. He disappears quickly into a room and afterwards he insists on being let out through the back door. Youth leader Von Schirach has been here on a number of occasions. He swaggers in, consumed within his own self-importance. He is another who prefers the youngest girls. I used to wonder if his Hitler Youth or his BDM girls were not good enough. I have never seen Himmler here but many of his SS staff are here quite often. Kaltenbrunner is another who makes full use of the benefits just next door. I've heard about him and he has the nickname of 'a few grunts and it's all over'. It could all be quite amusing if it were not so seedy. We don't always sleep well in our beds with sheets wet through. Our lives appear a dead end. A well-paid dead end.

On 17 July 1942 Pension Schmidt was damaged during an air raid on Berlin. It was decided that the whole prostitution operation would be relocated to the first floor of the building, where it would be safer. The Pension Schmidt was then renamed Salon Kitty, a name it retained until the end of the war in 1945. At the end of the war, Wilhelmina recorded one final moment in her diary. The faded, pencil-written narrative took some effort for even Rainier to read.

> The fighting started and liberation began. We were safe here in the basement. No clean water but lots of alcohol [...] There are Soviets everywhere and tanks everywhere. The Soviets have been through the building. They left me alone and took wine and cigarettes. They marvel at the stocks of champagne we have. They scurry away with arms full of bottles. Everyone else has left the building. There are clothes, bottles of wine, shoes, handbags, cigarettes and fur coats left strewn about the rooms. I pick up a coat and put it on and I walk out of the place. As I walk outside I take one look back. Then I am faced with the smell, the smoke, the rubble, the detritus of warfare, the dead dogs and cats and human remains, rotting beneath tons of smashed concrete. There is little trade for whores here. Where am I going? I don't know. Does home still exist? Orientation is difficult as buildings are now gone, and remembering where all of your old haunts once were is not as easy as it was.

In the years after the Second World War Katherina Zammit shed her Kitty Schmidt nickname, settling down to a quieter life. It is believed that Salon Kitty continued to operate as a brothel after the Second World War, when the business was handed over to Zammit's son and daughter. Zammit refused to talk about the running of Salon Kitty, or to reveal any information about her former employers. This appears somewhat odd when one considers how she was originally coerced into complying with her former employers' wishes. Rainier's great grandmother, Wilhelmina, was of the opinion that, even after the war, there were fears of reprisal from former members of the Nazi security services. Either way, the now-infamous brothel Madame of the Third Reich took her secrets to the grave when she died, aged seventy-one, in 1954.

It is believed that the Soviets recovered 25,000 recordings made at Salon Kitty. These recordings were retained as the property of the Stasi [East German Security Service] after 1945. Virtually all of the recordings have since been claimed to be either lost or destroyed due to their lack of post-war significance. How long after the Second World War Salon Kitty operated as a brothel is not known. In 1988 the former brothel was in use as a guitar studio. In the 1990s the building was turned into a refuge for asylum seekers, which soon closed due to protests from the local residents. Today, the grand-looking house still stands on the Giesebrechtstrasse in Charlottenburg. Its seedy history somehow lost in the mists of time and seemingly invisible to the many thousands of tourists who visit the area.

In 2003 Rainier retraced her great grandmother's footsteps to that grand house on the Giesebrechtstrasse. She stood outside for a few minutes, appearing to absorb some invisible energy. Taking an old photograph of her great grandmother from her jacket pocket, she said, 'It's weird to think that she was once here and that she came and went from this very building that I am now standing outside. I wish I was not almost seventy years too late. I wish I could go back in time. I wish I could just hold her and embrace her and give her some of the warmth and comfort that she had obviously been missing in her young life. There is no anger towards her, just a terrible weight of sadness.'

At this point Rainier sheds tears for the great grandmother she never knew. For a minute she sobs to the point where a passer-by asks her if she is okay. She explains she is fine and the young man continues on his way. She recalls of that day: 'I not only thought of how she had been a victim of some unforeseeable circumstance, now very long ago, but of all the evil that had walked up and down the steps of this place.'

Rainier kisses a single red rose she has brought with her, before carefully placing it down on the steps of the building that was once home of sorts to her great grandmother. It is the closing of one of the chapters of Rainier's life. She wipes the tears away from her eyes and makes her journey back home.

Chapter Seven

A French Adventure

By the summer of 1940 the two former BDM girls, Thelma Ortge and Gabbi Becker, whose friendship had begun during their school days in Berlin, were faced with some unenviable choices. Having been through Reich Labour Service, both girls now found themselves back home without jobs. Thelma explains:

We were at war, but only in the early stages, and we were doing well at this time. There was not a call up or anything then in 1940. You had the choice of just settling down to marriage and children or finding a job in a shop, or one of the cafés or something. In fact, the pressure to get married was greater than anything else. My parents were not too bad, but they felt that if I met a young man and got married I would be safely out of the reach of the Nazis in a quiet village somewhere. At nineteen I felt I was not ready for all the mess of babies and things. I knew it was something we would have to do, but at that moment I just wanted to have some fun in life. Gabbi Becker, my friend, felt exactly the same way. She had applied for a few positions, including one with a scientific research institute. They turned her down even though she was qualified for the post. There was a sense that there were prejudices against us just because we were young girls. I applied for various local jobs, including a job at a postal office. The man I spoke to told me, 'Look, this can be heavy work at times. You will find yourself working in the cold and the rain and the heat of the day. Would you not be better off at home with your mother, that's where you girls belong, not here doing a man's work.' I'm afraid I lost my temper with this imbecile. I was so angry I could not help it and I swore at him. 'Well, fuck your job, I will go elsewhere,' I snapped at the old fool. As I stormed off he shouted, 'And I will be telling your father of this behaviour.' I stopped, turned around, and just said, 'Oh, really. How are you going to do that then? You do not even know my father!' He just stood and watched me storm off in a mood.

It was Gabbi's parents who first heard that the Luftwaffe needed female staff in their canteens, and cleaners and things for their bases. The Luftwaffe airfield at Abbeville, in conquered France, was not a great distance from Cologne. Some phone calls were made and as I left Gabbi's house she was already excitedly packing a suitcase with things for the trip. I knew my parents would be angry about our plans. They were not happy with me being friends with Gabbi as she and her family supported the National Socialists. I felt an argument may be imminent so I walked into our house, quietly took a deep breath and sat in the living room with my parents. I told them I was going to Abbeville to work in the canteens at a Luftwaffe airbase. My father almost choked and said, 'You are what?' He then began to lecture me, 'Why, in God's name, are you going there? Do you know it's in a war zone? It's dangerous.' I argued that I wanted to work but men in this town don't want to work side by side with us women. 'Then stay here with your mother, for God's sake,' was father's answer. I explained I was going with Gabbi and father then started to moan about her, 'I might have known Gabbrielle Becker would have been something to do with this. Has that girl brainwashed you or something? Next thing you will be wearing a Hitler armband!' I tried to stay calm but felt my frustration boiling up in me again. I told my parents I was going and it was all arranged with Gabbi's father. As I went up to my room to pack, things were silent and frosty. I came downstairs with my bag and told my parents I was going now. Neither of them came to me to say goodbye, they just sat in their chairs ignoring me. I told them I would write when I got to France. Before I closed the door behind me, I said, 'Father, mother, I do love you, you know. I will write soon. I will be fine, I promise you.'

Gabbi's father drove us to the train station where we waited for the train to Cologne. We were both a little quiet as this was the farthest either of us would ever have gone away from home since our labour service duty. Gabbi seemed to sense when I was not happy or something was on my mind. As we sat waiting for the train to arrive she picked up my hand and held it in hers. Caressing my knuckles with her soft fingers, she said, 'Don't worry. Everything will be very good, you will see.' Gabbi's strong yet compassionate nature was such a contrast to her National Socialist views. The National Socialists condoned the use of violence yet this girl was kind, caring, funny, loving and very intelligent. She was just the kind of friend that you wanted. She would do anything for you.

The train to Cologne was not far away. We heard the whistles and the 'puff, puff' noise of the engine as it approached the station. We climbed aboard, engulfed in a silvery grey veil of smoke and steam. Like excited children, we ran along the carriage and took our seats. Gabbi sat opposite me and we both stared out of the window in anticipation of the adventure which lay ahead of us. As the train pulled away, a man in uniform came along and asked to see our travel documents. We presented them along with our tickets. He looked at us sternly then flickered the hint of a smile before thanking us and walking on to the other people. Gabbi remarked, 'Is it that out of the normal to see two girls travelling on a train these days?' We laughed to each other about this as everywhere we went people would stare at us. The journey was quite a steady one. The gentle rocking of the train was almost hypnotic and I found my eyes growing ever heavy. Before I knew it I was fast asleep. When I woke a while later I found that Gabbi had moved from her seat and was next to me with her head on my chest and her knees drawn up onto the seat. She was fast asleep. I put my arms around her, resting my chin on the top of her head and dozed off again.

We were both startled awake as the uniformed man shook us to wake us up. 'Are you two getting off or what?' he grunted at us. We quickly stood up, trying to gather our senses and grab our cases. Gabbi was still half asleep and fell over in the gangway like a drunk man. She fell onto her suitcase and there were roars of laughter. She angrily got to her feet, grabbed her suitcase and dragged it off the train onto the platform. We put our bags down and sat on a bench on the platform as we waited for the train to leave. Gabbi was still angry from falling over on the train and said, 'Idiots! How dare they laugh like that.' I remarked, 'Well, it was kind of funny, Gabbi.' She looked at me and tried to keep a serious face, but she couldn't. We both burst out laughing and when we calmed down we took out some sandwiches that Gabbi's mother had made for us. After eating them, we discovered the train to Abbeville would not get in until the following morning. Again the mood changed and Gabbi said, 'Oh, fuck! Well, that really is good, isn't it!' I told her she shouldn't be swearing like that and she just went on, 'Well, what do you expect? We come all this way and there's no train to take us the rest of the way until morning.' She then kicked her suitcase and shouted, 'Fuck, fuck, fuck and fuck!' I started laughing at her again as she really was funny when she got angry about something.

A voice from the platform then boomed, 'Hoi! Stop that nonsense this minute, do you hear me?' We didn't know who this man was but we sat back down and Gabbi calmed down after a while. The same man later came back and, seeing that we were still sat there, asked us our business. We said we would have to stay at the station all night as the train to Abbeville was not in until morning. We had nowhere else to go for the night. The man then told us, 'Pick up your bags. You can come and stay with my wife and I for the night. It's not safe for young ladies to be out alone all night.' We put our bags into the back of his car and jumped into the back seat. Just a short drive and we were pulling up outside a row of terraced houses at the edge of a small village. The houses were beautiful, painted white and with roses and other flowers in full bloom in the gardens. It was late afternoon by this time and we were invited into the man's home to meet his wife and son. They made us a hot coffee each, sat us down and asked where we had come from and where we were going. We explained we were going to Abbeville to work. The man and his wife were puzzled until we told them we were going to work at the Luftwaffe airfield there. 'Ah, yes,' the man replied, 'that's a pretty big one they've got there and a lot of action going on there too, but thankfully we're not on the receiving end of it!' He told us stories of the fighter planes and bomber aircraft he had seen in the sky around this area. We sat mesmerised by the stories he was telling us. Occasionally the man's wife would interrupt him, saying, 'Ernst, are you going to bore these girls with this all night?' That was the first I learned of the man's name. He explained he had been a war veteran of the Spanish campaign with the Legion Condor as it was called. He received multiple bullet wounds to his leg and shoulder and could no longer serve. He explained his job now was as a signalman at the station.

Gabbi and me were both fascinated, but it was getting late and we had an early start in the morning so Ernst's wife showed us to a room. She explained, 'We've only the one spare room so you will have to share, if this is okay with you both.' She explained if we needed the toilet in the night to use the candle on the small table in our room as it was outside in the yard. It did not worry us as it was quite warm and not raining. We both undressed and put our nightclothes on and squeezed into the bed, which was clearly not intended for two people. We were squashed together like sardines in a tin. Gabbi made me shriek when she put her cold feet on the backs of my legs. We lay there and giggled like fools for some minutes before wishing each other a goodnight and falling asleep.

Ernst's wife roused us at seven in the morning as our train was due in around nine and we did not wish to miss this one. We both lay and tried to stretch our legs but became tangled and tumbled out of the bed onto the floor. We were in hysterics of laughter again until Gabbi spotted a spider on the wall in the corner of the room. She shrieked, grabbed her clothes and ran downstairs. Ernst's wife came upstairs and threw the spider out of the window. 'There, it's sorted now,' she said. Gabbi came back into the room, sheepishly looking around her. We washed in the small basin in our room, got dressed then went downstairs. Breakfast was just superb. We had eggs, bread and butter, and bacon, which we scoffed down as if we were starving. We helped clear and wash up and put the breakfast things away before we were ready to leave. As the heat of the day began to build, we put the suitcases in the car and Ernst drove us down to the station. When we arrived we got out our bags and we both thanked him. He told us to visit if we were ever passing and that we would always be welcome. He told us to take care when in France and not to be silly as France was still dangerous and not everyone wanted the Germans there. Funny that he should remind us of that, but we heeded his warnings.

It was a huge relief to finally arrive at Abbeville. We made our way to the airfield on foot, stopping every so often to put our bags down and have a rest. We heard a vehicle approach and, as it drew closer, could see it was one of our Luftwaffe lorries. We did not have to wave it down as the driver saw us and pulled in. There was a screech of brakes followed by a huge dust cloud. A voice bellows 'Please jump in but be quick as I don't wish to be late.' We climb up into the cab of the lorry and this young Luftwaffe man introduces himself, 'My name is Holger Gefreiter. Holger.' We introduce ourselves and, as we have German accents and are carrying suitcases, he assumes we are going to the same place that he is. 'It's not that far, just over there,' he says and points to the fields and surrounding woodlands. As we approach the entrance to the airfield we are stopped, searched and asked to present our papers and work documents. For some minutes these are examined and the guard makes a telephone call before he returns and says, 'You are okay to go through, thank you.' We then drive on down a dirt track and see buildings come into view. They are a mixture of farm buildings and what look like hastily erected barracks. In the fields are rows of Messerchmitt Bf109 fighter aircraft. We can see the dispersal huts and the pilots sitting around outside reading their papers and books. It all looks so idyllic here we both think.

The lorry stops and we jump out and collect our bags. We are told to empty our bags for inspection and both our bags and clothes are thoroughly searched. Our papers are checked again and we are escorted to the main office. An officer apologises for the search but this is a necessity with all new arrivals. 'We have to be careful here, you understand,' he explains. We enter a small office and he pulls out a wad of documents. He says, 'Well, we have work for you in the kitchens or in the laundry, if you are willing.' Me and Gabbi both say at once that we want to work in the kitchens as we are excellent cooks. 'So you should be,' he says with a kind of sarcastic smile. He then insists on showing us to the hut where we will be sleeping with eight other women who work in the kitchen, canteen and laundry. We are given beds and then unpack our things and put them away. The officer then says, 'The others will show you what to do. I'm sure you will be fine once you have settled in here. If you wish to go off this site then a pass is required but we advise you not to go anywhere on your own. We have good reasons for this and we ask your cooperation in this matter. Is this clear?' We both nod, and he says, 'Good. I will wish you a good afternoon and the other girls will be back shortly. If there is anything you need to know they will tell you.' So we sit on the beds, wondering what the other girls are going to be like. Will they like us? Will they be nice to us? I guess pretty soon we will find out.

When the other women returned to the hut I was busy writing the events of the last two days into my diary. Gabbi was lying on her bed, staring at the ceiling deep in thought. As the women entered the hut I stopped writing, shut my diary and stood up to greet them. The women introduced themselves to us in turn, shaking our hands and offering a hug. There was one, however, who appeared to be distant compared to the others. She did not seem very interested in getting to know either me or Gabbi. After talking for a few minutes we were told that we had to be out of our beds before dawn. The fighter boys would need coffee and breakfast before commencing any operation. The eldest of the women, whose name was Diana, told us rather curtly, 'Be friendly, smile at them and be professional, and no flirting with them. Understand?' Me and Gabbi looked at one another, raising our eyebrows in the process. We were then shown where air raid shelters were located if we needed to use them. We were also told about etiquette when going into the nearby town. There were many dos and don'ts. We were told not to take French boyfriends or accept anything from strangers. We were told only to buy from legitimate shops. We were also told to go out in a large group if we went out drinking. I asked them why all the fuss and was told that the French people are dangerous and that there is a resistance movement operating here. We were warned that if we did not obey the rules we could end up being raped, murdered or kidnapped. After this brief we were shown where the latrines were and where we could wash. We were also warned to watch out for rats which frequented the airfield. I hated rats and so did Gabbi and we hoped we would not encounter any. If you saw one you had to hit it with a heavy club that looked like a piece of wood. I asked if any rats had got in here before and was told they sometimes did. That they ran across you at night while you were sleeping. I really did not think much to this at all.

The evening was as hot as the daytime and we sat outside our hut in chairs and talked amongst ourselves. The sunset was beautiful and we watched the sun go down and darkness fall. We were advised to go to bed as we would be up early and, as this was our first night, we may have trouble sleeping. Me and Gabbi had beds side by side, which was good. I felt I wanted her near me and she felt the same. Neither of us slept very well. The hut was very warm in the night and sleep was restless. I kicked off my blanket, despite the fear of rats scurrying over me. I think I must have fallen asleep an hour before we were woken up to start our day. I felt like shit but here we were beginning our adventure.

We washed, grabbed some breakfast and brushed our teeth. We were then taken over to the canteen. Me and Gabbi knew what we had to do and, once we found our way around and where everything was kept, we were soon busy preparing breakfast. The pilots started coming in before it was light. They noticed the two new faces and they were very nice to us and asked us if we were getting on alright and how good the food smelled. They were as ordinary as anyone else really. They looked so handsome in their uniforms and I thought how smart and well-groomed they all were. Soon the canteen was filled with cigarette smoke and the voices of the airmen as they talked about the coming day's operations. They sat making gestures with their hands, explaining to comrades the various manoeuvres used in combat. They ate their breakfast and sat drinking coffee and smoking cigarettes before slowly filtering out to their dispersal areas where they would await instructions. We never found out anything about the operations but most days large numbers of fighters would take off and head for England. Fleets of our bombers could also be seen heading towards England. We were later told that our Luftwaffe was engaged in a battle with the British Royal Air Force and that we were winning the battle.

When we finished serving the food, we had to clean everything and wash up and then prepare the food for the next meal. It was a never-ending process and we snatched an hour's rest here and there through the day. By the time we had finished it was late in the day and we were just ready to fall into our beds. We had our turn to have days off and me and Gabbi would join others and head into the town. We would visit the cafés and the bars and be there for most of the day and night. The French seemed to just ignore us and get on with their lives. Our soldiers were everywhere so we felt quite safe. Me and Gabbi paused to take photographs of each other near the various monuments and landmarks.

Our first night out in the town was a disaster. We had drunk much too much wine and by the time we had to leave to return to the aerodrome we were very pissed. We were helped into the back of a truck and off we went. We both felt thoroughly sick on the way back. The other women seemed oblivious and just chatted as if we were not there. When we arrived back at the aerodrome we had to produce our identity passes. Gabbi had problems finding hers and her drunken state did not help matters. In the end I pulled it out of her jacket pocket for her. We just wanted to go to bed as we felt so ill. Once inside the hut, the mixture of the warm air and spinning ceiling caused by our drunkenness meant we leapt out of our beds and ran out of the door. Neither of us made it to the latrines. We collapsed onto our knees and vomited for all we were worth. A sentry spotted us and shone his torch on us. He was stood there laughing at us, shaking his head in disbelief. I asked him, 'Please turn off that bloody light.' He then came over and asked us if we felt better and remarked that this was the first time he had ever seen two *Fräulein* drunk. He helped us up off the damp grass and escorted us back to our hut. I had to go outside two more times to vomit, then spent most the night awake as I was worried about Gabbi. I kept waking up and looking at her and checking her to make sure she had not stopped breathing.

When I told her next morning she said how sweet of me that was. Lucky for us we were not working the next day. We spent the morning relaxing and writing letters to our parents. We had not written to them in two weeks so we felt we should let them know how we were getting on. As we settled in, we would go, when we could, to watch our fighter planes take off, and we would count how many took off and how many came back. We found a nearby hill where we could sit and watch them. Often Gabbi would lie on her back reading a book as I told her what was going on. One day we were watching the Messerschmitts coming in to land. One of them caught my eye as it seemed he was approaching at much higher speed than the others. I tapped Gabbi on the arm, pointing to the Messerschmitt, and told her, 'Quick, look at this. I think something's wrong with that one.' Gabbi dropped her book, sat up and said, 'Fucking hell, he's going to —' but before she could say the word 'crash' the Messerschmitt ploughed into the ground. The plane seemed to concertina as it hit the ground. It went all the way in while the wings and fuselage separated and flew up in different directions. The propeller blades flew off into the air, then there was a huge explosion followed by an orange fireball which engulfed the aircraft. By now we were standing up, watching in disbelief as the other Messerschmitts circled the aerodrome, unable to land. They flew off to the satellite landing strips. We watched as the fire service rushed to the crash and began hosing it down. By the time the fire was extinguished it was perfectly clear that the pilot was dead. Me and Gabbi hugged one another. We did not want to see anything like that again. We made our way down the hill as the pilot's dead body was being removed from the mangled, burnt-out wreckage.

Crashes became more frequent and we witnessed our aircraft limping back home, trailing thick, black smoke behind them. We would count them out and see that fewer had returned from their missions. When I asked about this I was told that they had returned but had landed at satellite aerodromes due to technical problems. I found out later that this was a lie. The mood amongst the pilots changed too. Many new faces began to arrive, replacing ones who had vanished overnight. Our pilots steadily began to look exhausted. I asked one of them, 'What is it like over there?' He replied, 'It's like flying in a coffin, that is what it feels like!' We saw the damage on the aircraft that returned covered in bullet holes. We heard that the bomber crews fared far worse. Bombers would fly home, trailing smoke, their interiors splashed with blood and dead or dying crew on board. For the first time, Gabbi said to me one night, 'I don't get the feeling the war against England is going to plan!' How prophetic her words were, I thought to myself in the years after the war. During the relatively short period we were at Abbeville we had seen death on many occasions.

We worked hard for the boys to make sure we fed them well. Our experiences brought me and Gabbi closer than ever. We worked hard and we played hard. When we went out we would drink, but made sure we didn't get too drunk.

One evening we both found suitors in the form of two German flak boys. We couldn't take them back to our aerodrome but they suggested a friend's apartment in Abbeville. We agreed to go back with them, but only as guests, not prostitutes. As it happened the boys behaved like real gentlemen. It was quite a surprise to us and made us feel more compelled to let our hair down with them. We probably drank too much again. Gabbi admitted the next morning giving her boy a suck, as she put it. I had to admit to her that I had wanked off my boy. Gabbi was saying how she hated it when they came in your mouth. We both laughed so much on the way back to the aerodrome but Gabbi said, 'Well, he really did enjoy it, of course he did.'

We had written many letters home, sparing our families any of the sordid details of course. We arranged to return home so we could visit our families and be with them for Christmas time. This was all sorted and on the way we visited the kindly war veteran Ernst and his wife who we had met on our way here. We had some tea with them and again stayed the night at their cottage before leaving on the train the next day. While at home we said nothing of the bad things we had seen. Being back with my family was really very nice as I had missed them. The problem was I had spent so much time with Gabbi. I had worked with her, gone everywhere with her, and all I could think about while sitting in the living room with my family was Gabbi. It was weird. I just wanted to be with her, like at Abbeville. I hoped this feeling would pass during the few weeks at home. I lay in my comfy bed in my room at home but couldn't sleep. I lay there thinking about Gabbi for most of the night. I missed her so much it hurt.

I decided to call on her as she did not live too far from us. It was New Year's Eve 1940. The air was chilly but not that cold. I put on some nice clothes, grabbed my coat and set off for Gabbi's house. When I arrived her father was there and he seemed a little drunk, and somewhat surprised to see me. He asked if I was alright and if anything was wrong. I told him no, that I just wanted to come and wish Gabbi a 'Happy New Year' before midnight. I was invited in and Gabbi's father

called her down. As usual, she was sat in her room reading a
book. She almost fell down the stairs in the rush to get to me.
She threw her arms around me and said, 'What are you doing
here? Why are you not at home with your family? It's New
Year's Eve.' I asked her if we could talk and she grabbed my
hand and pulled me up the stairs to her room. As the music
downstairs played to the backdrop of drunken singing and
laughter, me and Gabbi sat down on her bed. I started crying
and she hugged me, asking, 'Whatever is wrong? What has
happened? Has something happened at home?' I told her it
was nothing to do with that, it was to do with her. She smiled
at me and asked, 'What do you mean it's to do with me? In
what way?' I replied, 'I'm not sure how I can say this, but
I just want to be with you. I can't stop thinking about you and
I think I love you.' She just sat and stared into my eyes and
said to me, 'God, do you know, I love you too. I always have,
but I am not going to jump into bed with you yet, Thelma.
God, this is really weird.' We sat and discussed things right
up until the stroke of midnight and the birth of 1941. It was
a surreal moment, suspended in time. As the strokes of the
chiming clock began, Gabbi held my hands we looked into
each other's eyes. We leaned forward, our lips brushing,
followed by a passionate, lingering kiss. As the party below
cheered and sang in 1941 we were there, kissing, in Gabbi's
room. Afterwards we smiled at each other Gabbi turned to
lock the door to her room. We undressed each other, then
Gabbi took my hand and led me to her bed. She threw back
the covers and, without going into every detail, we spent the
next hour making love. It was the most wonderful experience I
had at that time. Afterwards Gabbi walked me back home and
we agreed we would talk again soon.

After a few weeks spent back home with their families, and entering
into a passionate affair, Thelma Ortge and Gabbi Becker felt that they
were leading double lives, in contrast to how they had both been raised.
When the time came for them to return to their duties at Abbeville, the
long winter days and nights would prove as painful to them as their

conflicting emotions. As they boarded the train and were soon surrounded by familiar sights that they had not long left behind, they discussed their predicament. Thelma recalls:

> We did not know what to say to each other about it. We had dated boys many times but there was just this strong attraction we had for one another. It was not just sex, it was a strong, caring, emotional feeling. We deeply cared for one another yet we felt we were not lesbians. Gabbi was really worried about it all. Her family would kill her if they found out. Homosexuals and lesbians, in her family's eyes, were some of society's worst deviants after Jews and Bolsheviks. Up until a few months ago Gabbi would have told anyone the same. What a totally horrible situation we were in.
>
> When we arrived at Abbeville we tried to act as normal as was possible. The problem was that, with the other women around, we could not be intimate. We had to go out on walks and find somewhere quiet where we could hold hands and kiss one another. It was far too cold to do anything else outdoors during the winter so it was very frustrating for us as all we could do was kiss.
>
> After a few weeks it got easier and we got used to things. We would still go out on our days off duty. We would go to bars, drink too much wine and hook up with boys. There was one evening out that I remember. We met two very charming and nice-looking boys. They wanted to take us back to their apartment, so we agreed and went back with them. We were all in the same room, messing about, when the boy I was with began kissing me. Gabbi stopped what she was doing, grabbed my wrist and dragged me out of the room and out of the building. We left the two boys behind, shouting at us, 'What's the matter? Where are you going?' We just ran out of the apartment block and down the road. We stopped under the cover of a building. Gabbi had tears running down her face and said, 'I can't see you being kissed like that. If I can't do it then those fuckers can't either.' She was really upset and it surprised me, and it upset me too. I did not want to see her

cry ever again. The only thing we could do was to stop seeing boys when we went out. What a complicated mess we were in. The only way we felt easier about dealing with it was to just say 'let's enjoy it, and if it lasts, great, if it doesn't and it fizzles out, we'll still have our friendship'. Gabbi used to say, 'I am breaking the law of the state. We are both breaking the law of the state. This is quite insane, is it not?'

I also recall when Abbeville first came under attack from the RAF. It was just proof that all the efforts of the previous year had been in vain. New faces would join the other pilots for breakfast then be gone by dusk. It was becoming obvious to me that something was wrong. Then, when the attacks on the aerodrome began to happen, I knew that someone was lying. We were not really winning this war, were we? The biggest problem for me and Gabbi was winning our own personal war. Would we win our war? Would we still be alive after it all? If Germany won we might never have a future, if indeed we had one to look forward to in the first place. At night, when I tried to sleep, I could think of nothing else. I was feeling more and more depressed each day.

After several months of battling the depression, I could not go on. I suffered some kind of a nervous breakdown. It was decided I should return home immediately. I refused to leave unless Gabbi could come with me. There was no way I could leave her behind. I just told them that she was an inseparable friend and that I needed a good friend at this time. So she came back home with me. We arrived home to hear the news of Operation Barbarossa being launched against the Russians. It was on my father's wireless as I was being taken upstairs to bed where I was to rest and regain my strength. Our forces had invaded Russian territory and both the Wehrmacht and Luftwaffe were making excellent progress. Gabbi whooped for joy at the news. My father cut me a glance as if to say, 'I don't like this Gabbi friend of yours at all'. He didn't need to say it. I saw it in his eyes. He didn't like her or her family at all, but then I knew that. I told him she had really looked after me at Abbeville and I needed her as my best friend. When she left to go home, my father just reiterated what he had told me when we were back at school: 'Don't let them influence you. Don't be brainwashed. Just pretend and play the game until this war is decided.' I was not brainwashed, as father believed, as Gabbi never spoke politics with me. We were just ordinary, if that makes sense.

Returning to Abbeville was now something which we felt was out of the question. We would have to make other plans closer to our homes. The moments of privacy we were able to get were treasured ones. As our cities became the target for the Allied bombers we lived constantly in fear of losing one another. If anything happened to Gabbi, if she was killed, I don't think I could live on without her. We tried to work together where possible, and to share what time we could with one another. If I could have lived with her I would have done so, but it was not possible at the time. One evening, after the bombers had paid Cologne a visit, we watched an area of the city burn and felt so helpless.

We will continue Thelma Ortge's and Gabbi Becker's story in a later chapter.

Chapter Eight

A Keeper of Beasts

There was never any question of coercion in encouraging German women to volunteer for duty in the Nazi concentration camps. Many of the German women who entered the camp system did so to fill gaps caused by manpower shortages. As the Second World War progressed and Germany began to suffer greater losses, more men were required to fight on various fronts. It was a logical step to use women to fill the vacant posts. The reality was, though, that in order for any female to carry out her duties effectively within these camps there were certain prerequisites. Pity and compassion were emotions that would have no place in the camps. They were an assault on the senses. The sights, sounds and smells, combined with the manner with which one was expected to behave while working there, often attracted the very worst of individuals.

Many of the young women who became female camp guards were those with largely limited choices. They came from the lower classes of German society. Hairdressers, hospital matrons, tramcar conductresses, retired teachers and even operatic performers were all easily recruited via advertisements in newspapers. The advertisements, which often carried the headline 'Show your love for the Reich', were designed specifically to appeal to women. By 1943 many women, young and old alike, felt that they were still struggling to find their place in the Third Reich. The BDM proved a useful tool for the indoctrination of teenaged girls and young women looking to play their part in the Third Reich community. Throughout their indoctrination they were taught to feel no pity, remorse or compassion for those under their control within the concentration camps. Of course, there were a few exceptions to this rule. There were some who volunteered, full of enthusiasm, only to be crushed by the experience. They could not bear the sight of little children being led to certain death in the gas chambers.

To thrive in such an environment required a particularly hard, dedicated and ruthless individual. Ruth Goetz recalls:

> I was seventeen years old. I had been a useless student in my school years. I was the daughter of a factory worker and part-time nurse. We had virtually nothing and all we did have took hard work to gain. I just felt worthless and wanted to do something where I could hold my head high. I applied, and failed, to join the Luftwaffe auxiliary. The disappointment was crushing. I saw many of my friends going into the auxiliary but I could not follow them. Maybe my own self-worth issues were driving factors in me entering the camp system. I saw the advertisement in the *Volkischer Beobachter*. It seemed that no academic attributes were required so I applied. I was given a medical to ensure I was fit and then it was case of 'report here and they will take care of you'.
>
> I reported to the Ravensbrück camp in July 1943. The camp was located in quite a beautiful area of Fürstenberg, in Havel. Many things appealed to me about this. The recreational facilities, for one thing, would be wonderful, I recall thinking at the time. When I arrived at the camp I was issued a uniform and told to take great care of it. Keeping it clean and tidy was my own personal responsibility. I basically lived on the camp and one of the first things I did was accompany the senior SS women in escorting women labourers from their daily work duties. We would have to be up early and, as a result, some of the SS women were very what you would call grumpy. We would be waiting outside the gates of the camp. The work party would come to the gates and then we had the task of ensuring the workers arrived at their places. At the end of the day we would then escort them back through the camp gates.
>
> From the very beginning, the SS women were ones I looked up to. I admired them greatly, and the power they had over the Jewish and Eastern European slave workers. One told me, 'Don't be afraid of these people. Drive them mercilessly. Feel nothing but hatred for them for they are our enemy.' As I have said, in the early mornings we would be up waiting

at the gates for what one of the SS women guards called 'the scum' to arrive. When these women labourers came through the gates, depending on the mood, they could be kicked and beaten up. This was because the SS women were tired and angry about having to deal with these people. They took out their anger and frustrations on these slave labourers. One of them kicked a woman to the ground and, while another held her by the hair, they called me over. The SS woman then said, 'Go on, kick her.' I hesitated and was kind of stunned, not knowing what to do. I had never been in this kind of situation before. The SS woman then shouted, 'I will not tell you again! Fucking kick her!' So I just kicked the woman. The SS shouted at me to do it again and again after that. By the time I had finished the woman was in a poor state. The SS ordered the other workers to pick her up off the ground.

Honestly, I had always felt that I hated Jews, but after that I don't know. My views changed drastically about how we as a nation were dealing with the Jewish problem. Did we have to kill, enslave and starve them to death? Could we not just expel them? My thoughts were naïve, I know. I lay in my bunk that night, pulled the blanket over my head and began to weep. I was weeping for the woman they had forced me into beating. I didn't want to beat anyone, but I should have thought more about this.

We had days off where we could go home and visit family, or we could go walking in the forest or swim in the rivers and lakes. I did not go home as this was the first time I had been away from the gloom of a big city. I wanted to get out into nature and away from everyone else. I walked into the town and bought rye bread, salami and cheeses and headed out into the countryside. I would find a spot by one of the many lakes, put a blanket down and just stretch out and enjoy the sun and the quiet of it all. I would stay there for hours, sunbathing, in the summer. You could swim there and no one would ever bother you. As I got to know the other girls in the camp we would go out together and have coffee, beer or wine. We once took a boat out on the lake. We had drunk too much and were fooling around and ended up capsizing the boat. We tried to right it, but as we tipped it, it filled with water and sank. The owner was not too happy about his boat being at the bottom of the lake but we were all very drunk and could not stop laughing.

In time I made a lot of friends and the emotional side of me just kind of evaporated. I just did as I was told and carried out my own duties as best I could. If I was told to go and hit someone, I went and hit them. It was not easy at all but I was fed up with being a *Fräulein* nobody. I wanted to be in the SS and work to make my country the best in the world. I felt here that I had a future as such. Yes, I know that is a stupid thing, on reflection, but it was how I felt at the time. Beating inmates took more courage than you think for some. Initially, to be cruel and violent is very hard. Once you have done it a few times it's like anything, its gets easier to deal with. With each beating I gave it made the next one easier, and so on. We would hit them with sticks, a whip or anything else to hand. We were their masters, we could do to them as we pleased at the time.

I remember one Saturday in particular. Saturday was a half day and our weekend began at that point. A consignment of slave labourers arrived in railroad carriages around midday. We were going to offload these units, as they were referred to, but were told to stop. One of the male officers said, 'Leave them there until Monday morning. It's our weekend now and nothing gets in the way of our weekend.' So the labourers were left inside the carriages with no food or water until Monday morning. Many had died as a result of being left inside the cramped carriages. It was like animals being brought in for slaughter. Nobody cared about these people. Nobody cared if they lived or died. They were considered just units and more could be transported in from the places in the east.

Giselle Junghman, born and raised in the nearby town of Fürstenberg, recalled:

As youngsters we grew up with the knowledge of the Ravensbrück concentration camp for women. As a young girl growing up in Fürstenberg, I was neither shocked, surprised nor appalled by the presence of the camp or its close proximity to where we lived. My father was a serving soldier and he was our hero. There were six children in our family; four girls, including myself, and two boys. My father expected discipline at all times. If we did anything bad to upset him he would take off his belt and thrash us with it. He would have no crying or sulking afterwards either. We were expected to take the beating and show no fear, or that it hurt. Our father ensured that each one of us followed the same path. My two brothers were expected to focus on becoming soldiers. We girls, he said, could do more for Hitler than just having his babies. I remember one day father was driving his car along the road by the Ravensbrück camp. He looked over at me in the back seat and just said 'One day you will be working there. They will have a nice uniform for you too.' As a kid, I took little notice but smiled and said 'thank you, papa'.

In 1943 and 1944 there were requests for more German women to help by volunteering for duty in the camps. Not just Ravensbrück, but all over, and in the east too. My father ensured that, as the oldest, I enrolled first. I was supposed to go on a compulsory labour work course. I enrolled on this year of labour on my eighteenth birthday. After this I was influenced by both father and family to become a camp overseer. I was given a uniform and I remember when I first put it on, the women fitting it said 'Oh, doesn't she look sweet!'

All new girls in the camp were shown the ropes by the older ones who had been there longer. In fact, we met some pretty infamous names. Fräulein Binz was one I had taken instructions from on many occasions at the Ravensbrück facility. She was, how can I say, quite an attractive girl, but with a ferocious temper. She was by no means the superior as there were more notable names who were her bosses. Yet I think she outdid them on many occasions. She would seek out timid or fearful inmates and then she would go and beat or whip them mercilessly. I saw her slap, kick and whip female inmates many times. She once even stamped on an inmate's head until she moved no more. She could kill with her bare hands if she had to.

From my own experience we would compete with one another to see who could instil the most fear and gain the most respect from the women prisoners we were in charge of. Discussing this is never easy, but at the time I had been raised a National Socialist. I wanted to be a good National Socialist. To be a good National Socialist meant I would be obliged to hate certain racial groups. This was something I was brought up with. It was nothing exceptional and nothing out of the ordinary for me. I grew up to hate Jews, homosexuals, lesbians, gypsies and those from the east. If I suspected anyone I reported it to the authorities. My father expected me to contribute to the greater Germany and so I did.

I was at Ravensbrück for two years. Did women prisoners die from a result of beatings I gave them? The answer is no, I never killed anyone, but I helped direct inmates along paths into the gas chambers at the camp. They would be lined up and driven like a herd of cattle into a slaughterhouse. They were very nervous looking. I don't think all were convinced when they were told they were going into showers to remove lice and dirt and things. They would go inside, the door would be slammed shut, and death would follow shortly. Afterwards other inmates were made to remove the corpses. This is, of course, a degree of complicity in the murders of inmates at the camp. After the war we were all questioned about our activities. I told all I knew and what I had done but they were after much bigger fish than me. There were much bigger names given to the Allied authorities.

I remember when the camp was liberated. I was beaten up and I had much of my hair ripped out. I could have easily fought back against the inmates seeking revenge, but there were Allied soldiers there, ensuring I didn't fight back. I was threatened and told 'If you hit out, we will hit you with this', and they held up their rifles. I was lucky to escape the mob alive, and when the soldiers felt they had had their fun they pulled me up off the ground and pushed me away. When I arrived home I was half naked and my sisters and brothers barely recognised me. Our father was nowhere to be seen and we didn't know where he was. Mother was trying to tidy up the house as it had been turned upside down by American-speaking soldiers. When I walked in she screamed and covered her face. I was a mess. They had broken my nose, blacked both my eyes and broken several of my fingers. I also had a suspected cracked rib.

Over the weeks that followed we were constantly pestered by American soldiers. They would just walk in and ask the same old questions and I would tell them again and again. Our father was captured not far away from our town. He was held and underwent questioning, but they released him pretty quickly. I spent a couple of months recovering from the beating I had been given. In many ways I guess I was lucky, it could have been worse. They could have killed me in revenge and I would have understood that clearly. After the war we never ever spoke about these things. My father was of the view we would all have been better off dead now that National Socialism had gone. Later on, I even had problems finding employment. I managed to secure a job not long after, but the boss said, 'We have been told of your past, young lady, and we can't have any association with someone like you. It's not good for our business. I'm sorry but that is how it is.' At the time I walked away very angry and called them traitors under my breath. But with hindsight it's all understandable, is it not?

Dela Bachoulz was another young female who entered the Ravensbrück camp in late 1943. She recalled of her time there:

I really thought, how can this job be hard? It should be an easy, straightforward job with good pay. I imagined it would be far better than many of the shitty jobs going for young ladies at that time. I had never worn a military-style uniform before and I liked the look of it. I was excited by it all. Though it soon dawned on me it was not all about looking good in a uniform. I found the conditions at Ravensbrück nauseating. I supervised inmates in the laundry. Yet even that was unpleasant. There were all these foul, stinking garments which had to be deloused. Many of them were stained with foul-smelling fluids and excrement. On my third duty in the camp I was shown the correct way to beat an inmate. The woman instructing me was Irma Grese herself. Fräulein Grese took this stick and started to beat this one woman about the torso with it. She said 'You hit them here, where they feel the most pain. Hit them on the head and they may fall unconscious and they will feel nothing. This defeats the object, does it not?' She continued hitting the woman about the torso and legs until she begged for her to leave her. She seemed to enjoy doing this, which did scare me a little. When she stopped she threw the stick down on the floor. It landed by my feet. Fräulein Grese then said to me, 'Well, here you are. Now you do what I have just shown you to do!' I hesitated for a few seconds, but she was right on me and shouted, 'Go on! I don't have all day!' I picked up the heavy wooden stick and did as I was told.

The most striking thing about the testimony given by Dela Bachoulz was that, at the time she entered the Ravensbrück camp, she was just sixteen years old. She had been encouraged to volunteer by her Latvian-born mother and father. Her father often berated and bullied her as a youngster, calling her 'that useless child of mine'. She had also suffered sexual abuse from her father. Her mother was aware of the fact that her daughter was being abused, but would say nothing of it. Dela was given the position at Ravensbrück after lying about her age to the authorities. She was soon found out and they dismissed her from her duties.

Diana Hollberg was a tall, blonde girl with blue eyes and a strikingly beautiful face. Her looks would draw the attention of every male who saw her, according to her sister Magda. Diana died in 1989 from cancer but Magda, her youngest surviving sister, was happy to relate her story and the memoir she kept in a small leather-bound book.

My sister Diana was a beauty. I used to enjoy going out with her. Everywhere she went she would be offered drinks and things and I would always get special treats if I kept quiet and did not tell our parents. Diana became an SS *Aufseherin* [supervisor] in April of 1944. When she went into the camp at Belsen I saw less of her. She lived in at the camp with the other female guards. Occasionally she would come home, and when she did she would take me out to the cinema or to a café, or buy me sweet treats. She was twenty-one at that time and I was fifteen. I really loved her and looked up to her and thought how beautiful she was. She was far prettier than the rest of us [she laughs]. When she came home we always shared the same room. She would sit up in her bed and write things down in her brown book as she called it. I used to ask, 'What is that you are writing, dear sister?' She would reply, 'Oh, it's nothing for you to worry your pretty little head about.' She would look up at me and smile and carry on writing in the book.

She caused something of a crisis in our family some nine months later. She came home and was in a right state. I heard her crying downstairs and went to find out what was wrong, only for father to say, 'Go upstairs, this is not your business.' I went back up to my room and just sat on my bed, wondering what was wrong. It turned out Diana had been meeting one of the young men on the camp. He was one of the male guards there. She had obviously been sleeping with him as it was soon revealed that she was pregnant. My father was furious and made phone calls. I heard him shouting down the telephone at whoever it was on the other end. Either way, the boy who had made Diana pregnant never showed his face at our house or made any attempt to get in touch. It was probably just as well that happened as the war ended badly for Germany and had my sister still been at that dreadful camp she may not have lived for as long as she did. My father arranged for Diana to have the pregnancy terminated by a doctor who he knew very well. It was all done in secret and I know this was a traumatic time for my sister. She cried many a night afterwards and felt unwell for some weeks after.

Just two weeks before *Weihnachten* [Christmas Day] in 1988 Diana had been diagnosed with an aggressive form of bowel cancer. The cancer ravaged her body and by June of 1989 she was dead. It was a terrible blow to our family, and her husband and children. Her instructions on her death were that I have possession of certain things of hers. The small list included some jewellery, clothing and the brown book she had kept all those years. I had forgotten about this book. After the funeral, and as the shock of losing my sister abated, I sat down and began to read through it. There are some pieces I have vowed never to reveal to anyone but I am happy to let you use the following transcript.

We were today compelled with a vengeance to express our cruelty […] Here we need few weapons or guard towers. It is quite enthralling how the threat of a German shepherd dog being let loose can resolve virtually every disciplinary issue here in Belsen. I note that some inmates defecate on the spot at the mere sight of a growling dog […] With a large dog I can instil instant terror within these ideological enemies of ours. My dog would pull hard at its chain; it would foam at the mouth at the mere prospect of being able to savage one of these people. Fear was the best way to gain respect here in this camp.

You see mothers who have just given birth. Their offspring will soon perish here as they have no food with which to nourish themselves let alone an infant. Infants do not survive long here. If they do not die within a few hours then disease will often claim them. It is the kindest way in some respects. I hear that our doctors carry out medical experiments upon some of the women prisoners. They experiment with different methods of abortion. Often foetal material along with complete foetuses and other body parts are sealed in jars. I have seen them in the clinic, all neatly arranged in rows on a shelf.

There are also whores here to pleasure our own men. There are Eastern European girls, Jewish girls, lots of girls. Some of the really pretty ones are specially selected. These lucky girls are given a good clean up, followed by a medical, some new clothing and even make-up sometimes. They get fed better than the others too. They are escorted to where they are required. It is a kind of sexual black market and there are girls as young as fifteen involved. Senior German officers here are using these girls' services. One of them is a sixty-year-old I know of. He likes the very young ones; fifteen or younger. I just think 'You dirty old devil, you'. In a sense does this not contradict our own racial hygiene laws? If Hitler knew what was going on here he would have a seizure I am sure. Pure-German camp staff fucking these young female Jews and Bolsheviks is a disgusting thought. Some of the German women staff use these girls too. They think I do not notice, but I have seen girls arriving at their quarters, then coming out a few hours later. It can only mean one thing. I like this place despite the stink that surrounds it, despite the corpses. Dead bodies do not bother me anymore and better them than us I think! I hear all forms of funny rumours. I hear that *Reichsführer* Himmler requests samples of human skin for analysis, or tattooed skin being removed from some of the corpses. I am not aware of the substance but these things are laughed about amongst our staff almost every day.

This is certainly an interesting transcript and the only piece I was permitted to use from Diana Hollberg's personal memoir. I would have liked to have used more but Diana's sister was adamant that no more of her sister's words would ever be revealed publicly. The mention of human skin being removed from the corpses of inmates at the concentration camps is one that constantly appears throughout research into this area. I have doubted the authenticity of many alleged cases myself. Some tattooed skin thought to have been taken from the bodies of concentration camp inmates was later found to have been skin from a goat. The skin had been used to make lampshades or other items. Judging by the rumours of the many things that occurred in the concentration camps, it really wouldn't be surprising if there was some truth in them.

Elizabeth Hunsche worked in the camp administration at Auschwitz. Her role was in the economic administration department of the camp. Elizabeth recalls:

There were seven or so departments of administration at the Auschwitz camp. Ours was considered of high importance. I had the feeling that the female camp guards envied us girls as we had to use our brains whereas they used their violent tempers. We always privately viewed the *Aufseherin* as the plebs of the camp. They were mostly uneducated girls from poor or working-class homes. Of course, we never said anything to them and were always polite and had conversations with them. Overall, women were treated with immense respect. Any male who openly showed us disrespect could be punished severely for it. Everyone had to respect each other, no matter what department they were in or what background they came from. The only people who were not subject to this rule were, of course, the prisoners at the camp.

I lived in a small cottage with four other girls who worked with me at the camp. We rented the cottage from a man named Julian Messer. The cottage had been confiscated from Jewish owners. Their new home was now the camp I was working at. We had some very good times at the cottage. It had its own garden and the whole building was set in some woods. In the summertime, after leaving the camp at the end of our day, we would all go and sit by the stream at the bottom of the garden. We would sit and paddle our feet in the cool water. We would smoke our cigarettes and talk about the day [...] We used to go out to watch a film occasionally and we had parties every now and then. The parties were where we could let off steam the most. We would invite all the people we loved to the cottage and just let our hair down. We were very naughty at times and if my father could have seen some of the things we used to get up to he would have probably died from a heart attack. He would have dragged me home by the scruff as they say. The best parties were those we had in summertime. We found champagne and brandy, some of which came from the black market. We would get drunk and sometimes we would pair off with one another, if there were boys there we fancied [she laughs].

I remember one party I did not go to as I had been with my boyfriend elsewhere. He dropped me off at home later and the party was still going on. It was one o'clock in the morning. I came through the front door and there was a couple having sex on the settee. They did not even stop when I walked in.

I walked through to the back garden and there were guests still sipping champagne in the garden. I asked where my three friends, Kathi, Emmi and Ursula, were. One young man said 'they are down there', pointing towards the woods and stream. When I got down there I found Kathi and Emmi making love with one man while Ursula was a short distance away, groaning and moaning with this young man between her thighs. I thought 'My God', shook my head, and headed back into the cottage. I went upstairs to bed. One young man tried his luck with me by creeping into the bedroom and sitting on the end of the bed. I felt him stroking my feet so I said to him 'What are you fucking doing?' I told him to get out now or I would tell my boyfriend who would give him a good punching [she laughs]. I think I embarrassed him. He got up, walked out of the room, and I heard him go downstairs.

My friends finally made it to bed at three thirty in the morning. They came in very drunk, laughing and messing around. Emmi was repeatedly singing '*Fräulein Knickebein, Fräulein Knickebein*'. Knickebein was a magic crow of German folklore. And why she had made up this song I don't know [she laughs]. I think she was referring to a woman she worked with who she didn't like, but I am not sure. They jumped on me and started messing around. I was half asleep and I had Ursula sat on me, holding my arms down while the other two tried to pour red wine into my mouth. I was shouting at them 'For God's sake, fuck off and leave me alone!' But I started laughing, which made it worse. In the end Ursula fell asleep on top of me. I had to roll her to one side and I moved over so she stayed in my bed all night.

They were totally crazy at times but they understood life could end tomorrow. We were surrounded by death and the war was not going that well, so we heard. So we lived for the moment and had as much fun as we could before it all came to an end. Of course, when it did we had to get out of the cottage. I remember that last time I walked out of the door. I looked back at it with great sadness and thought I will probably never come back here again. I walked up the road with my three friends and we wished each other well. There were tears and kissing then off we went in different directions. I never saw them again after that and all I have now are the memories. I knew the place that I was working at was a death factory. It's no excuse that I had no involvement in the crimes there, I understand that. People will still say I am guilty of being a part of it all. It happened long ago now, for God's sake, and I feel that Germany has paid for its conduct during the Second World War. Just let her go. Just let her go, is what I keep saying.

To close this particular chapter I felt that Bernadette Metschuldtz's words were most fitting:

I volunteered for service in the camps as, in my opinion, I had no other choice other than getting married or finding some horrible job inside a factory. At twenty years old I felt confused, with conflicting emotions. I did not want to be stuck in a house with screaming kids, washing and cooking all day long and cleaning up after some man, like my mother lectured me I should be doing. All this shit in between the constant air raids, the shortages of even the most basic of goods. No, I thought […] I don't want that. It was like I wanted to decide my own destiny. If I could fit in somewhere with the Nazis that might be better than anything else. My parents hated my decision but I had made it. In the camp itself life was regimented and it had structure. We ate well and slept well, and we had our fun times too. On later reflection, did I regret my decision to go and work in the camp system? No. I had, and still have, no regrets. I felt what I did was right at the time for me. My mother and father didn't agree at all. After the war we used to argue over it time and again. My father would always shout 'Is it something you are proud to look back on? You were like some homicidal farmer; a keeper of beasts.'

Chapter Nine

The Devil's Daughter

Defining the purest manifestation of evil to have emerged from the Third Reich era is no easy task. By the end of the war an entire catalogue of the names of those who had perpetrated some of the most obscene acts of cruelty ever against other humans was known around the world. It is no surprise that some of the worst exponents of pain and cruelty came from the Nazi medical profession. The medical examination that young Berliner Anita Von Schoener was subjected to as a child was testimony to the humiliating, painful and intrusive nature of the Nazi medical profession. If these supposedly professional individuals were happy to inflict pain and humiliation upon their own German society then one has to ask what suffering those considered 'lesser races' were subjected to, especially within the concentration camps.

Back in 2003 I can recall sitting down with Anita Von Schoener to try and identify the woman doctor who was present during the unpleasant medical examination she underwent. At the local library we pored over many images of known Nazi doctors, and the female staff who had assisted them. It was, at that time, like looking for a needle in a haystack. The woman present at Anita's examination could have been anyone. Anita recalled her attitude and demeanour as being stern and sharp. Anita also suspected that this woman was a professional associated with the SS. She remembered how cold and clinical the woman's eyes were. We were almost at the point of closing the file when Anita suddenly said, 'That's her there. She was the woman doctor, or so-called doctor, who was there at my examination.' This female doctor's name meant nothing to me at the time. I had previously never heard of her, but our curiosity was now piqued. We opened the file and began to read about her. What we read was not surprising, yet it still horrified us.

Herta Oberheuser was born on 15 May 1911 in Cologne. There was little information on her childhood in order to try and understand where the evil that would emerge in this otherwise normal young woman originated. From research, I learned that she and her family fully embraced the National Socialist cause. At school she was described as a bright, intuitive, highly intelligent girl. She was not unattractive as a young girl, yet those who associated with her during her youth recalled that she possessed a wicked temper.

Kyla Pacchianoa, the daughter of Italian immigrants, recalled

> She was quite ordinary in every way and she had her friends, people she liked and who liked her. She had a very bad temper though. I recall her having a fight with another girl in the playground once. It started off, as things usually do with young girls, with name-calling and silly things like that. I could see that Herta was becoming very irritated. When she stared at someone in anger, her eyes were scary. She had scary eyes even when she was happy. In the end she beat the girls up and they did not bother her again. I do not recall her being involved in such trouble very often though.

Herta's personality was described as a little quiet yet amiable. She had become a member of the BDM [League of German Girls] before it had become compulsory for all German-born girls to register for enrolment. One would imagine she would have excelled in the BDM and very likely have been appointed as one of its group leaders. She had a keen interest in becoming a doctor from an early age. Herta received her medical degree in Bonn, in 1937, specialising in dermatology. Afterwards she enrolled into the Nazi Party as a medical intern. Although Herta had been through medical school, she did not have the full licence allowing her to practise medicine in any unsupervised capacity. Herta's rise to horrific prominence was a steady one by any account. Records confirmed that she had later served as a doctor with the BDM. It was also stated that her abilities as a physician were highly respected and trusted. It was undoubtedly around this time that she participated in Anita's medical examination.

Hilde Ahrens recalls seeing Doctor Oberheuser on two occasions during her BDM membership:

> We had regular health check-ups and inspections. Every so many months there would be a full medical inspection where we would each see the doctor. The doctor would examine you in fine detail. Your feet, hair, eyes, skin, ears; everything would be thoroughly checked. Heart rate and blood pressure were also monitored. I recall these 'big inspections', as we used to call them, very well. We didn't really like them much as we had to take all our clothes off and do all these things, then the doctor would put her cold fingers all over you and do all these tests. It just was not very nice.
>
> I am pretty certain I saw Doctor Oberheuser on two occasions. She had the kind of face you could not forget easily. She was a very stern-looking woman who appeared to be angry even when she wasn't. She was incredibly thorough, checking hands, feet, ears, eyes, hair, mouth, teeth, underarms and even private areas. She expressed special interest if you had blue eyes or fair hair. She would ask you questions about your parents' eyes and hair colour. I remember the second time I saw Doctor Oberheuser. She spotted a splinter of wood I had stuck in my finger. She was quite horrified by the sight of the splinter and said 'This must come out this instant'. She removed the splinter with a long, thin needle. She told me, 'Be still. It will only take a moment to remove.' Sure enough, she removed it very quickly and then insisted I wash the area where the splinter had been. She then wiped it over with a clear disinfectant liquid. She then carried out the physical examination as normal. She never really bothered me. Back then all doctors appeared a little [...] creepy. I preferred having her examine me rather than a man. Some of the men did examine us and they were always rough. There was nothing that told me that she was evil. I was quite horrified when I heard of her arrest after the war and the things she had done.

In 1940, Herta Oberheuser was appointed to serve as an assistant to Karl Gebhardt who was then Chief Surgeon of the SS and also Heinrich

Himmler's personal physician. It was in 1942 that both Oberheuser and Gebhardt arrived at the Ravensbrück concentration camp. Their objective was to investigate methods of treating various infections. The guinea pigs for their medical experimentation were the camp inmates. Oberheuser and Gebhardt would purposely infect wounds with foreign objects such as wood, rusty nails, slivers of glass, soil, sawdust and even human excrement. In the filthy conditions in the camp the outcome of such experiments upon the inmates would have been obvious. The deliberately infected wounds would be carefully monitored, along with the progression of infection and its effect on the victim. Deliberate wound infection often resulted in the wound oozing with thick, green pus. Fever and gangrene, followed by blood poisoning, yet the victim was still left untreated to suffer their agony until they died. Gebhardt argued that many of the experiments which he and Oberheuser had conducted were in the interests of learning more about the surgical management of grossly contaminated traumatic injuries such as those often suffered by soldiers on the battlefield. At that time there were many new antibiotic innovations available that rendered such barbaric medical practices totally unnecessary. The pair also conducted experiments into transplanting bone, muscle and nerve tissues.

Most of the experiments at Ravensbrück were carried out on eighty-six women inmates, seventy-four of whom were Polish political prisoners. Their medical experiments also extended to children in the camp. Oberheuser experimented on children by injecting them with oil and Evipan. The latter was used throughout the 1940s as an anaesthetic. It was known that Oberheuser injected children with Evipan then proceeded to surgically remove their vital organs and limbs. The time from administering the injection of Evipan to expiry of the victim was between three and five minutes. Throughout this terrifying procedure the child victim would be fully conscious, right up until the moment of death. Such medical experiments served no useful purpose whatsoever. As doctors, Oberheuser and Gebhardt would have been fully aware of the suffering they were causing. One can only assume that they carried out these so-called medical experiments for their own sadistic pleasures. It has also been revealed that Oberheuser and Gebhardt also injected adults and children with powdered glass.

The reasoning behind these injections has never been made clear, but they would have served no medical purpose at all. Oberheuser's butchery did not stop there and she continued to operate unnecessarily on inmates. Often her work left victims with wounds and exposed bones. The wounds were often left untreated and sometimes were concealed with casts. One of Oberheuser's victims recalled how she made a large surgical incision into her leg. Part of the victim's shinbone was left exposed. The leg was later encased in a plaster cast yet the victim was still forced to walk on the limb. The wound soon became horribly infected to the point where pus would run from out of the plaster cast. When victims cried out for a drink they were often given water contaminated with vinegar. It was clear that Herta Oberheuser enjoyed inflicting pain and suffering on her victims. It was also rumoured that she removed skin blemishes such as moles and birthmarks with a scalpel without administering any anaesthetic. The orders to carry out these and other vile experiments came directly from SS chief Heinrich Himmler.

At the Nuremberg 'Doctors' Trial' Herta Oberheuser was the only female defendant. She escaped the hangman's noose and, on 20 August 1947, was sentenced instead to twenty years in prison. This sentence was later reduced to just five years as time already served in custody was taken into account. She was released from prison in 1952 and again began to practise as a doctor. As soon as it was revealed that Oberheuser was working as a doctor, her medical licence was revoked by the court of Schleswig-Holstein. Unable to practise medicine again, Oberheuser drifted into obscurity and little was heard of her again until her death in a nursing home in Germany in 1978. Karl Gebhardt was hanged for war crimes and crimes against humanity on 2 June 1948, at Landsberg Prison in Bavaria.

The thirty-five women who survived the medical experiments carried out by Oberheuser and Gebhardt suffered life-long pain and disability. Many of Herta Oberheuser's victims could not comprehend how she had been able to escape the death penalty. One of her victims recalled:

I thought that this was it. I thought that the last thing I would ever see was her cruel face staring at me as I drifted into unconsciousness. Her face was partially obscured by her white surgical mask, yet her eyes were like knives. All these years on

I have had operations to try and repair the damage that woman did to my body. Yet still the pain of what she did is present and still her piercing, cold eyes haunt my dreams. Whenever I have had nightmares about what I went through it's always that woman's eyes I see. She had the eyes of a devil. She was pure and utter evil.

A young German nurse who worked at the Ravensbrück medical facility recalled Herta Oberheuser:

I would never have done anything like she did. I had no intimate contact with the prisoners. I was employed by the dentist solely to assist him with treating camp staff. I do recall Herta Oberheuser though. We used to laugh about her and one of the girls remarked that she looked like Martin Bormann in drag.

It is certainly true that men do not have a monopoly on evil but what caused an otherwise normal young woman to embark upon such barbarity and cruelty cannot always be clearly ascertained. She was by no means alone in her evil deeds, or in the gravity of her crimes.

Chapter Ten

When Our City Burned

Although the city of Cologne had been subject to aerial bombing by Britain's Royal Air Force from 12 May 1940, the most infamous attack on the city would come during the early hours of 31 May 1942. Operation Millennium was the codename given to the first thousand-bomber raid on Cologne.

Two of the primary objectives of this bombing raid on Cologne were firstly to wreak such destruction that it would knock Germany out of the war, and secondly to cause such terror among the civilian population that it would severely weaken the German morale. The raid would also prove a useful propaganda tool for the Allies. Up until this point the RAF bombing raids on Germany, though undoubtedly effective in certain areas, were not proving to be as destructive to the German war effort as expected.

The head of RAF Bomber Command, Air Marshal Arthur Harris, had been pushing the concept of strategic bombing for some time. A successful heavy raid on a specific German city might demonstrate Harris's theory that a sustained strategic bombing campaign held the key to defeating Nazi Germany. Britain's War Cabinet had proved to have been a thorn in Harris's side; neither prepared to listen nor put new theories to the test. There were even some in the Air Ministry who viewed Harris as rather like an angry dog that needed to be controlled. Harris was convinced that, with the correct resources, his RAF could help deliver the knockout blow that would shorten the route to final victory. Harris had every confidence in the men of the Royal Air Force, but the strategic bombing theory would not be without heavy cost.

The day of 30 May 1942 dawned as a slightly cloudy and windy one in Cologne. It was pleasantly warm and for many of the inhabitants of the city it was business as usual. Being a Saturday, the city soon became crowded with people buying goods or just out for a walk. There was no indication of the nightmare that would arrive later. Thelma Ortge recalls that day:

> I loved Saturdays and Sundays as they were my guaranteed days off. I would get up, wash and dress, and then arrange to go and meet Gabbi in the city. We had both managed to secure work there. It was not quite the same as what we did in Abbeville at the aerodrome but our parents felt we would be safer back home. I would usually grab a cup of coffee and then fly out of the door to catch a tram into the city centre. Cologne city at the time had been left relatively unharmed. It had been bombed but not heavily like some other cities. Mine and Gabbi's routine was more or less the same. We were as predictable as the trams that ran through the city [she laughs]. You could set your watch by our movements.
>
> On that day, Saturday, 30 May 1942, it was a mild day and we planned to buy some rye bread and salami and go and have lunch sitting beside the Rhine. We found a quiet spot to ourselves, in the shade of trees, and put a blanket down. It was nice and we ate our lunch and talked about everyday things. We both understood that this level of peace could not last for ever. We knew the war was going to arrive soon, in a way that might change our lives for good. It was a mutual feeling we had developed about things. Gabbi always bought more than one newspaper and she would pick out bits and we would discuss them. But distinguishing the propaganda from the reality was impossible. You did not know what were lies and what was truth. I felt that Gabbi believed it all but I didn't. Of course, I did not tell her this, even though we were what you would call lovers. There were things I could still not reveal to her for fear of her maybe telling the authorities on me. I didn't think she would do that, but at that time I did not want to risk it. I was happy and felt comfortable with her and I enjoyed the relationship we were having. It was different to being with men. I can't explain it, but we'd have been in the shit if we had been found out. Only in private would we dare to hold hands and kiss each other.

After having our picnic by the Rhine we went and had a walk around the cathedral. It was one of our favourite buildings in the city. We loved looking around its ancient structure and marvelled at its beauty. Would it survive this war was often the question we would ask each other. On that day we both stood gazing at it with tears filling our eyes. We both felt a bit depressed so headed for home. We caught a tram and went back to Gabbi's house. We sat in her garden talking for a while. When her parents and grandmother arrived and set up a table for their tea we went inside. We ran up the stairs into Gabbi's room. She locked the door, leaving the key in the lock, and put a gramophone record on. We helped each other undress and climbed into her bed. I took her glasses off carefully, placing them on her bedside drawer set. I then lay on top her and we kissed for some time.

By the time we had finished it was late afternoon and I had to go home. As much as we hated it, we got out of bed, put on our clothes and tidied our hair up. I shouted goodnight to Gabbi's parents and grandmother. I then kissed Gabbi on the cheek and told her I would see her Monday morning. As I walked off down the road, Gabbi stood and watched and waved to me. I felt happy and that the war was a million miles away that moment. If it stayed this way, I thought, the Nazis could wage their war forever. Just as long as it didn't touch us I would be happy.

When I arrived home it was seven in the evening. My mother and father were sat out in our back yard talking. I vividly recall my father saying, 'I don't like the feeling in the air. It's too quiet and that means something is up.' There had been some thunder earlier in the day and the wind had got up. We all stared towards the darkening sky and said nothing. Father then asked what I had been doing all day and remarked sarcastically that I spent too much time with Gabbi Becker and that I should do more to help at home. I said nothing as I did not want to have an argument and spoil an otherwise memorable day.

When we went into the house mother and father listened to their radio while I went upstairs to my room to read. I couldn't focus on my book. I was too busy thinking about the day I'd had with Gabbi. I was worried about what we were going to do. Would the passion we had discovered all fizzle out in the months to come or would we both go back to being just good friends and dating boys? I had no answers and it was troubling for me. How would we live if we continued the way we were? There were just so many problems to think about [...]

I tossed and turned, eventually falling asleep, only to be awoken by the howl of the air raid alert. It was startling at first but we had these alerts in the past [...] My mother came into my room telling me, 'Hurry up and get dressed. Get your coat. We have to leave now!' It was the same old story. Grab some clothes and run down the road to the communal shelters that were situated around the city. People were already leaving their homes as we walked down the road. I saw people carrying their sleepy children in their arms. Others grabbing their cats and throwing them back inside their homes before slamming their doors shut.

It had not gone long past midnight from what I recall. There was a warning that a large enemy force was approaching and they were around thirty minutes or so away. I recall seeing the searchlights switching on. They were already sweeping the dark skies above and I could see flashes in the distance as the flak began firing at the planes. We arrived at the bomb-proof shelter and could do nothing more than wait and see what happened. Were the bombers going to attack us or somewhere else? At the time we had no idea where they would bomb. I thought of Gabbi and hoped that she was also heading for safety with her family.

After thirty minutes or so had passed I could hear the distinct rumble of planes approaching. It was a kind of distant hum at first but became louder by the minute. Then the explosions began. It was a combination of the flak batteries around the city and the bombs exploding. You would hear the bombs whistle as they fell, then in rapid succession you would hear them go off – whoomp, whoomp, whoomp – getting closer with each one. That was the sound. It was like a 'whoomp' sound as they went off. The ground shook, lights flickered, people began to cry and panic in the shelter. The sounds of terrified children were the ones that would live with me the most. Their parents were unable to console them or convince them that they would be safe here. The little children often urinated in their clothes with fear and babies cried uncontrollably. The noise grew louder and louder and we all thought that this time we had had it. This was a very big raid and we were absolutely terrified. For over an hour and thirty minutes, maybe even longer, the noise and explosions were constant.

Then, after what seemed an eternity, it gradually subsided and the noises outside faded away. The enemy planes were becoming a distant hum once again. There were fears that a second wave of enemy planes was coming and we were told to remain inside the shelter, but this was soon dispelled. When we emerged from the shelter after the all-clear had sounded, it was getting light. We came out of the shelter to a scene from hell itself. All around us piles of rubble that were once buildings burned furiously. Firefighters fought heroically against the fires but there were just so many. We were told to go nowhere near the centre of the city for it had been destroyed […] Then there were bombs which had not exploded. I recall seeing one hanging in the branches of a tree. We had to walk right under it on our way to safety. The chemical plant me and Gabbi worked at had been flattened too. In the direction of Gabbi's home the sky was red with fire. I began to feel fear and panic and I wanted to go and see if she was safe. I was told, 'No, you cannot go down there. Please move on.'

We arrived back home to see that our house was still standing, but many in our street had received some damage. One of our back windows was smashed and a door blown open but no other damage. Mother and father told me to get some rest, but I couldn't rest. I wanted to know if Gabbi was safe. I went out again later and made the journey to her house. I did not even get three streets close to where she lived. I was confronted by smoking rubble as far as the eye could see. The police would not let me go any further. I pleaded with them to let me go, but they stopped me. I asked about the street Gabbi lived in and was told, 'There is nothing there now apart from rubble.' They just kept telling me, 'Please go home. Announcements will be made as soon as we know.' They were referring to death notices. I stood there and burst into tears. One of the police came and put a blanket around me and consoled me. One of them escorted me back home and I sat in the living room staring at the floor.

Over the days that followed I received no word from Gabbi or any news of her or her parents. There were so many rumours of this family being killed and that family being killed that I did not know what to believe. The raid had struck such fear into the people of Cologne and many began to filter out of the city itself into the surrounding countryside. We were advised to leave the city even though we were not in the centre of it. Refuges were set up at farms further out in the countryside. Barns were converted into places where people could live in safety. My parents were reluctant to leave our home, but as other residents of our neighbourhood left we felt it best to follow.

This was the first time the war had directly affected our lives. We decided we would go and stay outside the city for a few weeks and see what happened from there. We stayed with people from our own neighbourhood on a cattle farm. A Hitler Youth camp was situated nearby and the Hitler Youth boys and girls helped cook and feed everyone and make sure we all had somewhere to sleep out of the elements. The Hitler Youth were magnificent in their uniforms and helped everyone.

I asked everyone I met about the Becker family and if they had made it. Nobody knew where they were or if they were alive. One of the BDM girls told me the area where the Beckers lived had been totally destroyed. Three BDM girls came round handing out bread and cups of hot soup. As I took the soup and bread they asked me if I was alright then saluted and said 'Heil Hitler' before going on to the next person. They looked after us well and kept everyone fed, making sure

(*Right*) Thelma Ortge and Gabbi Becker. (*post war photo courtesy of G.Becker*)

(*Below*) Thelma and Gabbi pictured here with the crew of a Stug in late 1944 somewhere near Cologne.

(*Above left*) Bertha Wuremfjeld in the BDM. (*Courtesy Wuremfjeld*)

(*Above right*) A young Sofia Weiss pictured here with her aunt. (*Courtesy E.Bohn*)

(*Below left*) Traudl Junge Hitler's youngest secretary. (*The War in Pictures Archive*)

(*Below right*) Hellen Giehl on left in photo with friend in the BDM. (*Courtesy Giehl*)

(*Right*) Dr Jutta Rudiger head of the BDM. (*Courtesy Wikipedia*)

(*Below*) 'Arsing around' BDM style. Dagna Baier standing on the right with her friends in the BDM. (*Courtesy M.Koen*)

(*Above*) Dana Hahn sitting
at front in the middle.
(*Courtesy Ingeborg. Lischt*)

(*Left*) Vaida Raab. A post war
portrait. (*Courtesy V.Raab*)

(*Right*) A young Ellie Kauffmann poses with her younger sister. (*Courtesy Kauffmann*)

(*Below*) Katherina Zammit aka 'Kitty Schmidt' (on left) poses with her daughter. (*Source unknown*)

(*Left*) Only the prettiest girls were procured for service in the infamous 'Salon Kitty'. (*Source unknown*)

(*Below*) The former 'Salon Kitty' premises as it is today. (*Wikipedia*)

(*Right*) Ruth Goetz standing
third from front during
a BDM sports afternoon
(*BDM Yearbook photo*)

(*Below*) Bernadette Metschuldtz
lying down on right in the
photo. (*BDM Yearbook image*)

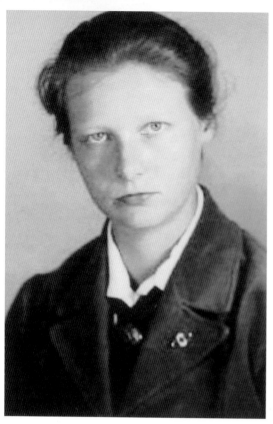

(*Above left*) The Devils Daughter-Herta Oberheuser pictured here in her BDM uniform. (*Wikipedia*)

(*Above right*) Matilda Weyergang with her back to the camera on left in the photo, which is a still from a BDM activities film reel used for propaganda purposes.

(*Left*) Selina Mayer pictured here standing in background with friends. (*Courtesy Mayer*)

(*Right*) Kathi Frier (on left) with Gertrud Lehnt. "They used to say I looked like Eva Braun"!

(*Below*) Hanna Burowitz on the left in the photo. (*Courtesy Burowitz*)

Olga Kirschener being bounced in
the air during sports practice in the
BDM. (*Courtesy Vatner*)

The cutest gurn in the Third Reich.
SS chief Heinrich Himmler's daughter
Gudrun. (*Source unknown*)

Another candid portrait of Gudrun
Himmler who Traudl Junge
described as "one of the prettiest
little girls she had ever seen".
(*Source unknown*)

Two sisters in the BDM. Many
young girls like these faced a grim
future in Adolf Hitler's Third Reich.
(*Source unknown*)

The female 'Aryan Ideal' so
beloved of Nazi propaganda.
(*Source unknown*)

Hilde Hartmann on right kisses
her friend. Whether in jest or true
emotional context relationships
between women did flourish
within Hitler's totalitarian state.
(*Courtesy Hartmann*)

(*Right*) Emma Klein.
(*Courtesy Johann Pohl*).

(*Below*) War Games with big brother. (*Source unknown*).

Berlin ablaze following a visit from the Allied air force. (*Source unknown*)

The carbonized remains of a woman and child collected by BDM girls in Berlin. Human remains were collected up in buckets and bathtubs after bombing raids. (*Courtesy E.Barnard*)

(*Right*) Annalise Soetzer who attempted to rescue a Russian crewman from his burning tank. (*Courtesy Soetzer*)

(*Below*) The diminutive figure of twenty-year-old Doris von Knoblock emerges from the packing crate she was hiding in after her discovery at Rhine-Main air base 2 October 1947. (*Courtesy Stars and Stripes*)

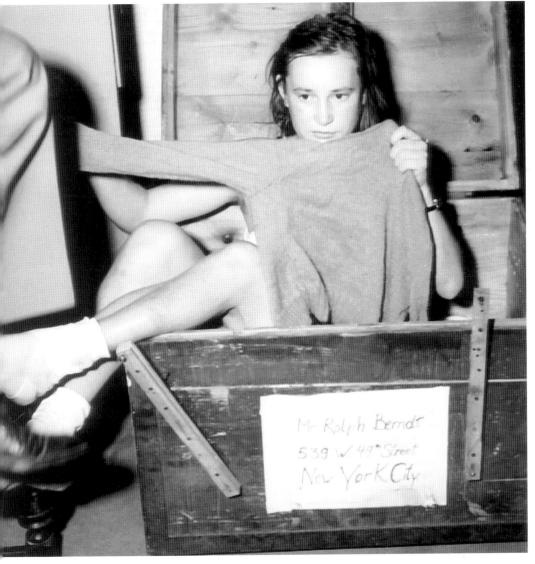

Mr Ralph Berndt
539 W 49ᵗʰ Street
New York City

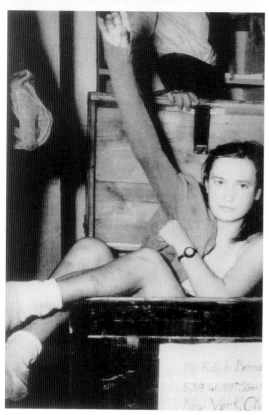

Doris von Knoblock pulls on a cardigan before emerging from the wooden crate. (*Courtesy Stars and Stripes*)

Doris poses by the crate she had been hiding inside during her attempt at joining her Jewish fiancé who left Germany to live in the USA. Had she been successful in boarding an aircraft in the crate she would have almost certainly died on the flight. (*Courtesy Stars and Stripes*)

people had blankets and things at night. We lived in what had been a barn for cattle. It had been cleaned out and fresh straw put inside with tables and benches. It was actually a very cosy place to sleep in, but I couldn't sleep. Every time I closed my eyes I saw Gabbi's face. I had dreams about her and during the day I could think of nothing else.

Two weeks later I had still found out nothing of Gabbi or her parents. I took a walk along the lane from the farm to a bridge. I just wanted to go and sit alone with my thoughts. I did this most days. There was the odd trickle of people still coming in from Cologne city. I would watch them walk by, hoping Gabbi would be with them, but she never was. I felt heartbroken by it all. I began to hate the British RAF for what they had done. I felt myself becoming a Nazi more and more with each tortuous day.

One such day, while I sat on the bridge, I noticed people walking up the lane to the farm. I was leaning over the bridge, watching the water and spitting. I would watch the spit bobbing along until it disappeared under the bridge. As the people approached I looked up and my heart began to pound furiously in my chest. I was sure I could see Gabbi. I began to walk towards them and then I could see it was her. When she noticed me she screamed with joy and ran towards me. She almost knocked me off my feet. We hugged each other and I had to keep pulling away from her to look at her face, saying 'It is really you, Gabbi', and 'I can't believe this is happening.' Gabbi explained that her parents were behind, helping her grandmother along, which is why it took them nearly all day to get here. I took her by the hand and we ran off up to the farm to my parents. We were so excited when we rushed into the barn and I said to my parents 'Here's Gabbi! She's alive!'

When her parents arrived we just sat and exchanged stories. Gabbi's father said that the grandmother had refused to leave the house the night of the big bombing raid [...] At that point several bombs hit the neighbourhood and they ran out into the street, leaving the old lady inside the house. Gabbi's father ran back into the house and brought the old lady out against her will and cursing furiously. They ran through the streets until they came to a shelter. The door was shut and they began banging on the door to be let in. The door opened and a soldier grabbed them and pushed them into the shelter, calling them 'imbeciles'. Gabbi explained that their home had been destroyed and was no more than a burning pile of stones now. After the raid they went and stayed with her father's boss, but her father did not want to outstay their welcome and felt they must leave with all the other homeless people until things were sorted out.

I didn't care about the house or anything else, I was just elated at having Gabbi back with me. That night we slept side by side in the barn, vowing we would never leave each other's side again. We held hands under the blankets and if Gabbi got up in the night to answer the call of nature I went with her. We were totally inseparable and, although we both knew it was wrong, we were hopelessly in love.

The next afternoon I took Gabbi out into the fields where we walked and talked. We sat down beside a bomb crater in one of the fields. We looked around to ensure no one else was around and shared the first kiss in weeks. The feeling of her soft mouth against mine was so exciting. The feeling of her tongue against mine was just too much. We got up and made our way into a small coppice where we undressed beneath the trees and made love to each other. It felt so right. Afterwards we talked about things. We agreed we should live for the moment. At any time we could be killed. We would have to live a secret life and see what destiny held for us both when all of this horror was over. Afterwards we walked back to the barn and the Hitler Youths were there again. They were asking for volunteers to assist the fire service and other emergency groups in and around the city. Anyone could help as long as they were aware that it would be dangerous. Anyone who volunteered would be performing a valuable duty to the Reich.

As former BDM girls and auxiliaries we felt we could help in some way and the work would occupy our minds rather than sitting around the farm twiddling our thumbs all day long. So me and Gabbi volunteered our services. There was much to be done in the city and the surrounding areas. Salvage operations had been underway more or less as soon as the bombing had finished. Bodies had to be recovered and a mass burial pit had to be dug. Any material in the bombed-out factories had to be recovered, ready for reuse. So here we went again into another adventure. We agreed that if we were going to die in this war then we would die together rather than alone. Gabbi looked me in the eyes and said, 'If there is to be another life after we die then I want to go to that other life with you.' We went and told our parents who protested vigorously, until the Hitler Youth reminded them that 'This is not an obligation, it is in the Führer's service'. We told our parents we would return and not to go off without us. Then we left with the Hitler Youth.

The city of Cologne had been devastated during the raid of 30–31 May 1942. In just ninety minutes almost 1,500 tons of bombs fell on the city; two-thirds of which were incendiary [fire] bombs. It was only the steadfast action of the city's firefighters and the wide streets that prevented a firestorm developing. Most of the damage had been caused by fire rather than by high explosives. It was reported that some 600 acres of the historic medieval city were in ruins. Some 45,000 German citizens were rendered homeless and 469 killed. The RAF had lost forty of its aircraft during the raid, equating to less than four per cent of the total aircraft involved in the raid. British Prime Minister Winston Churchill, who authorised the raid, telegraphed US President Franklin D. Roosevelt with the words, 'I hope you were pleased with our mass attack. There is plenty more to come.'

Thelma Ortge and Gabbi Becker joined recovery teams and headed back into the city. Thelma continues her story:

The bridge we had to cross to get back into the city was suspected of being damaged. So we went across the river by a barge-type boat. The idea was we would try and salvage any goods, medical supplies, clothing and food items we could.

The hospital had been bombed and the remains were scoured for any medical supplies still intact. Other teams went through the rubble to recover bodies. It was a horrific sight. Even our beloved cathedral was now in ruins and only its two spires remained, defiantly standing from the devastation all around. It was a ghost city. There was no water, electric or gas supplies. We were there for a few days, trying to salvage anything useful and searching for any survivors who may have been trapped in the rubble of their homes. Sadly we found not a soul alive. All we found were the corpses of men, women and children, and dead cats and dogs. There were arms, legs and other human remains scattered all around. The smell was terrible from rotting bodies buried in the rubble. I once saw a dog feeding on the corpse of a woman. I picked up a stone and threw it to make the dog run away, but it came back and tried to drag the corpse to somewhere quieter to continue feeding. Danger was everywhere in the city. Buildings would collapse without warning and gas explosions were frequent due to the ruptured mains. In reality we had come too late to feel that we had tried to save the city. We were now attending its funeral. It affected us both very much. When we returned to the safety of the farm we both began to have nightmares. The other people would moan at us for waking them up in the night. How could they understand?

Pressure began to mount on German cities as a result of the Allied bombing campaign, and female firefighters were once again recruited into the *Feuerwehr* [fire defence service]. Women had served in the *Feuerwehr* during the First World War and had been active in this role mainly in Berlin and Breslau. German women were encouraged once again to volunteer for the fire defence service throughout the Second World War. Matilda Weyergang was just nineteen years old when she volunteered as a driver for the Berlin central *Feuerwehr*. She recalls:

My parents went berserk when I told them I had volunteered. They were not happy at all. 'Leave it to the men,' my father said to me. I had been in the *Bund Deutscher Mädel* and

Landjahr so how would this be any different, I thought. I had to feel that I was doing something to help. I was fit, strong and was not scared of anything. In the past I had learned to drive tractors, cars and even motorcycles. I was competent at driving and was given a driver's job in the fire defence service. The kind of vehicle that I was in charge of was a Mercedes. It was known as the Light Fire Truck L1500S LLG. It was not a very large vehicle and was easy to drive. It had a ladder attached to the roof and a small box-type trailer would be towed from the back. The box trailer contained all of the appliances that were needed for firefighting. The vehicle could carry seven people including myself. It was not exactly fast and had a maximum speed of fifty miles per hour, though driving around city streets at that speed required concentration and skill.

I began my duty in the winter of 1943. The bombings became horrendous and the dangers we all faced were very real. We were out in the thick of it as they say. My job was to get to the scene of the nearest fire as quickly as possible. High-priority buildings were to be saved first, we were told. I would drive the truck with the bombs falling all around us. Steel splinters from the exploding flak artillery rained down on us too. You could hear them landing on the roof of the truck. Pieces of these splinters could often be found afterwards lodged in the tyres. When we reached a designated fire, the men would jump out and connect the hoses and begin to fight the fires. All the time bombs were falling and exploding around us and steel fragments fell from the sky. You had to wear protective helmets. If a steel splinter hit your head without you wearing a helmet it could kill you easily. I found it frustrating just pulling up and letting the men do all the work while I sat in the driver's seat. Against the rules, I often jumped out and began helping them, or watching their backs as they worked. These men were some of the bravest I have ever met in my life. We were all in the frontline, out in the thick of it day after day and night after night. We could have been killed in an instant and we lived with that.

One thing that stands out in my mind was after one particularly bad raid on Berlin. We had been out all night fighting fires in the city. By dawn many fires were still raging, but we had managed to put many of them out or get them under control. There was this building that I went into. Inside were the charred remains of two children and a woman. They had huddled together and the smoke had probably killed them long before the fire incinerated them […] I went out through the back into a long passage way and saw something moving ahead of me. As I got closer I could see it was someone's pet cat. Its pitiful cries filled me with sadness. I coaxed the frightened animal to me and, when I picked it up, it gripped me like a terrified child might. Its eyes were wide with terror and it was trembling. There was no way I could leave it behind in this hell. I carried the cat back through the house and put it in the foot well of the truck where it stayed without moving. When the men climbed back in the truck they asked what it was and I told them 'It's a cat and its mine now.' They probably thought I was mad, but they didn't try and stop me or anything. When I got home later that day I brought the cat in and straight away my brothers and sisters crowded round to fuss over it. I gave it some food and some water and checked it for any injuries. Apart from some slightly burned fur he was fine. When I went up to bed the cat followed me and slept on my bed with me. Whenever I was home the cat would follow me everywhere I went. Do you know that cat lived for over sixteen years with me? When he died I was distraught and felt as if I had lost a family member, or a part of me. It was one of the good memories of my time with the fire defence service.

Most of the memories are of death; seeing my friends die, burned bodies of men, women and children and little babies. We often found whole families dead in their cellars. They had been trapped down there. The fire took away their oxygen and that, combined with the smoke, was the main killer. By the time the flames and the heat had burned them they were, mercifully, dead. Those who had burned to death often had the grimace of pain etched into their faces. They were like the dead but still screaming out. The children were the worst sights. Seeing them clinging to their mothers who had tried to protect them, those were the nightmares I had in the years afterwards. Terrible dreams night after night. Bodies were often reduced to carbon, so that when you tried to move them, bits would break off in your hands. I married after the war, but we soon separated as my husband could not deal with me. He tried his best to understand and support me, but I suffered such terrible mood swings and after just one year he left. We remained friends up until we divorced but from then on I lived alone. It's the curse I carried from the days when our city burned.

Emmi Dorr was a nineteen-year-old resident of Cologne. She had enrolled in the fire defence service just three months prior to the thousand-bomber raid on the city. She gave the following account:

The aftermath was the worst part of it all. The sheer devastation and death that had been caused was just horrifying. Dealing with the fires was one thing, but having to deal with the other things was equally difficult. The burned bodies had to be removed and buried. Then there were parts of bodies that had been caught in explosions. We would walk around with buckets in our hands, picking up pieces of human beings. I found a young child wandering around, crying. I asked him, 'Where are your mother and father?' He just kept repeating, 'Mother and father dead'. I said to the boy, 'Be brave. Hold onto my hand and I will take you to your relatives.' I knew the boy had grandparents and, from making enquiries, I discovered they had survived the bombing. It was heart-warming being able to reunite that child with the last remaining family he had. The problem was there were so many like that child and, as much as I wanted to, I could not help every one of them.

I saw the bodies of whole families that I had known in the city. One was a young woman with a five-year-old girl. The husband was away fighting in the war. I found the body of the little girl with her legs missing and she was still clutching a small plastic doll in her arms. The doll had melted in the heat and the plastic had fused to the little girl's skin. She had died a horrible death. The mother was found several hundred yards away. She had been literally blown in half. She had probably been carrying her child when the explosion occurred. As I knew the family I helped comfort the husband when he returned home after the war. He asked me how his wife and child had died. I started to cry as I couldn't tell him the awful nature of it all. I had to write it all down for him. He sat with his head in his hands and sobbed. Just a few weeks after I met with him he took his own life. The grief of losing the wife and child he adored was just too much for him.

Vaida Raab recalls a similar scene in Berlin which became all too familiar as the Allied bombing progressed.

The girls of the BDM had to go out and collect up any human remains we could find. We were given various containers in which to put the body parts we found. The best things to use were the tin baths everyone had. We would work in pairs and walk around looking for body parts. I once spotted what I thought was the burnt remains of a small child's toy doll. I bent down and picked it up, but dropped it in the same instant. It was not a child's doll but the charred and shrivelled remains of a baby. We found the remains of its mother just a few yards away. They were so badly charred that both fitted in the tin bath we were carrying. It was horrible. I saw some Hitler Youths break off limbs to get the bodies to fit into the containers they were using. I was told the remains we collected would be put into a single mass grave. I could never forget the sound of those enemy bombers approaching. It was the sound that death was on its way. It was like a deep, vibrating hum that became a continuous growling sound. Then the bombs would begin to fall. We lived each day not knowing if we would be alive to see the dawn next morning. In quiet moments I would sit and think to myself, 'Men and their fucking wars. Why can they not live on this planet in peace?' Surely the answers are there somewhere?

I have a special admiration for those women involved in helping to fight the fires that engulfed Germany's cities during the Second World War. Those who worked in the Fire Defence were confronted with walls of flame and hellish scenes that are quite unimaginable to people today. They did not retreat; they stood firm and fought the fires that were consuming their people and destroying their cities. Many of these women paid with their lives.

Chapter Eleven

Rotes Kreuz

The *Deutscher Rotes Kreuz* [German Red Cross] was instituted in 1864 by Dr Aaron Silverman of the Charité Hospital in Berlin. Known as the DRK, it was a highly professional and efficient organisation involved in all areas of the medical and nursing profession in Germany. During the First World War the DRK was active in assisting Germany's military forces. Behind the front lines they operated mobile first-aid stations, setting up and operating surgical units for badly wounded German soldiers. There was a carefully organised medical logistics system put in place whereby even the most severely wounded soldiers could be treated and then put on a train home to a hospital to recuperate within hours. DRK staff would ensure all those wounded were cared for every step of the way. As a result many men who should have died from their wounds were often saved.

At the end of the First World War, under the terms of the Treaty of Versailles, the DRK was prevented from having any association with the German military. As a result of this policy, during the Weimar years the DRK became involved largely in social welfare due to the privations in German society at the time. It was officially acknowledged by the Geneva Convention in 1929. After the Nazis came to power in 1933 it was made clear that the DRK would once again play a role in assisting Germany's armed forces. Nazi Reich Interior Minister Wilhelm Frick said of the DRK: 'The DRK is something like the conscience of the nation. Together with the nation, the DRK is ready to commit all its strengths for the high goals of our leader Adolf Hitler.'

By its very nature the DRK should have been a politically neutral organisation but, by the outbreak of the Second World War, it was subject to the political and social ideology of the Third Reich. Many of the DRK's staff were already thoroughly indoctrinated individuals, fully aware of their racial obligations. Jews were not only expelled from positions of employment in the DRK but also denied treatment. As Germany inched towards war in 1939 the DRK were more than prepared to support any military action its army would have to embark upon.

Selina Mayer was just eighteen years of age when she began her work with the DRK. She was working as a maternity nurse in the hospital at Spandau, Berlin. She recalled:

> I liked working with children. I came from a large family and was used to helping my mother with the care of my younger brothers and sisters. Working in the DRK was a natural progression for me career wise. In the hospital my work did not just evolve around looking after the babies and children in the hospital. There were many elderly people in there too who we had the task of caring for. Drugs and medicines had to be prescribed to them. The medicines and drugs were given to me and I would then take them and administer them to the patients. It was all fairly routine and things never got to the point where the staff could not cope.
>
> I remember the policy after 1933 was that we were to treat and care for Germans only. If any Jews required treatment for anything they were to be refused. Refusing Jews medical care was seen as a logical way of getting rid of them. In fact, many would die as a result of being denied basic medical care. What did I think to this policy of refusing Jews medical care? Well, as an eighteen-year-old raised under the National Socialists I complied with their wishes. Had I been difficult and given them problems I would have been dismissed from my services and I did not want that to happen. Yet my conscience was also affected by this. A Jewish family came in once and they begged us for help. One of the children had been suffering from seizures and a young Jewish girl with the family was five months pregnant. I had to turn them all away as I was forbidden to give them treatment. They walked out of the hospital, resigned to the fact we would not help them. People in the hospital looked at them in disgust as they walked out. As they reached the exit door some of the people coming in spat at them. Some orderlies were told to disinfect the floor where the 'dirty Jews' had

just walked. There was this terrible paranoia that Jews carried disease, like rats. This was a universal opinion. Our country had taught us this and we feared Jews like a contagion. A sign was placed outside the hospital warning all Jews to stay away under the racial hygiene laws. Soon all the Jews steadily disappeared from the area. In later years I had regrets about it. But it was not my fault. I just did as I was told.

Diana Urbacher was typical of the average German girl who aspired to enter the DRK and she recalled:

The Hitler Youth for the girls, or BDM as it was called, taught all aspects of first-aid. The BDM was adamant all of the girls under its charge be proficient at dealing with a wide variety of wounds, breaks and injuries. It seemed to me we were, in some ways, being prepared for a war. We would be shown how to treat basic things like cuts and burns. Then we went on to learn about how one should diagnose and treat a broken limb. Then it would progress to head injuries and all this included treatment, bandaging and care methods to be used for each casualty. Amputation was also discussed and we had to practise the use of a tourniquet for loss of limbs or assisting a doctor with amputation procedures and things. If you had a love for this work then you aspired to join the DRK. The more proficient you were within the BDM, the better it would be for you going towards a nursing or medical career.

I learned all of the basics then was shown how you assess and treat a gunshot or shrapnel wound. Shrapnel wounds produced massive damage to the body. You could not always see the internal damage so you had to understand the signs and what to look for. Generally, a high velocity bullet will make a clean entry wound in a victim, but where it exits there will be a huge hole. Sometimes shrapnel will be so hot that it will cauterise the wound as it penetrates flesh. I was taught how to assess if shrapnel was still inside a wound and things like that. I also did much in the field of childcare. I helped midwives to deliver babies and then helped the mothers afterwards. We got to see both sides of it all you see. A few years of that kind of teaching and you can deal with a great many things. This is why girls of the BDM were the German nation's most precious resource. We were taught so many skills, from the traditional to more advanced. We even learned survival techniques and to us girls it was all one big adventure.

I had already made up my mind that I wanted to enter the medical profession. It was something I wanted to do for a living. When war broke out in 1939, my heart sank as I thought I wouldn't be able to realise this dream with our country at war. I need not have worried as, on the contrary, it proved useful to my ambitions. As the war progressed, our country needed more and more medical staff, some of whom would be serving right behind the battlefront. Men were needed most of all to fight. Men who were surgeons and doctors were not sent to out to fight and stayed in their professions. Those of us who volunteered to be nursing staff and assist surgeons and doctors needed a strong stomach. The sights of war are not something that every female could stand for long periods. You either took to it like a duck to water or you didn't; it was as simple as that. Often you learned on the job and there was no such thing as a day off. You took time off when conditions permitted.

I was posted to a mobile hospital unit just after Barbarossa [the name given to the German invasion of the Soviet Union in 1941]. As I was told I would learn on the job, it would be intense at times, I would see men live and I would see men die. I would see some horrible things that might cause me sleepless nights, but I still wanted to do the work. We followed as our armies pushed deeper into enemy territory. Most of the German soldiers we treated at first were gunshot wounds and then artillery injuries would come in. Gunshot wounds could be operated on and dealt with fairly easily, unless the soldier had been shot in the head and the brain had been injured. Artillery fire created the most devastating injuries of all. It would blow an arm or a leg off. Sometimes a soldier would be brought in with both legs and an arm or both legs and both arms missing. We would work immediately to stop any bleeding and prevent the soldier from going into shock. You couldn't let them sleep sometimes so they would pick the prettiest nurses to sit with them and keep talking to them. I myself had to do this on countless occasions. I would finish my work with my uniform covered in blood, feeling drained of all energy. Saving lives like that requires so much of your energy. When I was not working I just slept. I wrote letters home to my parents to let them know that I was alright. I never once let on to them how exhausted I was becoming.

We expected casualties as we were in a war, but when winter started to arrive with the cold and snow even some of us nurses fell ill. I came down with a bout of influenza and was confined to bed for almost a week and a half until I felt fit enough to work again. My colleagues looked after me, bringing me hot drinks, bread and soup all the time. I found myself longing for some apple cake. I loved the apple cake my mother and grandmother made back home. They sent me one in a parcel, but how could I not share it with my colleagues. I cut it up equally and we sat and ate the cake with our coffee and it was like heaven, a little piece of home. I asked my mother to please send me more apple cake whenever she could. I still love apple cake to this day and taught both my son and daughter how to make it.

That winter of 1941 was a horror story for us. The men were dropping like flies. They had no proper winter clothing issued to them, much to the shame of the authorities. They were living in holes in the ground at times and many just went to sleep and never woke up. What they call trench foot was the biggest problem, apart from the effects of hypothermia. So many trench foot cases came in and they were utterly dreadful. I had to cut both the boots from one soldier's feet once. I cut through the rotted leather with scissors. The boots were no good for the wet, cold and freezing conditions here. As I pulled off his socks the flesh came off his feet with the socks. Many of the toenails were missing and some of the toes had turned black. This was the worst possible scenario of all. It often meant that the black toes had to be removed surgically through amputation. Sometimes the foot, or even both feet, had to be amputated as gangrene had set in. The not so serious cases were still a huge problem. We could clean and dry the soldiers' feet and treat them properly, but as soon as they went back out into the fighting their feet would become cold and wet again and the feet could not heal. Trench foot could mean being sent home from the battlefront, for if a soldier could not walk or run he was of no use. It could take many weeks for trench foot to clear up. Some would have lasting physical problems because of it.

I said to my superiors once, 'When are the winter boots and clothing for our men going to arrive here?' One replied, 'When Goering gets off his fat fucking arse and lives up to his promises, Fräulein!' I could not believe the contempt that the higher powers had in allowing our men to be exposed to temperatures of minus 40 to 50 with no proper clothing. We girls huddled around a small fire in an abandoned building. We talked about the situation while smoking our cigarettes and drinking our steaming hot coffee. One stood up and said, 'I feel so fucking guilty, you know. Here we are, sat in the relative warmth of this hut with our coffee and cigarettes while our men are all but twenty or so miles ahead of us, slowly freezing to death!' We sat and said nothing as we knew she was right. But what could we do? We did keep reminding the officers that the men needed adequate footwear and clothing for the conditions. They would reassure us that everything possible was being done. The situation was exacerbated as the enemy went on the offensive. They knew we were struggling with the conditions. It was normal to them as it was their land and they were able to fight in this weather. We could have fought, but Herr Hitler should have ensured that the Wehrmacht had the resources to get the job done and win the war. They were some very brave boys. Some were just kids themselves, seventeen, eighteen, nineteen years of age. Many wore Iron Cross ribbons on their tunics.

I recall some enemy soldiers being captured on one occasion. Some were obviously wounded but still able to walk and some helped by their comrades. I just assumed that we would treat their injuries and they would be sent to be held as POWs [Prisoners of War]. I went to one's aid but was pulled back by an officer. The officer wore the runes of the SS on his collars. I said to him, 'It's my job to treat the wounded whoever they are, is it not?' He barked back, 'These men have no need of your services, Fräulein.' They were pushed on and I watched them until they were out of sight. Minutes later I heard the crack of small arms' fire from the direction where the men had been marched. I don't know if those Russians had been executed as I was prevented from going to investigate. They threatened to dismiss me if I persisted in interfering in the affairs that were the concerns of the SS and the state. They threatened me with arrest. That's what they said to me.

As the Second World War progressed, German cities came under increasingly heavy attack from the air, particularly from the United States Eighth Air Force. The German Anti-Aircraft defences were increased to the point where they were even situated on the rooftops of hospitals. Such measures made these hospitals fair game for the bombers. One nurse from East Prussia recalled:

I was not a Nazi and did not sympathise with Hitler. As a nurse working under the DRK, I felt that, as a human being, I should help anyone who needed me, regardless of their race or colour. Of course, this was not easy to do under National Socialism. I defied them at every opportunity and many of my colleagues did the same. Jews had been sought out and removed to concentration camps in parts of Germany and the east. If you were caught assisting anyone regarded as racially inferior under the Nazi laws then you faced the possibility of being executed or sent to one of the concentration camps yourself.

The thought of hospitals being bombed was horrific. The hospital I was working at was bombed, which was inevitable as it had guns on the roof. We helped get as many patients as we could out. The dead were buried in a mass grave around the back of the hospital. Bits of bodies lay all around and these had to be collected up too. We evacuated before the Russians arrived. We had heard all of the horrible stories about them and, yes, we were afraid of what they would do to us. There was a huge effort to remove all the women from our area to prevent the Russians from raping them. The strange thing was my attitude was that I would treat anyone, regardless whether they were civilians, Waffen SS, or even Russians. Compassion was my trade in a sense. Had I lacked compassion I would have been just another of Hitler's monsters.

Emma Klein entered the DRK in December of 1943. Emma was an extremely pretty girl though not the typical blonde-haired, blue-eyed Aryan type so beloved of the German propaganda machine. Emma wore her brown hair in the traditional plaits and while on duty wore her hair in a bun. She often wore spectacles while on duty, but she would still receive admiring comments on her looks, particularly her hazel eyes. Emma recalled:

I was a nineteen-year-old and, for a short period, I was in Minsk with our forces in Belorussia. I was working with a surgical unit helping the doctors and surgical teams. I did various jobs there such as sanitising and preparing surgical instruments ready for operations. I remember the fighting there had been quite intense and we were kept busy most of the time. The times I had stood and watched bullets being pulled out of the heads, legs, arms and bodies of soldiers was something I soon lost count of. Those in charge of us were of the opinion that any wounded enemy brought in should be left to die unless they had information which may prove useful to our army. Only then would they be given treatment that could save their lives. You will be surprised at the number who offered to squeal in order to spare their own lives. They clearly had no scruples about the lives of their comrades. Yes, I was a National Socialist and I was a German. In my capacity as a nurse I would have treated anyone, but I was not making the rules. There were German officers and ordinary soldiers who disagreed with some of the Reich's policies regarding the treatment of enemy soldiers. There were equally as many who 'did not care a fuck for the enemy'. I was once given a leaflet reminding me of my duty and not to feel any sympathy for the 'apes'. The enemy were often referred to as apes, or as sub-human.

My happiest memories were of some of our boys. There were some that we would fight for hours to save. After operating they would be left to recover. I would see them and care for them every day and grew to know many of them. Some were repatriated back home to Germany when they were fit enough. Others were sent back to the battlefront. Many would receive bravery decorations in their hospital beds. There was one young man who was rather cheeky. He tried the touch-my-backside trick then made out it was an accident. How could I be angry with him? I just laughed at him. I warned him to behave himself in future. I became quite good friends with him and would sit and talk with him. He was a couple of years older than me. He actually asked if he could take me out for dinner when the war was over. I told him I would have to think about it. I was with him the morning his officer arrived to present him with his Iron Cross Second Class and a wound badge. His legs were in a pretty bad shape and it would take a long time for him to regain full use of them. Before he left to go home to his family I told him to persevere with the treatment and do as he was told and he would recover. He would never be fit enough for the army ever again, though I never told him that. He asked me for my address before he left so I gave him two addresses, including that of my home back in Germany. He left and I continued my work. Some of the injuries that I saw horrified me. One German soldier came in with half of his own steel helmet embedded in his skull. A mortar had landed close by and the blast forced the metal rim of the helmet into his head. He died on the operating table shortly after the helmet was extracted from his skull. Had he survived I have no doubts he would have had severe brain injuries. Where would such an injury have left a young man like that in our society? I heard one surgeon say, 'Better a cripple dies here on the table than return to the Reich a burden.'

We moved around a lot over the next few months. The conditions were not pleasant as we lived in large tents. When it rained, the water came in as floods along the ground. The snow and cold in winter was utterly intolerable. I hated the weather in that place. Even in summer it was bad as the heat brought with it clouds of biting insects and flies. The flies got in everything. It was a nightmare to live in. As a nurse I was very particular about my hygiene, but you could not keep clean, living like this. When things began to turn badly for our forces we were suddenly retreating under Russian artillery fire. For the first time I witnessed incoming artillery and the effect of blast and shrapnel on human bodies. I saw people blown apart into what looked like casserole steaks. So we were constantly retreating backwards. No one asked questions; we just did as we were told. One morning a Junkers aircraft arrived and we were told to get our most important things, leave anything else and get on the plane. 'Don't ask questions, Fräulein, just do it', was the order. So I picked up my small trinket box, a coat and some shoes and got on board the Junkers. We were being evacuated from the front, as I could see as we flew over our troop positions.

When I arrived back in Germany my parents were excited to see me. They told me that a bundle of letters had arrived for me. Once I had rested and had some food they brought me the letters. They were from the soldier I had treated in the east. I sat down and began to read through them all. Some of the writing made me smile. I wrote a letter back to the boy, agreeing that I would go to a dance with him. A few weeks later we met up and he took me to a dance. I had been to a few before with friends of mine from the DRK but this was very pleasant. He would not let go of me all night, even though his legs were clearly still giving him much pain. 'For God's sake, rest those legs,' I told him and took his hand and made him sit down. We met a few more times after that but there was nothing naughty going on [she laughs]. I wanted to be sure his intentions were entirely honourable before I would allow things to go any further. My girlfriends in the DRK would always ask, 'Have you not done it with him yet?' I would tell them every time 'no'. We would all laugh about it as it was funny in some ways.

I started working at a local hospital in my home city so was soon busy again. But my boyfriend took me to another dance and afterwards I invited him back to the apartment I shared with some other girls. After three months I felt I was ready and he spent the night with me. I would say he certainly enjoyed it [she laughs]. We discussed marriage as I had really fallen in love with this boy. My parents expressed concern at me marrying a man who may be an invalid and unable to support me. I reminded them, 'This invalid, as you call him, is only an invalid through fighting for this country.' When they met him their opinions changed, of course.

His legs improved a lot over the months that followed. We eventually married in 1948. The defeat of our country and the mess it was in at the end of the Second World War meant all plans to marry had to be shelved until everything had settled to a degree. After the war I worked again as a nurse as the new West Germany needed nurses and medical staff with experience [...] After the war the whole structure of the DRK changed once again. There were no more racial laws, no more discrimination and we went back to being human again.

Kathi Frier and her best friend, Gertrud Lehnt, both enrolled into the German Red Cross at the same time. They were friends virtually from kindergarten and had come of age under National Socialism, joining the *Jungmädelbund* and BDM through the late 1930s. Kathi takes up her story:

Both me and Gertrud grew up in Leipzig, a beautiful German city that lies close to Berlin. We fulfilled all of our obligations for the Reich and, as both of us liked it, we volunteered to train in nursing. We both ended up at a sanatorium that was being used for wounded soldiers to recuperate in. I think

Gertrud made a bit of a gaffe when we arrived and I vividly remember her saying something like 'Where are the lunatics?' The director of services was not happy at all at the remark, '"Lunatics?" What do you mean "lunatics"?' She shook her head and told us both curtly to follow her. We were taken into a room and given a uniform each. I suspected the woman didn't like us as we were given all kinds of shitty jobs like emptying the soldiers' bed pans and things. I found it all quite repulsive and not quite how I imagined it. At night many of the wounded soldiers would have nightmares. They would scream the place down and their screams echoed around the silent corridors. I always got put on night duty and I found the place really creepy. There were soldiers who couldn't sleep and, to pass the time, I would sit and talk with them. They talked about their service and how they got wounded and their concerns about how the war was going for Germany. They expressed great fear for their families. I was told to keep this quiet as things were not going the way our leaders had anticipated. Gertrud had to do her fair share of night work too and she hated it as much as I did. I had an argument with the director one evening and I just thought to myself that I didn't want to do this shitty job anymore. I walked out and Gertrud resigned the next day and followed me. We just got sick of the doing all the dirty jobs while the others did all the real nursing work. That hospital was later struck by bombs and people lost their lives there. I think it was abandoned after that.

Not all the hospitals were bad though and we soon found other work where we were actually applying our nursing skills. Again we were more often than not dealing with wounded soldiers. There were so many wounded coming back from the east. It was slightly alarming. We would travel to the train station and help remove the wounded from the train. They would be transported to hospitals and another train would come in and we would do the same. Injuries ranged from broken bones to gunshot wounds, shrapnel wounds and amputations. I recall one of the patients had been exposed to phosphorous during a shell attack. I had to sit and watch him all night as there was a danger that phosphorous residues still in his skin could spontaneously ignite and not only burn him to death but set the whole place alight. It was just awful.

We saw the true horrors of the war in that place; what weapons could do to a human being and how they destroyed lives. In the beginning we supported the reforms brought into effect by Hitler, but by the end we were suffering a war of conscience. The worst thing of all was that people used to say, 'Fräulein Frier, you look just like Eva Braun'. Eva Braun was, of course, Hitler's lady at the time. Whenever me and Gertrud went out to socialise I would be pestered by men who just wanted to sleep with me because I looked like Eva Braun. One young man I had met was different, I thought. We went out a few times for drinks. Things went further one evening and he took me back to his house. We were making love and he suddenly started to say to me, 'Oh, Eva! Oh, Eva! I adore you, my Eva!' I just wanted him off me at that point but I couldn't get him off until he had finished. After that he rolled off and I got up straightaway and slapped him. He told me to get out so I got dressed as quickly as I could and left.

[…] We had to leave the city ahead of the Russian advance. We just left everything behind in blind panic with everyone else. The rule was to keep heading west and not stop. After the war we didn't quite know what to do with ourselves. We joined rubble gangs and helped clear up, and we helped out on farms with crops and things. Neither of us really wanted to go back into nursing. There were too many bad memories. We took whatever menial work we could and saved up our money so we could go off travelling. We went all over the place and even went to Goa in India. It was the height of the Flower Power thing and everyone was smoking marijuana. We both tried smoking it to see what all the fuss was about. It was okay, but to be honest I preferred normal cigarettes. We returned to Germany and I began working at a hair salon while Gertrud worked for a car sales company. We both met people and later married. We kept in touch for some time then drifted apart. I just have the memories and a few photographs now.

It would appear that many of the young girls and women who enrolled for service in the DRK were struggling with their conscience, torn between their support for their National Socialist leadership and that of remaining racially impartial where medical matters were concerned. The reality was that it was difficult to be humane under the direction of Nazism, whatever your chosen profession was.

Chapter Twelve

There be Monsters

The sexual excesses pursued by leading figures in the Third Reich hierarchy are now well documented. What remains one of the darkest and most sinister elements is that of the rape, abuse and paedophilia that substantial sections of the German female populace were subjected to between 1933 and 1945. It should also come as no surprise that the rape, sexual abuse and exploitation of young Jewish girls and women was far more prevalent than it was previously thought to have been.

In the concentration camps the abuse of Jewish females of all ages went on largely undetected. The perpetrators, aware of their racial hygiene obligations, were opportunist predators. Only when they were certain that their crimes would not be detected did they attempt to carry them out. There were, of course, those in higher office prepared to turn a blind eye to a camp guard abusing or even raping one of the female inmates. This practice was far more commonplace than one might expect. It was even more commonplace amongst the foreign volunteers employed by the Germans during the Second World War. Bribes in the form of money, tobacco, alcohol and jewellery were often enough to secure the silence of senior officers. It was a form of corruption.

Sexual abuse and exploitation take place in every society and culture and victims often suffer in silence, living in fear of the ridicule and stigma associated with it. When addressing this issue with former BDM girls I was not surprised to discover that almost all of them, at some point, had experienced some form of abuse and exploitation, or even worse. While Jews were totally at the mercy of those who viewed them as nothing more than vermin, the girls of the BDM were Germany's future. The Nazis took much pride in their League of German Maidens so why were so many of them subjected to derogatory remarks and sexual abuse? To even begin to explore this dark area of German Third Reich history made me feel very uneasy. I knew that I would probably hear many things that I hoped I would not. Many of the abusers are long dead, but the effects of their deeds live on in their victims. The courage displayed by many of the women, who, as young girls, suffered abuse, is exemplary.

In this chapter we will address both German and Jewish perspectives on the sexual abuse of women in the Third Reich. It is by no means an exhaustive study. There are thousands of cases that could not be included in this narrative. We begin with the account given by Klara Wyborny, a resident of Berlin.

> I was an excited fifteen-year-old in 1936 and I was present at the rally at Nuremberg. This was a very big Nazi rally and I was there with the League of German Girls. It was known as the 'Rally of Honour' and [...] represented the restoration of honour to the German people. My parents were with me, but not all of the time during the day. I remember there were so many photographers there who wanted to take pictures of us. It was after we had finished a sports routine that it happened to me.
>
> There was this man, a German man, who told me he was a photographer for the *Völkischer Beobachter*. This was a big Nazi newspaper of the time. He was a tall, balding man who I would say was in his fifties maybe [...] He had this big camera around his neck and asked if I would pose for a photograph for his paper. I trusted him and had no bad feeling initially about him. He said there was a setting he wanted to use as a background for his shots, so I went with him. Back then there were no warnings about strange men. This was Third Reich Germany. The Jews, we were told, were the bogeymen, not German men like this.
>
> We walked a short distance to where there was a stream and trees. He asked me to remove my gym shoes and socks and step into the stream. I did as he asked and he began to shoot some pictures. I asked if that was it and could I go back now, but he said no, he had more pictures he wanted to take of me. He asked me to lie down as if I were sunbathing. I did not feel comfortable lying down with him kneeling beside me but I did

as he asked. The minute I lay down he removed the camera strap from around his neck and sat astride me. He put a hand over my mouth and told me that if I cried out I would get into very serious trouble, that no one would believe me as he was a respectable family man and a member of the Nazi Party. I was terrified and obeyed him. He pulled up my sports vest and began feeling me while pleasuring himself with his other hand. After he had finished he got up, fastened his trousers and warned me to keep quiet about it or there would be very big trouble for me and my family. He then walked off quickly. I got up and used some water from the stream to wash his semen off my stomach and breasts. I used some grass to try and dry myself. I got my gym shoes back on and headed back. I felt in shock and kept looking around to see if I could see the man, but I never saw him again. I could not have reported what happened to anyone. I was terrified no one would believe me and so I kept it secret.

Girls of the BDM – as has been revealed in *Hitler's Girls: Doves Amongst Eagles* and *In Hitler's Shadow: Post-War Germany and the Girls of the BDM* – were often pressured to have sex with their male counterparts. The fact that some were even raped is even more shocking. The sad fact is that rape happened frequently and girls felt obliged to keep these attacks quiet. Only in very recent years have many courageously decided to speak out.

Elise Marschmann was a twenty-one-year-old gymnast in attendance at Nuremberg in 1936. Her account is very typical of many rapes that went unrecorded and unpunished in the Third Reich.

We had always been the subject of attention and sexual remarks. That was something we girls lived with. We never imagined that anyone could overstep the mark as they say. I certainly did not feel that way until Nuremberg. There was a lot of drinking and a lot of drunk men around. Young men of the Hitler Youth had spent most the day drinking in some cases. The authorities were not concerned as long as there was no fighting or breaches of the peace. We mixed with these young men all the time on such big occasions and at tournaments.

One of them seemed very nice and we started chatting. He told me he came from Nuremberg and was a Nuremberg Hitler Youth through and through. Over the few days that followed he showed me some of the sights around the city, so when he asked me to join him for a picnic I said yes. I had no suspicions of him not behaving in an appropriate manner at that time. I had had a boyfriend so was used to being around boys. I never felt that I was going to end up being raped.

It happened on the picnic. We had, up until that moment, quite a lovely time together. After the picnic he started paying me compliments about how nice I looked. He then asked me if I had ever had sex with a boy before. I told him it was none of his business. So he says, 'That means you have then.' He tried to kiss me and I told him to stop it and behave himself. He would not stop and, as I tried to get up and walk away, he pulled me back down. He was then on top of me and I just tried to get him off me. He kept saying, 'It's not good you trying to stop me, Fräulein. You will soon tire, so stop fighting me.' I kept fighting him even as he was pulling up my skirt and pulling down my underwear. He became angry the more I struggled. In the end I had no strength left to fight him off. I had to lie there as he forced himself inside me. I had to just close my eyes and wait for him to have his fun with me and then maybe I could go. After the rape – that is exactly what it was – he got up and asked me if I had enjoyed the afternoon. He asked if we could do this again tomorrow as I only had two more days left in Nuremberg. I was so angry I tried to hit him, but he grabbed my wrists and snarled in my face, 'Don't you ever try to hit me! No woman ever hits me!' I just ran away and left him standing there laughing. Yes, he thought it was all very funny.

After that my whole opinion changed of the way we were living in Germany. You couldn't go and tell a policeman as the man's word was always against the woman's and the woman would be blamed for leading the young man on or whatever. They would say, 'You probably encouraged the boy, look at how you are dressed', things like that. Girls and women were treated like shit by their leaders and menfolk. I told my husband about the rape, but I did that before we got married. He wanted to try and track the culprit down. He wanted to go to Nuremberg and search for this fellow. Had he done so, he might have been put in prison for murder. Oh yes, he would have probably killed him. It takes time to get through things like that. For a woman to be raped, it is the worst possible violation she can face in life. It did cause both me and my husband problems over the years, but he was a good man, dear and understanding. I am thankful for that. As for the boy who did that to me, he was just a beast preying on a defenceless girl. That is nothing whatsoever to be proud of, is it?

Inge Gursche was another former BDM girl who decided that she should finally speak out. Talking to me via a live link in early 2003, she recalled:

Even when I was just fourteen I had boys of the Hitler Youth and old men ogling me everywhere I went. It was always worse when you were in either gym clothing or your uniform. I think these things kind of turned them on. It was not funny though and it felt threatening when you got older boys and old men coming up to you telling you what they wanted to do with you in their beds. One of the Hitler Youth boys I knew used to say, 'Look, Inge, if you give me what I want I will give you this.' They would have money or other things and try to bribe you into giving them hand relief or oral sex. I was once grabbed by a boy five years my senior. He had a grip like a vice and I had no hope of being able to get away from him. He frightened me. I knew that if he wanted to he could have thrown me down and done whatever he wanted to do with me. I shouted out, but there was no one around to hear me. He cupped my breasts with his hands and was saying things like 'Hmm, this is really good.' I could feel him getting excited. It was only after I kicked him as hard as I could with the heel of my foot that he let me go. I went straight to one of the Hitler Youth boy leaders and told him what happened. All he said was, 'I have no time to hear your romantic stories. Now go away. Go on, get out of here.' It was dismissed just like that. I should have told my parents, but to tell them was out of the question. They would probably have beaten me for aiding in the betting [sic] as it is called. I had done no wrong yet the boys got away with these things because they were the superiors. They were seen as the fighters, the warriors of our race. What choices did we young girls have back then? No, it was not good, and when things like this happened it made you question everything, including your loyalty.

There were also numerous wealthy benefactors who used their positions to attempt to exploit young girls and women. The powers that these individuals had over ordinary citizens and the influence they had over local government could be very intimidating. Klara Binz, a Berlin BDM girl, aged sixteen at the time, recalled:

There were some very powerful individuals within our community. We were to give these men and women full respect at all times. They were wealthy German business people and respected contributors to the Reich finance offices and banks. Most of them were old, or rather they appeared old to me back then as I was young. They would come and give us talks and we would be invited to see their houses. They used these things to get close to you and to win your confidence. They would tell you how they had dined with Hitler and things like that. They knew such things would impress us. You did not really understand what was going on until it was too late. They would get you into their houses and give you sweets and things. Maybe I was foolish, but I fell for it.

I was offered violin lessons but the man's wife was never there when I went for the lessons. I was not immediately suspicious as he was a highly respected man and had a wife and children. You don't always realise the dangers, do you? I was shown how to hold a violin in the correct way and he would always hold my left hand and position my fingers on the strings. After around three lessons he did much the same thing, but instead of letting go of my hand he held it and kissed it. He kept telling me what a beautiful young girl I was. He then leaned forward and kissed me on the lips. I don't know, I was just shocked. He embraced me and pressed his lips against mine again. I told him, 'You shouldn't be doing this. You have a wife and children who will be back here soon.' He said, 'What my wife and children don't know doesn't hurt them, does it? If anything is said it could only have come from you, girl. You will not say anything, will you? If you do, you realise what trouble you would be in by creating silly tales about me.' In other words, if I said anything he would say I was telling lies and blackmailing him. I was just totally shocked. I had this old man pawing me, running his hands over my body, kissing me on the lips and asking me to do things to him that repulsed me. He threatened that if I did not do as he asked he could make things difficult for me. On the other hand, if I were a good girl I could go far in the world. It was the fear that made me go back and keep doing these so-called violin lessons. I was given tuition so I did learn the instrument. For an hour it would be violin tuition and then giving in to this old man's sick fantasies. He would always lock the door. I would have to undress, kneel down and suck my thumb. That is what he wanted me to do. It was like acting out his fantasy. He would sit in a chair in front of me, masturbating. He seemed barely able to finish and would say to me, 'Here, girl, finish me off.' I would then have to masturbate him.

I hated it and it only stopped after six months when he was taken ill one night. He had suffered a stroke and was quite ill. I made a point of going to see him in his private clinic. When I went into his room it was just me and him. He could see and understood all what was going on around him, but could not move or speak. I leaned down and whispered, 'I hope it hurts and I hope you die you [...] old pig.' I smiled at him as I left the room and walked out of the clinic. Three hours later he suffered a second stroke, which killed him off. To me that was justice. I would love to have gone and told his wife and children. I almost did after the war, but felt it would not have been fair on them. They had enough troubles of their own at that point.

Vaida Raab, whose experiences were included in my second book *In Hitler's Shadow: Post-War Germany and the Girls of the BDM*, verified the authenticity of the above accounts with one of her own. Vaida recalled:

The men […] were obsessed with sex. I knew of men who liked young boys and I knew of men who liked young girls. Today these men would be called paedophiles. I knew of one old man in the town where I lived. He was a librarian and he adored books and his collection was amazing. He had many antique works. I loved books, so when I was invited to see them I was thrilled. I was an excited, naïve thirteen-year-old and I looked up to this man. We were alone once in his library when he started going on about his wife. He said, 'I have a wife, but that's all she is, a wife. I have lots of money so I can have what I want. My wife is old and old women are not good. They are not athletic. They have wrinkled skin, corpse-like fingers and puckered vaginas. Being intimate with them is like being intimate with pigs.' I was nervous of his coarseness and told him I had to go. I am not sure what he was trying to get at by telling me what he did.

Only in later years did I think back that, had I continued going to his library, he might have tried to do something. After what he said I felt uncomfortable and had no desire to go back. It annoys me to think this went on in our supposedly pure culture. I heard that at Nuremberg in 1936 a lot of girls had sex. It wasn't just Nuremberg in 1936 though. There were instances where male Hitler Youth camps were positioned near to female BDM camps. Although promiscuity was frowned upon in the public context, it was secretly encouraged midway through the Second World War. Girls were easily exploited and influenced by the males, not because we were stupid, but because if anything went wrong it would always be the girl's fault. Believe me, life was no bed of roses if you were a girl in Hitler's Third Reich. It was a dog's existence and sadly many of us only truly understood that when it was all over.

It has been said that after the 1936 Nuremberg Nazi Party rally 900 girls of the BDM returned home only to discover later that they were pregnant. The Third Reich at this time, unlike later in the war, were pursuing a policy of 'controlled sexuality'. The horror of these young girls' parents is all too imaginable. The consequences of finding oneself pregnant outside of the sanctity of marriage would have been severe. Many girls in this predicament often gave up their babies to the *Lebensborn* homes, where there would be no questions asked. This was often done at the request of the girl's parents.

BDM girl Bella Schonn had a friend unfortunate enough to find herself pregnant after meeting up with a boyfriend. Bella remembers vividly what happened to the girl:

> My God, did she receive a beating. The father beat her black and blue. He was furious that his daughter could bring such shame on the family. The family sent her away and she only returned after giving birth. The baby was taken away and that was it. She never learned what sex the child was or where it was taken. Her father made her go to church every weekend without fail. He also made her read the Bible every night. I know the BDM were informed about what had happened and they did not seem to act until much later. Someone was sent to the house to threaten the father. They told him, 'If your daughter is being taught that God is greater than the Führer then we will have you arrested for treason.' She never spoke about it again. It was all forgotten, like it had never happened.

Former BDM girl Kirtsen Eckermann remembers certain BDM group leaders who expressed an unhealthy interest in their charges.

> I am sure there was one leader of our troop who was a lesbian. She had the power as she was the leader so what could we do? She would often come round when we were washing and she would look at you in an abnormal way. You could almost read her mind by how she looked at you. I once bruised my leg. It was nothing much, but she insisted I let her look at it. She made me take my shoe and sock off and began massaging my

leg. She started at my foot. She said 'What a pretty foot you have here,' and began working her way up. In my opinion she went too far. Her fingers went up between my thighs, which made me flinch. She just remarked, 'Does this not feel good to you, girl?' I told her, no, it didn't. She let me put my sock and shoe back on, but only after digging her nails into me in anger. It was as if she was trying to make a point like 'you are mine, and I can do what I want with you'.

Anna Dann also recalled the inappropriate behaviour of certain BDM leaders. She remarked:

Back then there were a few of what you would call 'dykes' these days [she laughs]. It wasn't really funny at the time. Some of them were big, butch types with bad tempers. They liked to manhandle you and I am sure some were inclined the other way. Did they take advantage? Oh yes, they did take advantage, and at every available opportunity. There was one we nicknamed 'Big Bertha' after a famous World War One artillery gun. Big Bertha seemed to enjoy watching girls undress and she would stand there, looking intently at you. One of my friends told me she had forcibly kissed her. It just made us all wary of her. When she left we didn't miss her at all. The leader that replaced her was fine though.

If abuse and exploitation flourished within the BDM it is unimaginable how young Jewish girls and women fared at the mercy of their Nazi captors. Some of the worst things I have ever heard during my research were, rather unsurprisingly, perpetrated against Jewish girls and women in the Nazi concentration camps. As slave labourers, they were regarded as property of the Reich. No one cared what happened to these girls. No one cared whether they lived or died. Young Jewish girls were the subject of horrific sexual abuses, some of which are only now coming to light.

Celina Earhart was a young Jewish girl who found herself in Auschwitz. She felt lucky in being selected as suitable to work as a labourer in one of the factory workshops on the site, for, as long as she remained fit, it meant she would escape the gas chambers. She arrived at Auschwitz in 1943, aged seventeen. She recalled the nightmare that soon began to unfold during her time there.

When they made the work selections they looked at me closely. I joined a line to go on work duties in the camp. I saw other lines of people going off in other directions. Obviously I later learned they were going to their deaths. The brutality of the guards was always a problem. If they beat you up too badly and you couldn't work you were sent to your death. I was sent to work in a chemicals workshop. I just did my best to get on with what I had to do and maybe survive this hell.

It was just a few weeks after, in the early hours of the morning, they came for me the first time. I was taken from where I was sleeping with the other women. Two guards took me out of the block and blindfolded me and bound my hands. I asked them what was happening and told them I was frightened. They said nothing and led me outside and we entered another building. Once inside this building they took off the blindfold. I could see it was some kind of office room. There was a bed against a wall and a sink and toilet down a small corridor. A desk stood in the centre of the room. There were three of them in the room. I asked them what they wanted and why I was here. I was told to take off my clothes. I obeyed because I knew what would happen if I said no and if I resisted them. You could not bargain with these beasts. They were drinking alcohol from little bottles. As I removed my clothes they complimented me on my body. They told me I could almost pass for an Aryan, that I did not look like a Jew at all. One of them then walked forward, lifted me up and sat me on the edge of the table. He then pushed me back and shouted for me to lie still. I started to cry, but was told to shut up. He then put on a condom and I knew exactly what they were going to do with me. The one with the condom on then lifted up my legs and continued to enter me. I could do nothing at all to stop him. Once he had finished the other two then raped me. All I can say is that it hurt both physically and emotionally. When they had finished I was blindfolded again and taken back to my block. As I was pushed back in through the door no one said anything. I found a space to lie down and cried myself to sleep. In the days afterwards I considered eating poisonous chemicals. I could not get what happened out of my mind. Every night after the rape ordeal I tried to sleep, wondering if they would come for me again. I lay trying to sleep, in terror.

A month later I was taken again in the same manner. There was just one man in the room this time. The two that had taken me from my block waited outside. This man was old, probably in his sixties, and was wearing a military uniform, but I had not seen him before. He made me pleasure him for some minutes and when he was ready he told me to lie down on the small single bed in the room. I lay there, fully conscious of what was going to happen, while this filthy old Nazi creature gratified himself upon my body. This rape seemed to go on and on and was like he would never stop. When he finally finished I had his sweat in my mouth, hair and on my body. I was going to get up and get dressed and he said 'No, no, lie there. Don't move.' So I lay back down and he walked over with a cigar in his hand. He opened my legs and pushed the cigar inside me and then lit the end of it. He roared with laughter and just said, 'Do you know that I have always wanted to do that?' He left the room and I was ordered to get dressed. Before I was taken back to my block I was given some German cake and a small cup with some hot coffee in it. Why they did this I don't know. Maybe they felt guilt, but I doubt it.

After the liberation of Auschwitz I began searching for my parents. I was lucky they were found alive, although in not very good condition. We spent the next part of our lives trying to come to terms with it all. I told them everything that had happened to me. I recall the first real hot bath I had after the liberation. My mother washed my hair and body and just said to me, 'Celina, the world is a sea and in that sea there be monsters. Never ever forget that.'

Chapter Thirteen

Surviving our Youth

By the end of 1943 the writing was certainly on the wall for Hitler's Third Reich. Germany had suffered irreversible, catastrophic losses, particularly on the Eastern Front. This, coupled with the entry of the United States of America into the Second World War, meant Germany was now fighting a war of on two fronts; one that Nazi Germany could not possibly hope to win. Great efforts went into the production of propaganda aimed at convincing an ever more fearful civilian population that Germany would win. With bombs falling on their cities day and night around the clock, only the most ignorant of individuals could not have foreseen the disaster which was now looming. With quite remarkable resilience, the German population continued as best it could with their lives. With the same defiance shown by Londoners during the Blitz, young German women were determined they would not be terrorised or bombed into submission. Hanna Burowitz recalls:

As the Allied bombing campaign against German cities intensified, measures were taken to protect the children and the young of Germany. The *Bund Deutscher Mädel* and the Hitler Youth had established special camps outside the cities, in the countryside where it was considered safer. Many of us were happy to be evacuated from the danger areas of Berlin. The camps were very good and provided us with everything we needed. We were a youth community and we worked as a community to support each other. Our camp was near a farm where some of the buildings were taken over by the Hitler Youth. After some work, the brick outbuildings became our second home.

As a fourteen-year-old girl it was, of course, all very exciting. In these camps the teaching and other Hitler Youth activities could be continued in relative safety from bombs. We would hear an air attack coming before the warnings had even sounded. You could hear the distant rumble of many engines. Also the outer flak belts would engage the enemy planes so you could hear the flak firing in the distance too. We would take cover, but we always wanted to see the action. We would watch from the farm building or beneath trees as all these white trails high up in the sky would sweep over our area. Our fighter aircraft would be chasing them all the way and you could just about make them out as they weaved in and out of the bomber formations. The localised flak would start shooting at the bombers too. It was quite a spectacle to watch. When the danger had passed we would sneak off to look for souvenirs. We went off with the boys and looked around the fields. You could pick up hundreds of bullet casings from the aircraft, along with pieces that had been shot off aircraft during the fighting. We would collect flak splinters and see who could find the most.

I remember one morning some of the boys came and woke us up early to go and see something. They always came and woke me and my other two friends up as I knew they liked us, they thought we were pretty and they liked having us along with them [she laughs]. The boys took us down the fields and it was quite a hike from our camp. Eventually we came to a field with a large pile of green-painted, twisted metal in it. It was the remains of an American bomber. The bodies had been removed so there were no dead inside it. We just wanted to have a look for more souvenirs. I climbed inside what was left of the fuselage section. I was a skinny girl so I was able to get in where the boys couldn't. They were outside, excited, saying, 'What's in there? Is there anything good? What can you see, Hanna?' I went in further and there were lots of bullets so I picked up a few handfuls and threw them out through a hole for the boys to see. I heard them saying, 'Yes, this is great. Hanna, can you get us some more?' So I am inside this very confined space throwing out handfuls of potentially dangerous bullets. The bullets were pretty big and some had bent in the impact of the crash. Many still had parts of the belt that held them in place in the gun boxes. The boys then said, 'Are there any guns in there, Hanna? Please see if there are any guns.' I am on my hands and knees now, crawling along, but I can't see any guns. I find parts of a radio set and throw them out to the boys, along with what looked like a measuring ruler or something. The best thing I found was a hand-sized piece of a map of Berlin. It had obviously been torn up in the crash. I put this piece of map in my pocket as I wanted it for myself. I was trying to go further back in the wreckage when I found a flying boot. When I grabbed the boot and pulled it towards me I noticed it still had part of a human foot stuck in the bottom. I remember seeing the bone sticking up inside the boot. I quickly threw it back and made a funny noise like kids do when they see or pick up something nasty. The boys and the two girls outside were going mad, 'What is it, Hanna? Let us see!' I told them what it was and that I was coming out now. The boys kept saying, 'Bring it out with you, I want to see.' I told them, 'If you want to see, go in there yourself.' I had seen dead bodies and bits of human shrapnel many times so such sights did not really frighten me. They were just not very pleasant to see. As I crawled out of the wrecked fuselage the boys were filling up their pockets with the bullets I had thrown out for them. I had my piece of map and a radio part.

The piece of map was safely in my pocket when we heard a voice shout, 'What are you doing here, you scoundrels?' It was a soldier from a nearby flak battery. He came over, really irritated, and grabbed the boys and made them tip the bullets out of their pockets. 'Do you not know how dangerous these things are?' he said, 'If one of these goes off in your pocket it will blow you in half. How might you others explain that to your parents?' He made the boys empty their pockets until he was satisfied that all the bullets had now been surrendered. The piece of radio which I had in my hand was taken off me. He asked me, 'Do you have anything else on you?' I lied and told him 'nein' [no]. He just said, 'Fucking kids! Now get out of here and don't come back. If I catch you here again there will be big trouble. I will kick all of you up your arses!' He stood shaking his head as we walked off back down the field to our camp. I looked back and saw him lighting a cigarette and sitting down on the wreckage. One of the boys said to me, 'I can't believe that wanker. I bet he will go and have a look and take something for himself.' When we got back to the camp I pulled out the piece of map and showed the others. Being caught like that did not stop us. We were a very daring little gang and us girls were as adventurous as the boys.

By 1943 the war was becoming more personal to us. We were warned to be very careful when outside playing. The main threat came from Allied fighter aircraft. They had a habit of attacking anything that moved on the ground. They would escort the bomber aircraft in and, once they had done their job, they would fly down to lower altitudes searching for targets on the ground. We were forbidden to go anywhere near flak, radar or any other military installations due to the danger of them becoming a target. We were taught how to recognise the Allied planes. Most of the ones that were attacking people on the ground were American, so we were taught. We were told many horror stories to ensure we complied with the rules. We were encouraged to go about our lives yet at the same time to be alert at all times. If we were out in the fields and we heard aircraft coming we were told we must lie flat on the ground and not move, or hide in a ditch if there was one nearby. We were only to move after we were sure the planes had left the area.

We knew where all of the flak positions were around our area. It was at least an hour's walk to the nearest one. There was one Saturday when we had finished the tasks we had to do. Our gang decided we would go and have a look at a flak site. We heard it had been moved so we thought we would go and see if the soldiers had left anything behind. We were breaking the rules, but once we were off that was it. The walk was quite pleasant and on the way we stopped to climb trees. We climbed as high up the tree as we could. This gave us views across the countryside. This was something we had learned through the

Hitler Youth. As the eldest of three girls in our gang I was always the first to do something. I think the boys really liked me for that.

As we approached the site where the flak guns had been we could see sandbagged dugouts and empty shell cases stacked up on their sides. We crept along through some trees, looking around to make sure the site was abandoned. We watched for a few minutes like Red Indians in the Wild West [she laughs]. The site was definitely abandoned so we stood up and had a walk around. We were hoping we might find some food or sweets. We spent a while looking around in the small dugouts but didn't see anything worth taking. The boys were picking up shell cases but I told them, 'You can't take any of them back. We'll be found out.' They dropped them with disappointed looks on their faces. We sat down and shared out some biscuits we had brought with us. One of the boys found an army helmet so he sat down and stuck it on his head. We just laughed at him. We sat there eating our biscuits in the peace and quiet. There was a small stream on the site and we went to get a drink. Using our hands as cups we scooped up the refreshing water. After that we just sat in one of the dugouts, resting our heads on each other's shoulders. We had not a care in the world [...]

We got up and started heading back to the camp. We had not taken more than twenty steps when we heard engines in the distance. We panicked for a moment, looking around to try and find which direction the engines were coming from. They were definitely aircraft. I took the two girls by their hands and ran towards some trees. We threw ourselves down and waited. The boys went in another direction and jumped down into a hole. The engines grew very loud and when I looked up I saw eight Messerschmitts in formation, passing overhead at low level. When they passed I stood up and shouted to the boys, 'It's alright, they're ours. Come on, we need to get back.' As we were coming out of the trees the boys crawled out of this hole covered in what I thought was wet soil. It was not soil though and as they got closer I could tell it was shit. They had only jumped into the pit that the flak gunners had been using as a toilet. The smell was terrible, but we could not stop laughing at them. The boys were not happy at all. We helped them wash in the stream but their shirts and trousers were just so heavily soiled you could not clean off the shit. We realised we would have to explain how they got into this state and we had to think of a suitable story. As we walked back we swapped ideas for what we could say. The only thing I could think of was to find some animal shit and smear it over the human shit and tell them to say we were fooling around and they fell into slurry. We found some cow shit and used that.

When we returned to the camp we told our parents what had happened. I don't think they were convinced we were telling them the truth. The boys had a smack around the head from their fathers while we girls were interrogated. We all stuck to our story that we were chasing each other around when the boys fell into slurry. Our story fell apart after a member of the military arrived to inform the adults and the Hitler Youth leaders that some Luftwaffe pilots had spotted a group of children at a flak artillery site some six miles to the north of our camp. The pilots had radioed in to warn that we might be in danger if Allied aircraft came into the sector. I knew we were in for it now. We all had a thrashing from our parents. My father hit the back of my legs with his belt. He was furious with me for disobeying the safety rules. After the hiding we received from our parents we had a tongue-lashing from the Hitler Youth leaders. We were made to sit and listen to a lecture then we were all given extra duties as punishment and forbidden to leave the immediate area of the camp in future. It seemed out little gang had been on its last adventure. We became bored and restless very quickly with the new routine and discussed amongst ourselves how we could change things. We talked about sneaking out at night but the threat of being caught by the Hitler Youth SRD [*Streifendienst* or Hitler Youth Police] would have made such an attempt far too risky. We had to be content with sitting out the rest of the war in the confines of the farm and camp.

By 1944 we were practising fire drills in case any incendiaries were dropped on the farm. We had to form lines with buckets, pretend to fill the buckets and then run with them to the point of the imaginary fire. I had the feeling that the authorities knew more than they were telling us. We were told the war would be won even though Allied aircraft were gaining superiority in our skies. We were told war-changing weapons would soon be entering service and we should maintain faith in our leader, Adolf Hitler.

The fears that we might be attacked came true late in 1944. Fighter bomber aircraft came in low across the trees and fields, firing their machine guns as they came in. They hit grain and animal feed storage areas and destroyed the water butts we were using for our own water storage. One of the old farm buildings, which was largely wood, was set alight by incendiary bullets. We flew into action filling buckets of water, as we had been trained, and formed a human chain, throwing water onto the blaze. Despite all our efforts we could not contain the fire and the building was lost along with everything inside it. Why we were targeted remains a mystery even today. Maybe they thought there were soldiers garrisoned at the farm. I don't know. They could have just been trying to starve us. I say this because the day after, cattle were fired on in the pasture and they were all killed. The animals were used only for milk and it was a sad sight to see their corpses lying motionless in the fields.

The attack was reported up the chain to the Luftwaffe station in charge of air defence in our sector. It made little difference as the planes kept coming back and shooting at farm buildings and storage units. In the end even the farm was no longer safe and we were forced to move further away into the woods and forested areas. There were no more animals. The enemy planes had killed them all so we had no more milk. What grain we had was destroyed by fire. Another problem was finding new supplies of even the most basic food, like bread. Anything that moved on the roads in the daytime would be attacked without warning. Near the end we had to go out for supplies at night.

Anna Dann has recollections of going out with friends to search for items of food to add to their meagre rations late in 1944. She recalled:

Our gymnastic abilities certainly came in useful for some of these little trips we went on. There were a few army training centres in and around our city. Most had been abandoned after the training had been carried out. Most of the soldiers training there had left for the battlefront in the east. We would get up early and meet up. There would sometimes be as many as eight of us, boys and girls. Some of the abandoned camps had quite high fences around them with locked gates. We used to climb the fences using the gymnastic routines we had done while in the BDM. The tallest girl would kneel down and we would then take off our shoes and climb onto her shoulders. As I was the smallest I would climb up last. I would reach the top of the fence and then use the holes in to climb down the other side. The others more often than not would scale the fences on their own. Once I was over the fence the others would throw their shoes over to me. Once we were all over we would then look around the buildings and in the bins to see if there was anything left behind that we could eat or take home. Anything we found, like pots, pans, coins, cigarette lighters, cutlery, we would take back home. Anything that could be used or exchanged was of value to us. We would always find food scraps, including fruit, and we often ate these on the spot. The soldiers must have had plenty of food to have left things like this behind.

I remember one morning one of the boys found a large circular metal item. He pulled it out of a wooden box from a shed he had been looking in. I knew what it was straight away as my brothers, Franz and Josef, had small books with these things listed in them. I shouted at him to carefully lie it down and leave it alone as it was a land mine. I am not sure if it was a dummy or not, but I did not want to find out so I called the boy away. He went very pale in the face when I explained that what he was dragging along the ground was an explosive mine. It could have gone bang at any moment and killed us.

We often found bullets lying around the compounds and we found the target practice walls where the soldiers fired to practise their marksmanship. The walls were pitted with bullet holes and the sand traps below full of lead bullets. I remember one boy wedging a rifle bullet into a tree then looking around for something to hit the detonator of the bullet with. He found this nail and used a stone to hit into the back of the bullet casing. He struck it twice and nothing happened. The third time there was this almighty crack as the bullet exploded. There was a flash and puff of smoke. It scared the hell out of the boy, who had dropped the stone and the nail in fright and ran a distance away before stopping to look back. He had a small laceration on his hand. A small piece of the brass case had torn off and hit his hand. It was not that deep but it bled a lot. I actually sat down and took off my socks and gave him one of my socks to wrap around his hand. I told him 'Don't you forget to give that sock back.' [She laughs].

These army training camps could be very exciting, but they could be dangerous too. We once found these small chemical containers. The boys never stopped to think about anything, they would just grab them and wrench off the lids to see what was inside. This one made a loud hissing sound as the boy removed the lid. There was like a cloud of steam coming out of it. He threw it down and we all ran like hell. He complained that it gave a kind of burning sensation as he had inhaled a tiny amount of the steam. He coughed for a while afterwards but it did not have any lasting effects. What was in that container we never knew. When I mentioned it to my brothers after the war they went mad. They said it could have been poison gas for controlling pests or military use. That is how we lived our lives before the war arrived on our doorstep. Had my mother and father known half the things I got up to I would have

been in a lot of trouble and they would have stopped me from
going out.

Theresa Moelle, another former BDM I had great pleasure in talking
with on many occasions in the past, recalled that even in the countryside
danger was never far away.

> I remember Allied aircraft would sometimes jettison their
> bombs over the countryside. I don't know why they carried out
> this practice. Surely they should have been dropping bombs on
> the real targets. I know they bombed flak positions that were
> not far from our home. We would hear these bombs going off
> and, even at a distance, they often shook the ground.
>
> I remember one summer's afternoon in 1943, my sisters
> were down the field with the horses. I looked out the window
> of my room and saw them throwing stones up at a tree. I just
> thought to myself, 'What are they doing?' So I went down the
> field to see what they were up to. At first I could see nothing
> and my youngest sister had just thrown a big stick up into
> the tree. I asked them, 'What are you doing? What are you
> throwing things at?' They all chirped up at once, 'That
> thing up there.' I walked closer and looked up into the tree,
> and wedged halfway up was an unexploded bomb. It was a
> 500-pounder from what I could see, and absolutely dangerous.
> I told them, 'We must get away from here right now! Come
> on.' I took them all back up to the house and told my father,
> who then alerted the authorities.
>
> When the army came to have a look it was very difficult for
> them to get at the bomb because of where it was. The soldiers
> discussed blowing it up where it was. The problem was it was
> quite high off the ground and if they blew it up it would have
> an airburst effect. This was far more dangerous than it going
> off on the ground. One of their men had to go up the tree and
> defuse the bomb. He was up there a while and soon as the
> bomb had been made safe a winch was brought up and it was
> taken down from the tree. Had that bomb fallen out of the tree
> while my sisters were playing around with it they would have

all been killed, no question about that. It made me very angry indeed.

There were other dangers too. I would sometimes find unexploded flak shells littering our fields. Their fuses sometimes failed to detonate in the sky and they would fall back to earth. Some of these shells had a calibre or bore diameter of 10cm or more. These were full of high explosive. I would also find smaller flak shells that had not detonated or struck a target. The most dangerous ones were the high explosives. I often found the 2-cm flak shell heads where they had fallen without going off. If you stepped on one or picked one up it could exploded and kill you instantly. A cow was once killed after stumbling onto a shell near the stream in the bottom field. The cow's stomach had taken the full impact of the explosion. I remember there was blood, guts and cow shit everywhere. It made a right mess of the animal. Every time I saw something like a shell I would find something, like a stick, to put in the ground near it and then the army would be told. They did not always have the time to come and remove these things though. I know some shells remained in the fields where they fell for years after the war.

Kirsten Eckermann also recalls inadvertent brushes with danger during her youth under Hitler.

Kids never really quite understand danger in the same context as an adult does. I used to do things I would never even think of doing now. I once found one of our incendiary bombs in a wood. We knew they had cases made from magnesium material. We made a small fire using some twigs and lit it using methods we had learned in the BDM. Once the fire was lit one of the boys with us showed us that if you scraped the metal casing with a pen knife as the bits dropped off into the fire it made the most beautiful sparks. We were doing this for some minutes when an older Hitler Youth boy came along and saw what we were doing. He ran over shouting, 'What the fucking hell are you doing with that. Put it down this instant.'

We dropped it down into the fire. The Hitler Youth boy went berserk and kicked it from out of the fire. 'Fucking fools! What are you trying to do? Just get out of here now!' he barked at us. We just thought him a spoilsport until we later learned that the incendiary was live and full of phosphorous material. Phosphorous is deadly and will burn right through you if it gets onto you. It ignites at very high temperatures, which is why they used it to manufacture fire bombs. I can honestly say back then I did not think of danger. If we were going to do something then we would just go and do it. Only now do I look back and think 'you daft girl'.

Olga Kirschener recalls being thirteen years old and effectively living in a war zone.

We were bombed most days and nights so we were in a war zone constantly. It was all very exciting to me at the time. There was a boy I was friends with and I used to help him go looking for shrapnel after the air raids. The stupid thing was it was always me who had to do the dangerous stuff.

We once spotted a large piece of what looked like a bomb fin. It was up on his neighbour's roof, wedged between the chimney pots. He said to me 'That is way too high for us to get at.' Me being the BDM girl not wishing to be outdone, replied, 'It's not that high. I can get up there.' In fact I was more concerned about him looking up my skirt as I climbed up rather than falling [she laughs]. I told him, 'Don't you dare look up my knickers.' There was this small wooden ladder in the yard so I climbed up onto the outhouse roof and told him to pass the ladder up to me. He then joined me up on the roof. I told him, 'You hold this steady and don't you dare let it go, okay?' I took my shoes and socks off for a better grip then I climbed up as far as it would reach. The cast iron gutterings of the houses were very sturdy so I rested one foot on the edge and pulled myself up. I inched my way up the tiles and actually managed to grab the piece of metal and throw it down into the yard. It made such a noise as it landed on top of a metal coal box. The noise startled his grandmother, who then came out to investigate. She came out into the yard and almost had a heart attack. She stood there and shouted, 'Olga! Get down from there right away, you stupid, idiotic child!' By this time the grandfather had also come out of the house to see what was going on. He dropped his pipe in disbelief as he watched me coming down from the roof of his house.

When we were back down in the yard safely we both got a right telling off. They went round to my parents and told them what I had done. My parents went mad at me and would not let me out to play with my friends for nearly three weeks. I was told, 'You are never to play with that stupid boy ever again.' For all our efforts that day the piece of metal I pulled off the rooftop was confiscated by the boy's grandfather. I don't know what he did with it, but neither me nor the boy ever saw it again. I think they probably threw it out afterwards. I wasn't scared at the time. Back then, at that young age, few things really scared me. When I look back on it now though it sends shivers through me. If I had fallen I could have been seriously hurt, even killed.

Katherine Rumfeld was a twenty-two-year-old factory worker who also has reminiscences of a reckless wartime youth.

When the sirens went off you were supposed to go to one of the main air raid shelters in your allotted area, or if you had one in your garden you could go in there. You were meant to stay inside until the all-clear was given. The all-clear sounded after a raid to let you know it was over and that it was safe to come out. I remember one heavy attack in 1944 at Emden, where we once lived. I was in a shelter, which was on a small allotment. It was only a couple of minutes or so walk from our house. We were all inside when the attack came in. It was the usual routine of just sitting in that damp and cold shelter trying to get comfortable as the world around started to erupt into bedlam. That's what it was like, pure bedlam. The noise was loud and violent and, by God, it was terrifying. We got used to it, but if anyone said they were not afraid then they were liars. My father was a giant of a man and, at sixteen stone, he was no weakling. Even he was shaking on this particular attack.

I was sat complaining about the cold and the fact that we had left the coffee inside the house. We had a small paraffin-type burner we used to make hot drinks while in the shelter. Maybe I was behaving like a spoiled child, but no Allied raid was going to come between me and my hot drink. I got up and, despite the shouts of my family, I ran to our house, determined I would get the coffee. I went through the back door and picked up the small bottle of coffee. The house was in darkness and I could hear shell fragments falling down the roof and drainpipes. I left the house then sprinted the short distance to the shelter holding the bottle of coffee like it was my only possession. I had almost reached the shelter when it felt as if a brick had landed on my head. I fell over and for a minute or so was dizzy, just sat there like a defeated boxer after receiving a knock-out blow. Next thing my father is running over to me, throws me over his shoulder and runs to the shelter with me. I complain that the bottle of coffee is still on the ground and he hasn't got it. Back inside the shelter I feel something warm on the top of my head. I put my hand on my head to see what it is and I feel a jagged cut. I see my own blood on my fingers. My father is furious with me, shouting obscenities until mother persuades him to calm down. The cut is not serious but will probably need a few stitches. The first-aid kit that every German family keeps in their shelter is used for the first and last time. Father puts a bandage on my head and after the raid I am taken to a first-aid post where the wound is cared for professionally. Two stitches are put into the wound.

What had happened was a common occurrence. A flak shell had exploded in the sky above and a fragment had landed on my unprotected head. As I said, it was just like a blow from a brick. I had a good telling-off from everyone and learned my lesson. It could have been much worse. I later heard stories of big flak shells falling down to earth and exploding on the ground, killing people. A fire defence crew were all killed when a 12.8-cm shell fell amongst them as they fought a blaze. Their remains were discovered a short while after and one of them had been decapitated in the blast. I was told the head was never found.

The above accounts are so typical of those of girls and young women in Nazi Germany during the Second World War. It seems almost surreal that, for the survivors, they were living their childhood while at the same time trying to survive the war going on all around them. Thankfully, none of the abovementioned suffered any serious injury.

Chapter Fourteen

Shoot Straight

The Allied landings, which took place on the beaches of Normandy on 6 June 1944, were met with fierce resistance. For a few tentative hours the invasion of Nazi-occupied Europe could have gone either way. There were many factors which contributed to the success of 'Operation Overlord'. As the Allied invasion was taking place Adolf Hitler was sleeping peacefully in his bed. No one dared to wake the Führer to inform him of the events unfolding in Normandy. The fear of taking command initiatives without his consent meant many commanding officers had to wait until Hitler woke. In those critical first hours of the Allied invasion the Germans had lost the initiative before the firing had even started.

The German forces were much like a boil being squeezed from both sides. The Soviets were making good ground from the east and now the Allies were attacking from the west. With ever dwindling resources at her disposal, it was now only a matter of time. Germany's death would be a slow and painful one. However, the old adage that a wounded beast was still capable of being a threat was very much in evidence as Germany's forces quickly rallied to the challenges they now faced. As more and more men were called to the battlefronts in the east and west so more girls and women were required to replace them. The women of the Third Reich were now in the factories, the Red Cross, Luftwaffe and flak auxiliary, the Fire Service, communications and postal services, as well as fulfilling numerous other home defence roles within their communities. Without the efforts made by its women, Germany's defeat might have come about sooner.

At this stage of the Second World War, girls and women in Germany had already been indoctrinated with the ethos of defending the fatherland. In Hitler's view, if the people failed – women and girls included – then no one deserved to survive. He was of the opinion that if Germany could not win the war then it would have to face certain annihilation and cease to exist as a nation or as a society. The skilled use of propaganda encouraged the German people to prepare. Propaganda minister Josef Goebbels' speech of 18 February 1943, at the Berlin Sportpalast, was a pivotal moment. Goebbels demanded support for total war from the German people. In response the German people gave its blessing. This now infamous oratory masterpiece should have convinced even the most optimistic Nazi of the reality that Germany was losing the Second World War.

As Maria Kottinger from Munich remarked: 'When the men of any society start calling for the civilian women, children and old men to prepare to fight then, all has to be lost.' Maria recalled:

I was a thirteen-year-old in the *Jungmädelbund*. The whole mood in Germany slowly began to change from 1943. It felt as if she was becoming this frightened animal that was being backed up against a wall, weighing up its options. It was an animal that knew it was unable to escape yet knew that it had little option other than to fight its tormentors.

They brought round leaflets at a Saturday meeting for the Hitler Youth girls. The leaflets described in detail how we, as Germany's future, could take part in the great salvation of the German race. Even young German girls could learn how to build barricades, dig holes in which mines could be placed and assist the soldiers in creating traps to kill the enemy if they arrived in our towns, villages and cities. I was frightened by this, but they would tell you, 'You don't need to worry, the enemy will not come here. He will be vanquished in the fire of an enormous and decisive victory.'

They also brought in various weapons that could be used for home defence. These were very simple devices such as the *Panzerfaust* ['tank fist']. The *Panzerfaust* was a weapon used mainly against tanks, but it could also be used against enemy infantry. It could be armed, aimed and fired in seconds. They brought in these wooden replica versions and we were called up and each one of us was shown what to do to fire the weapon. Then we had to go through the motions of arming and firing it. They said, 'It is really quite simple. If an old man or woman can use this, then there is no reason why you can't use it too.'

They also had these metal bracket things that you could attach to trees. You would slot a grenade inside them and attach a piece of fine wire. You would place the wire across doorways or other entrances. If an enemy walked into the wire the force exerted on the wire would operate the pull cord in the grenade. The grenade would then be detonated by the unwary enemy. It was a steady and methodical instruction. We were told that only if the time came would we form into groups and carry out these tasks as instructed. We were told if we all carried out this task as required the enemy would sustain tremendous losses and his attack would stall and we would be victorious.

Another thing we were shown was what they called the S-Mine. This was a mine that you would set into the ground. It had a pressure fuse in its top. When triggered, a small propelling charge fired the mine out of the ground to a height of around 3-6ft. The mine would then explode, spraying steel splitter [shrapnel] balls over a wide area. You had to ensure you were not within the danger area. If you were lying down on the ground it would not always guarantee you would not be hit by the steel balls from the mine. Using and preparing these types of mine for operational use required careful and intensive instruction. They only let you do it if they felt you would do it properly.

As the war progressed, more and more of the population of Munich moved out of the city. It was so heavily bombed that trying to live there became impossible, unless you wanted to die of course. As we moved out of the city we cried. It was just so sad to see all those beautiful old buildings that had stood for hundreds of years now in ruin. We felt such sadness, but then came the anger and the urge to avenge what had been done to our city. I vowed if that, if the time came, I would sew a harvest of death for the enemy. Even if it meant me working all day and night I would place as many mines as I could for the enemy. Yes, I hated the enemy then, but how would you have felt had it been your town, city or village being blown up into towers of rubble?

Barbie Densk, a fifteen-year-old BDM girl from Aachen, told me during an interview back in 2005:

> It really irritates me when you get these historians today who dispute the facts. They say stupid things like, 'Oh, BDM girls didn't fight', and, 'No, they couldn't use guns like they say they did'. These people weren't there so what do they know? There is this general misconception that women have to be weaklings, that they can't do what men can do. Well, we already proved we were equal to most of the males in our society by the tasks we had to carry out in the BDM and on the home front. Using firearms was nothing new to me at all. A young girl, even a child, can be taught how to fire a gun. The only limitation you face as a child is how heavy the gun is and if you are able to carry it. Pulling the trigger is the easiest part of killing someone.

Magda Heppel, who lived in Berlin, recalled how girls of the BDM were encouraged to learn how to use rifles, grenades and *Panzerfausts*.

> There was conflict within the BDM leadership as to the roles girls could play in the defence of the fatherland. There were those who totally opposed having females, particularly young girls, involved in military matters. The problem we faced was, at that time, our neighbourhoods would soon become part of the battlefront. So what do you do? Go and hide somewhere or do you join the fight? All the Hitler Youth boys made it clear they would fight so why shouldn't we? It didn't matter what anyone thought in the end. The propaganda called for everyone to join the fight. Either fight or lose the war and end up as slaves. So, faced with something like that, you wake up and think 'I must do this for my country'. You don't think of being killed or wounded.

The most common weapon that we used in the home-defence role was the *Panzerfaust*. There were thousands of these weapons stacked up all around the city. They were not difficult to find and they were easy to use. Rifles were only issued to those females who could use them properly. I had always wanted to learn to shoot so I volunteered and it turned out to be a lot of fun and very exciting. It was the most excitement I had in a long time. I was shown how to aim a rifle properly and how to compensate for longer distances when taking a shot. I was told, 'We don't really need marksmen shooting for an enemy's head. If an enemy presents himself, shoot him full on in the centre of his upper body. This presents a better target, and if you don't kill him you will put him out of action.' I was also told never to waste ammunition firing on tanks as rifle ammunition will have no useful effect against a tank. There was also the threat of counter-fire to consider. We were told, 'Find somewhere secure to shoot from that gives you a degree of safety, and consider your escape routes. Don't try to shoot from trees as you will almost certainly be killed if you do that.' Basically we were to form into groups, look after one another and try and fight a guerrilla war in our city. We would use hit and run tactics. It was exciting and frightening at the same time.

What was worse was the threat of being taken over by Russia. No German wanted that to happen. They used to say 'Better dead than red'. That was the main propaganda slogan. Fear then is a very good motivator. The Hitler Youth leadership understood that young people have an inherent lack of fear; that they will do things many adults might be afraid to do. The reality was we did what we felt was the right thing at the time. I learned to use a rifle and I found it fun, and I would be ready to use it, if and when the time came.

Kirsten Eckermann remembers the mood in the city of Berlin and how everyone was asked to do their bit for their nation's very survival.

I watched as old men and women were taught how to use rocket launchers. The mood in Berlin was one of defiance, that we would not go down without a real fight. Some of the old people being shown how to use these weapons were hopeless. This made us young people more determined to step up so that maybe they would not have to fight. I recall one old woman, dressed in fine clothes, saying, 'Here, let me have a go. If a man can do it then so can I!' She proved a bit too clumsy and almost fired the rocket launcher into her feet. It was quickly taken out of her hands and then her husband pulled her away. As she was pulled away I could hear her protesting and cursing. It was a very surreal scene. I heard one *Volkssturm* [People's Militia] member cursing, 'Fucking old fool almost killed me!'

The city of Berlin and its surrounds covered a vast area. Most of the inhabitants of central Berlin had moved out due to the dangers posed by the Allied strategic bombing offensive. It was in the peripheral areas where most of the girls of the BDM and boys of the Hitler Youth were trained to use weapons for the fighting that was to come. BDM girl Heidi Koch recalls some of the training:

I watched as girls and other women were shown how to shoulder a rifle and then fire it. They fired against the wall of this old rundown cottage. Then there were these dummy stick grenades given to us for training. It was probably the simplest thing you could use. You would unscrew the base, pull the cord, throw it, then take cover. There was no shortage of the stick grenades, and I remember seeing a huge pile of them waiting to be distributed. We were effectively a rearguard. We were behind what was left of our armies, and as they were pushed back so we would be pushed back too. We would end up back in the rubble of the city, from where we would then attack the enemy. It was either that or surrender to the Russian forces. No one wanted to do that after hearing some of the horror stories we had been told about them. Had it been the Americans, people would have not been so fearful and would have probably been happy to surrender. I know I would have.

Theresa Moelle reflected on a time where Berlin was in chaos and children were preparing to fight alongside soldiers, old men and *Volkssturm* fighters.

> We were told we must form into groups and fight as 'Werewolves', as they became known. Everyone was given a leaflet with detailed information on how you could attack your enemy and cause him problems by sabotaging his equipment and fuel supplies. We learned all the information by heart. We set up tripwires that were wired up to grenades, and we were also told that if the enemy comes we should try and lure him into traps. The traps were just ambush points where soldiers or *Volkssturm* would be waiting with machine guns or grenades. The idea was to jump up out of cover, wave your arms at them and then run like hell toward the ambush point. The pursuing enemy would then be fired on once you were safely out of the way.
>
> It was very risky, but anything risky or naughty attracted me. I was not really a 'girlie girl' as they say, so I thought this was great. I learned how to fire a machine pistol or sub-machine gun, whatever it is you call them in English. These weapons were said to be highly reliable, but the one I was given jammed after barely firing a few shots. The *Panzerfaust* was the best weapon. It did require courage to use it effectively. It could destroy any tank and it was so easy to use. Anyone could learn. We fired a few of those in live practice as there were so many available. I know many BDM girls were taught to use air rifles to get them used to the feel of a rifle. It was not a problem for the older girls like me to learn these things. The younger girls, if they couldn't pick up and use a rifle, were shown pistols or stick bombs. Anything that went bang, that could kill or injure the enemy, was a suitable weapon. The training was not always very thorough but it was enough.

Sophia Kortge has an amusing recollection of the first time a German army Mauser rifle was handed to her:

> I was not a big girl and I wrestled with it, desperately trying to prove that I could handle it [she laughs]. I was hopeless with

it and almost ended up dropping the damn thing on my foot. They took the rifle off me, which made me feel a bit pissed off as you say today. Yes, it made me very grumpy. There was this new BDM group head who then suggested giving me a pistol. So I was given a pistol. It was a P.38-type handgun and very modern looking I recall. I found it easy to handle and could point and squeeze the trigger with no problems. The empty gun made a loud click and that was it. This new leader was nicknamed 'The Beast' due to her short temper and lack of humour. She placed the pistol on the table and proceeded to take it apart. She ordered me to watch and listen as she dismantled the pistol. Then she handed it to me and said, 'Right, now you do what I have just shown you to do.' I was bloody hopeless at first and I could not get it right. I tried several times then 'The Beast' started to get really angry. I knew I had to get this right and thankfully I did. I didn't want to hand the pistol back, but we were not permitted to be in possession of weapons at that time. I handed the pistol back and 'The Beast' smiled and said, 'Don't worry, your turn may well come yet.' I was quite pleased with myself that I had learned how to operate and take apart a pistol. Over the weeks that followed I was taught to shoot by 'The Beast'. There were a lot of persistent rumours about that woman. One was that she had been selected by Gertrud Scholtz-Klink to help train girls of the BDM to use weapons.

Sophia Kortge recalls the varying degree of proficiency and skill displayed by girls of the BDM in their weapons training:

Dear God, some were quite terrible. I saw one girl trip over a rifle she had been given. She had a habit of using it as a kind of leaning post. The others roared with laughter but were soon told off. She was a very good shot with that rifle though. I recall they played a trick once after this Hitler Youth boy was caught mocking the girl as she practised firing the rifle. The boy's leader ordered him to sit down cross-legged on the ground. A can was placed on top of his head and the leader said the girl was going to shoot the can from his head. A blank cartridge was loaded into the rifle, which the girl knew but the boy didn't. I've never even seen the face of an enemy look so terrified as that boy's as he sat there while this girl took aim at the can on top of his head. When she squeezed the trigger and the gun went off the boy dived to one side. It scared the hell out of him and we all laughed so much we were in tears. The boy's Hitler Youth leader then told him the cartridge had been a blank and quite harmless. It made him look stupid, but it taught him a very valuable lesson. To be fair, most of our girls were very good at shooting and some better than others. We all found the idea very exciting at the time. We did not really think of the consequences of killing someone, or what it felt like to kill someone. Nothing can train you for that, believe me.

Melissa Schroeder remembers the first time she had ever handled weapons that she had only previously seen soldiers carrying:

I have vivid memories of that morning. I had retired to bed early the previous evening as I had a stomach ache. I spent the whole night tossing and turning. I could not get comfortable or settle. I did not wish to make a fuss so I just lay with my eyes closed trying to sleep. I tried everything. Goats jumping over a mountain; I must have counted thousands and I was still awake. I must have drifted off to sleep at some point. When I woke up it was daylight. I kicked off the bedclothes and was horrified to see blood on my mattress. I began to panic, thinking there was something very wrong with me. My older sister stopped me running half naked down the stairs and explained to me what was happening. She then went and told mother and she came and talked to me too and helped me to wash.

I was not feeling good but I wanted to go the BDM meeting. We had been told that special tasks were going to be discussed. The special tasks were to do with the 'Werewolf Project' as it became known. There was nothing really that special at that first meeting. They were just asking for volunteers to act as Werewolves should the need arise. I thought initially this was not serious, that it was all a joke, but it was not. We already had a people's army in the *Volkssturm*. These were men who were unable to fight on the frontline due to their age or physical condition. There were also women in the *Volkssturm*. Pretty soon anyone could be a *Volkssturm* fighter, it didn't matter; man, woman, girl, boy, whatever. The Werewolves were different. They were the most dedicated members of the Hitler Youth and BDM. The Werewolves were something quite special.

Hilde Hartmann was sixteen years old in 1944 when she volunteered for the Luftwaffe as a flak auxiliary. Her memories of that time were not all happy ones:

I had to first apply to the Wehrmacht before I could then go onto the Luftwaffe auxiliary as a helper. You had to be in the army before you could be considered for our Luftwaffe. It sounds stupid, I know, but that is how it was. I also had to leave my parents and my younger sister, Adelen, behind. Me and Adelen were very close and I hated being away from her and my parents. I felt that the flak auxiliary would mean I would not be away from home much, that I would be near home, but I was wrong.

I had some initial training, but by that late stage of the war it was not much at all. I was sent to Rechlin and was informed that more defences were required around this valuable Reich resource. I didn't know much about Rechlin at that time but soon discovered it was an air base where many new Luftwaffe flying projects were being carried out. They also carried out flight tests on captured Allied aircraft. I was billeted there as the journey home was nearly two hours and too much to travel there and back each day. I didn't know any of the other girls there so felt like a stranger.

We were sent out to man a flak artillery gun on the far perimeter of the base. The gun was a single-barrel 37-mm weapon and there were seven of us to operate it. All I had to do was keep the gun firing with eight-round clips of ammunition. This was pretty easy but it was monotonous. Sometimes we spent hours just hanging around waiting on the alert. Sometimes we were on night duty, which I hated. The noise of the planes in the daytime and people moving around and all the alerts meant it was hard to sleep properly. You couldn't relax for fear of a raid alert and then having to run off to a shelter.

The 37-mm gun was no use against high-flying aircraft. We were there more for ground support or low-altitude targets. I recalled the incessant drills and the shouting of 'Shoot straight! Shoot straight!' During one firing drill I dropped a clip full of ammunition. They shouted at me, 'You bloody fool! Are you trying to blow us all up? Pay attention!' The few good times were spent alone and I would watch the aircraft taking off from the base. I once watched a captured Spitfire being put through aerobatics. It was a magnificent sight and I thought what a beautiful looking aeroplane it was. As I was not getting on too well I was taken off the gun and put with some other women on a rangefinder site for an 8.8-cm flak battery. There were a couple of girls who showed me what I had to do and taught me what I would need to know. They were very nice compared to the others I had been with. We were a battery, set out with four 8.8-cm guns in a square formation, and there was a fire control unit connecting the batteries. The fire control section was the most complex as it took five of us girls to operate. The rangefinder had a computer that made elevation and azimuth predictions for the guns. This is why the 8.8-cm was so effective and accurate. They never let us near the guns though; the men took care of that.

I was getting on alright but was missing my sister so much. It affected my concentration on numerous occasions, to the point I was sent to the medical officer. I spent some time talking to him and ended up in tears. He diagnosed me as suffering from depression and advised me to go home and rest. When I arrived home my parents were shocked and said I had lost so much weight. My little sister was at her friend's house but when she came home we both screamed with delight. We had some food then went to bed and spent some time reading our favourite fairy tales to each other. Our favourite books were always the Grimms' fairy tales. I found these books to be so much like our reality as it was back then. In those Grimms' fairy tale books Little Red Riding Hood always got eaten by the big, bad wolf. It was like the Third Reich, where evil would always prevail over good. I never went back to Rechlin and for the remainder of the war I worked in the mailing service.

Ursula Schiemer had joined the BDM in 1942. She was now seventeen and found herself with Hitler Youth boys and girls preparing for the defence of Berlin. It was a sign of the madness to come that young girls were being openly encouraged by their BDM troops to effectively volunteer their lives for what was now a lost cause. Propaganda speakers blared out endless messages across the city about the coming 'Red tide'. People wandered about the ruined city in a state of unease, contemplating the coming battle. Women scurried down into cellars clutching babies and holding the hands of their young children. Others cowered in the ruins, their faces expressionless. Ursula Schiemer recalls:

They had taught us how to use light flak artillery against the Russian army. We had been shown this under the new emergency defensive measures ordered by the leadership of the Hitler Youth. The guns could be placed on vantage points on rooftops and hidden up alleyways; anywhere an enemy could be ambushed. We were taught how to operate a 2-cm gun. It was very simple as it had just one barrel, but fired large bullets filled with explosives. The older boys of the Hitler Youth were given charge of us and they had the job of teaching us how to operate the gun. It was not that difficult going through the drill, but we had nowhere we could practise firing it, so we had to pretend. Pretty stupid when you think about it after.

As some of our soldiers began to arrive in the city they said, 'What the fucking hell is this?' The Hitler Youth boys told them, 'We are waiting to kill our enemy and we are doing it for the Führer.' They would then salute with a 'Heil Hitler'. I remember the soldiers laughing sarcastically at us and saying, 'We couldn't stop the enemy so what makes you think that you can?' There was tense silence for a few seconds before the soldiers became serious and said, 'Why don't you all go home? There's nothing you can do about this now. If you stay here you will be killed, so just go home to your mothers and fathers.' We stood in silence looking at each other as if one of us had an answer. Then one of the Hitler Youth boys shouted, 'We are going nowhere. We stay here and we fight.' Another soldier asked us, 'Have you fired that thing yet?' We replied, 'No, but we are trained and ready.' Before the soldiers moved off they again repeated their warning, 'When nightfall comes leave this thing here and go back home.' The soldiers moved off, then one of the Hitler Youth boys threatened us, 'No one is going home. We stay here and we fight, if and when the time comes.' He had a small pistol in his belt and got it out, waving it around, saying 'If anyone tries to leave I will shoot them dead.' The thing was he was totally serious. I think he would have shot us had we turned and walked away. So here we were, ready to fire a flak gun built to shoot down planes at enemy soldiers. The main thing was we were ready. We were motivated by fear and, if the time came, I guess we would do as we were told; stand firm and shoot straight.

Chapter Fifteen

Maidens of Iron

Cologne proved to be a relatively quiet affair for Thelma Ortge and Gabbi Becker. After their initial forays into the debris of the city with the Hitler Youth to recover any useful material, the girls returned to the farm. There was an ever-increasing influx of refugees from the fighting at the farm. It had now become an extended camp. Thelma recalls:

We had reports that the Americans had broken through into the city. They had made rapid progress due to the relative lack of resistance they encountered. I was not sure just how much of this was propaganda or rumour at the time. I remember hearing the noise of the fighting in the city. These were just normal sounds by then. When I say 'normal' we would hear gunfire and artillery all day and night so it was nothing unusual to us.

We stayed on the camp at the farm and just spent time helping others. I remember one morning a formation of American aircraft coming over at low level. The planes circled us for some minutes before flying off in an easterly direction. The American planes had no opposition and there was not a Luftwaffe aircraft to be seen. From this we guessed that the rumours must be true. Me and Gabbi talked about what we would do if the Americans came. It was at that point that Gabbi said to me, 'You are not really a supporter at all, are you?' I replied, 'Don't be silly. What do you mean?' Shen then said, 'I've known all along that you haven't really supported our government. I'm not stupid, you know. It hasn't changed the way I feel about you, if that's what you are thinking.' She then asked, 'But what do we do when this is all over?'

Our conversation was interrupted by a commotion. Some young Hitler Youths were trying to force men to join them in an armed fight against the approaching American soldiers. They were pulling old men around and pointing pistols at their heads, threatening to kill them on the spot if they refused to do their duty. They were also threatening boys that they would be shot if they didn't join them. I said to Gabbi, 'This is getting worse. Everything is collapsing into chaos here. I really don't like it.' The arguing and threats went on for thirty minutes or so until some of our soldiers came and sorted out the Hitler Youth. The two with pistols were disarmed and given a hiding by the soldiers. The others were told to shut up and warned that if they caused any more trouble the soldiers would have them strung up from the nearest tree. The soldiers seemed reluctant to offer resistance. Some officers turned up and they talked amongst themselves and looked at maps, pointing towards Cologne. At the time I recall hearing something about them being told not to fight or resist the American forces. We were all instructed to stay here in this camp and not to be foolish. I went to one of the soldiers later and asked him what was going on. He looked at me with his haggard face and tired eyes and he smiled and said, 'Fräulein, we have lost this war. We can't possibly win now. All we can do is try and survive.' I went back to Gabbi and told her, then we told our parents.

The end to Thelma and Gabbi's war would not come until after mid-April of 1945. The two girls were lucky not to have had to witness the full fury of a battle. When the Americans arrived at the farm they were confronted not by hell or fury, but hordes of wretched people who were more in need of food, shelter and medical attention than revenge. The American forces searched the buildings and all the young men in the camp. A handful of weapons were found, but there were no incidents. In many cases people were relieved that their war was finally at an end.

For Ursula Schiemer the events in Berlin, in April and May of 1945, are a painful scar on her memory to this day. Ursula, now an elderly

lady well into her eighties, takes a deep breath and begins to relive
the battle:

> It was like hell itself. When darkness fell, the fires in the city
> created dancing shadows everywhere. Even the Hitler Youth
> boys were now showing signs of fear. We fired the 2-cm gun
> at enemy soldiers who were not even there. All there was
> at that stage were the eerie shadows and the sounds of an
> approaching battle. We stood at the ready by the gun, staring
> out into the gloom ahead. I told the one boy that I needed to
> piss. He picked up a steel helmet and threw it to me, saying,
> 'Here, you can use this to piss in. Just go behind the gun and
> do it there.' I was concerned about them watching me and
> before I went behind the gun I told them, 'None of you had
> better try to look!'
>
> The boys then began playing cards. One of them took a
> pack out of his pocket and asked, 'Anyone want to play cards?'
> It seemed like a good idea to take our minds off things, so
> we sat around the gun and the cards were dealt between us.
> It was hard to see in the semi-darkness and only the light
> from nearby fires made it possible to see. Near the end of the
> game I was out and I sat watching the remaining players. One
> stood up and shouted, 'Bollocks! That is not right. You have
> cheated me!' The other replied, "'No, I did not!' I told them
> 'For God's sake, will you two stop this.' They had been playing
> [...] for cigarettes. They broke the cigarettes in half and used
> them rather than money, which we didn't have anyway.
>
> There were no more reports of the situation coming in.
> We felt isolated, as if we were the only ones out here. My mouth
> felt dry and I had a headache and I wanted a drink of water.
> One of the boys went out to a ruptured main and came back
> with some brackish-looking water. Whether it was fit to drink
> or not I didn't care. I just craved something to moisten my
> mouth. We all had a few swigs from the metal water bottle. That
> small amount of water wasn't enough though. I then saw what
> looked like fireworks going up into the dark sky. They looked
> like little sparks in the distance. One of the boys shouted for us

to get down as they were incoming artillery rockets. Seconds later the explosions began; a long series of explosions behind us. They were landing around a block away and our view was obscured by the huge rubble pile that was behind us.

We saw figures moving in the dark ahead and immediately we prepared to fire. We fired a burst and were met with a string of expletives in German. One of the boys shouted, 'Keep firing! They could be German-speaking Russians.' We could see their silhouettes against the fires in front of us. They were Germans. We stopped firing and shouted at them to come to us. They were not happy at being shot at with an anti-aircraft gun and one of them hit one of the boys. 'What the fucking hell are you doing here? Get away from here now!' they said to us. They were in a panic and out of breath. They just kept telling us to get away from there. We demanded to know where the Russians were. The soldiers pointed all around us and one said, 'They are everywhere. This city is lost and you need to get away from here now or you will all be killed.' The Hitler Youth with the pistol told them, 'We go nowhere. We stay and we fight for the fatherland.' The soldier laughs at him and said, 'Fatherland? There is no fatherland anymore. This is over.' They climbed the pile of rubble behind us and disappeared out of sight.

It was quiet for a few minutes then machine guns were fired at us. You could see the tracer rounds as they zipped towards you. Some bounced off the rubble behind us. On hands and knees we scurried back to the gun and began firing at the muzzle flashes ahead. We could see soldiers moving in between ruined buildings and piles of rubble. They were carrying the sub-machine guns that many Russians used in Berlin. We fired and fired at them. Some of our own ammunition ricocheted back towards us and hundreds of feet into the air. The noise was deafening. I could hear nothing but the constant firing of the gun. We had many magazines of ammunition, but the gun jammed. As we tried to free the stoppage we were charged. We were thrown down and guns were pointed at us. We were searched while more Russian soldiers ran all around us, advancing over the rubble pile behind. The Hitler Youth with the pistol had his gun taken off him. He spat at one of the enemy as he was being searched and received a punch in the face. I told him to stop being such an idiot and do as they asked. He just kept fighting them, saying, 'Never, never!' He was pulled up by the scruff of his coat and taken away. I never saw him again. We were all searched and moved away from the gun. The Russian soldiers knew exactly what they were doing. They tossed three grenades at the gun and once they had exploded the gun was useless. We watched the scene from a distance. Satisfied we had no more weapons, a Russian gestured for us to follow him. We did as we were told, with our hands in the air. We came to a building with a cellar and they gestured for us to go inside and stay out of the way. Then they moved off and we were left alone as fighting continued ahead. We crammed ourselves into the doorway to the cellar and watched as many more soldiers came running past us. It was like we were not even there. They did not give us a second glance. The odd one would stop look at us and wave his hand as if to say 'stay down' and that was it.

The rest of the night was just gunfire, explosions and flashes. It was well after first light that we saw the next Russian soldiers. These were a little different to the first we had encountered. They stopped, dragged us out of the cellar doorway and looked at us. They looked through our pockets and then went into the cellar. They kicked things around with their boots and came back out. They looked us up and down again and then went into the building next door. I watched them work their way along, going into every building they could get into. They came out of one building holding a screaming woman by her wrist. They took her with them but I cannot say where or what they did with her. We began to feel real fear for the first time. There were five of us and we tried to stay together. We stayed where we were, too afraid to move. More soldiers came and we watched several tanks roll past us.

It was well into afternoon the next day when a Russian told us in broken German, 'The war is over. You can go home, if your homes still exist.' We looked at each other and climbed out of the cellar. My mother and father had gone to the main air raid shelter. I decided I would try and walk there. As I walked over dead bodies and piles of rubble and empty shell casings my mind was void. I felt the gaze of the victorious Russians on me as I walked past them, but they never touched me or hurt me. Many of them were celebrating with looted alcohol. I was spat upon once, and one threw a lump of stone at me, but that was it. I found my mother and father outside the main shelter. There was a large crowd of civilians there and Russian soldiers directing them. My war ended in the arms of my parents who thought I was dead. They were very angry with me but relieved I was alive. We all walked off into the unknown.

Elise Pfaff had been a member of the BDM since 1943 and came from a working–class family who were dedicated National Socialists. She reflected on 'Operation Clausewitz', the codeword for the implementation of the defence of Berlin.

No one was excused the duty of defending Berlin. Orders were issued to everyone to fight until the last round of ammunition had been fired. We were all hyped up and the bloodlust was certainly very high. We had been given what some of the soldiers nicknamed 'The Führer Drug'. Its proper name was Pervitin. They offered it you and said, 'This will help you defeat the enemy.' I had some in my pocket, but after seeing how those who took Pervitin behaved, I decided not to take it. When the Russian attack penetrated into the government district of Berlin there seemed to be no real cohesion and it soon became confusing. Old men, children and families were running around in a state of hysteria. Bands of Hitler Youth girls and boys were trying to find suitable places in which to mount their ambushes on the enemy.

I was there and I did fight. I am not ashamed to admit to it. We were in the vicinity of the Wilhelmstrasse. The noise of battle was deafening and it was a strange mixture of sounds:

explosions, gun fire, the shouts of the wounded and the dying, all mixed up together. The smell never leaves you either. It's the worst possible smell imaginable on this earth. Rotting bodies, blood, dirt, smoke, sweat; it's horrible. Some of our older Hitler Youth boys had scaled partial remains of a collapsed building. They began shouting across to us, 'Enemy at one thousand metres.' They advanced very rapidly and had brought armour with them. The armour formed into a single column, approaching us from a westerly direction. We knew they had armour as we could hear it moving along. The young men on the building were yelling at us to move forward and throw grenades at them. We crawled forward and found ourselves on a huge slab of concrete. When we peered over we could see the enemy soldiers. All we had were grenades, but we threw them at the soldiers. We all turned and ran towards the building that the young men were on when it vanished in a huge ball of choking dust and smoke. A few seconds after I felt a hammer blow to my right arm. The force spun me off balance and I fell over. It was impossible to see anything with dust all around me. I felt warm blood running down my arm and it dripped out of the sleeve of my coat and onto my hand. There was a small hole in the arm of my jacket so I knew I had been hit by something, either a bullet or shrapnel.

Out of the gloom and dust I saw figures crouching down and moving forwards towards me. They had guns and were stopping to look at the bodies on the ground. They stopped and searched them then continued. I stayed sitting on the ground and the next thing there's an enemy soldier standing over me. He doesn't say anything, just leans down and pulls me up. I yelp in pain as he grabs my injured arm. He points to the route they have just come up and I think he is trying to tell me to go there. He pushes me to make me move and I follow his instructions. For the first time I am frightened and I think of taking the Pervitin. Maybe it will block this entire experience out so I don't know what is happening.

More and more Russians appear. Some stare impassively at me while others ignore me completely. I keep walking past them until I find a large group of Germans being held. The group are circled by Russian soldiers. I am pushed in with the group and I sit down and remove my coat to see what damage has been done to my arm. It's sore but the damage is not bad. It was what they call a scratch or a flesh wound. Whatever hit me in the arm had caused a deep slice. It was nothing serious and one of the Russians saw me trying to bandage it with a sock. He actually bandaged it for me. He did not say much, but in broken German he said, 'War is finish for Germany. Germany is now Mother Russia's.' We were all frightened, but the Russians did not hurt any of us. They were not friendly, but they were not bad either. The group guarding us changed after a few weeks. Then these Russian women took over guarding us. They were different all together. They often spat and swore at us. One of them said to me, 'How would you like me to fuck you with this?' and held up a bayonet in her hand. You had to just take it and keep quiet. Provoking them was not a good idea. They were full of hate for us. We were the losers and we were at their mercy. I began taking the Pervitin to try and block it all out. When I ran out I tried to find more.

Adelen Muller was a sixteen-year-old girl who became embroiled in the struggle to save Berlin. She recalled:

I had never intended to fight. It was always the belief that girls and women did not fight; that fighting was a man's job. In the last desperate battle our leaders were suddenly telling us to pick up guns, grenades and bazookas and fight to the death. I saw German soldiers and French-speaking Waffen SS soldiers cowering in their holes in the ground. I looked at two of them hiding in their hole and I had no words for them. I shook my head at them and uttered the word 'cowards'.

We stood behind barricades made from vehicles. It reminded me of cowboys and Indians, only this was real. Funny thing is, I thought back to when I was a little girl with my mother sitting next to my bed reading me fairy stories; ones where the beasts were real and not always destroyed by the hero in the story. I thought of that as I stood waiting. I had a *Panzerfaust* 60 next to me, but one of the *Volkssturm* men came over and said, 'I will take this. Here, you have this instead.' He then took the *Panzerfaust* and put a rifle in its place. I said to him, 'Hey, I don't know how to use this. Give me the bazooka back.' He snarled 'shut up' and walked away.

I was about to follow him and continue the argument when a young man pulled me back. He showed me how to use the rifle and reload it, and how to use the sights when firing. It was very simple really. I calmed down and we began to talk about things. We talked about food, sausages, apple cake, potatoes, bread and hot cups of coffee, and how we yearned for these simple things that we had not eaten in a long time. The young man introduced himself as Walter and told me to stay by him and I would be alright.

Our supposedly safe position was at the end of a road. At the top we had placed anti-tank mines across the junction. Anyone trying to skirt around would also fall victim to mines we had placed all around the area. The Russians brought forward heavy tanks. One triggered a mine we had laid and I watched it blow up. For almost a minute it smoked then it just exploded into a huge ball of flames. Another tank drew up behind and slightly to its left and the turret was pointing directly at us. It was not in range of the *Panzerfausts* but even so, people with us fired at the tank. Their bombs fell short, exploding in front of the tank. I heard panicked shouts of 'Bring that thing up here', followed by three Hitler Youth boys wearing caps. They had what we called a *Panzerschreck* [an anti-tank rocket launcher]. They aimed and fired it and knocked out the second tank, which exploded just like the first. We began to feel like we could win this fight easily. When their soldiers appeared at the top of the junction we began to fire at them with rifles. There was so much adrenaline that I hardly noticed the enemy firing back at us. There were just puffs of dust and the sound of metal being struck by bullets around us. Just seconds later they began to mortar us. The explosions hurt your ears and I saw people fall to the ground, killed by shrapnel. We had no choice but to surrender. An old man walked forward holding a piece of white cloth. He began to wave it in the air. He was shot and fell backwards to the ground. The enemy came down the road and they took all the weapons from us. I looked around for Walter and found him lying on the ground a few yards away. I checked to see if he was still alive, but he was dead. Those of us who were left were prodded in our backs with rifles and then led away. Some of the Russians could speak German and shouted obscenities at us […]

The captivity that followed was a nightmare of threats of violence and beatings if we failed to tell them what they wanted to know. We were all questioned and once they were satisfied they left us alone. We didn't have much food or water over the weeks that followed. We became sick through drinking contaminated water. We had lice in our hair and we stank like pigs. One man that was with us told me, 'It is better you stink then maybe they will leave you alone.' I asked him what he meant and he replied, 'Well, if you are lucky they will not violate you like they have done with so many young women of ours.' I sat and again thought of my dear mother reading me those bedtime stories in happier days. I just wished I was back with my mother and father right now. My war was over, but this was still a fight for survival and to hopefully return home to them. We heard rumours that we would all be sent deep into Soviet Russia where we would be forced to work in factories, quarries or mines. All I could do at the time was hope these rumours would not become a reality. In the end the men were separated from the women and girls. We were allowed to leave but the men vanished and we never saw them again. Maybe they were sent to work as labourers in Russia. I don't know.

Twelve-year-old Gertrud Soetzer was with her family who were trying to get away from the fighting in Berlin. She recalled:

We were just trying to get away. We were running down a road when a tank appeared. The tank stopped and I heard someone shout 'Run! Run!' We scattered and there followed a huge explosion. I saw a man trying to climb out of the tank. It seemed as if something had hold of his leg, preventing him from escaping. My sister Annalise ran forward and jumped onto the tank and tried to pull the man out by his arm. I watched as the flames just consumed him. My sister had to jump down. My father was screaming at her hysterically, 'Get back here! That thing will explode!' She ran back and we crouched down inside the remains of a shop. I remember thinking that only a BDM girl possessed the courage of a soldier. She had burned her hands trying to pull the man out of the tank. None of us realised in the heat of the moment that the tank was enemy; it was Russian. I don't know, but maybe the Russians saw what she did. When they came into the place where we were sheltering they gave us some water. They talked amongst themselves then threw some food down into our laps and they stood outside the shop shouting and waving, then they all moved off.

Thora Weber was nineteen when she first handled a military rifle. She had undergone training to act as a rearguard with other girls of the BDM in the winter of 1944. She recalled:

I was a BDM leader so it was more or less expected of me to rise up and inspire the others to not feel fear but to fight to defend our nation and our honour. I was nineteen and a half at that time and I had never used a rifle before in my life. Other BDM leaders were sought out and encouraged to learn to use a rifle. The idea was we would be behind the soldiers operating purely as a rearguard to protect their rear and their flanks. On 9 April 1945 we were ordered to move out of the city and take up positions behind our forces near the Seelowe Heights.

Thirty of us moved off on foot in the darkness. In front of us we saw the flashes of artillery shells. We were going into the unknown and we didn't say much to each other as we walked through the darkness. We stopped occasionally for a rest and a swig of water from our canteens before moving on again. It got to the point where I thought 'how much further have we got to go?' We continued into the darkness until told to stop. We were to form a semi–circular line across a hill and be at least thirty-five paces away from each other. Then we were told to dig holes. So we were thrown these folding shovels that the army used and began to dig our own little trenches. Each trench had to be deep enough to totally conceal us. This was annoying and we were not too happy about having to do this. Once you had dug out your trench you made yourself as comfortable as possible and tried to get some rest. If we were needed we would be told to stand ready.

You certainly knew that war was approaching. The Russian artillery, which at first sounded distant, was becoming more and more audible from where we were. On a map we were shown where our main forces were in relation to where we were. It looked quite some distance away. Some food was handed out, but it wasn't much. It didn't fill you up at all and had to be eaten cold. It was just a cold, watery soup and some stale, brown rye bread. I began to take cigarettes as smoking seemed to deaden the hunger pangs. We were occasionally given sweets, but again these were not enough.

On the evening of the 15 April 1945 we were told to get our things together, that we were moving back. I asked, 'Are we going back home?' The soldier who was telling us this seemed very irritated and angry that we were there. There was some serious arguing going on behind us as we prepared to move back. The soldier told me, 'Yes, you are going back home, Fräulein. Now, please get a move on.' We began trudging our way back to the edge of Berlin, from where we had come. We were tired and bewildered, but we talked as we walked and one of the women said, 'This is good news. If they don't need us then things must be going well for us.' We all agreed this must be the reason for the order being given for us to move back.

Once we had reached the outskirts of Berlin we began to encounter large gatherings of civilians and men wearing

Volkssturm armbands on their coat sleeves. There were also Hitler Youths cradling *Panzerfausts* in their arms like babies. Among them were girls of the *Jungmädelbund* and BDM. I was shocked to see some of the girls had *Panzerfausts* too. I saw a few with rifles slung over their shoulders. Every so often they would swap them over to their other shoulder. It was obvious these guns were maybe a little too heavy for them to have to carry for long periods. In a sense it was a depressing scene to witness. If things were going so well for us, what was all this about?

At that point I just wanted to find somewhere I could lie down and sleep. I ended up spending most of the next day sleeping in a tent with eight other girls. Was the war still coming? Would we fight? Not knowing was the worst thing of all. Back near the city I was woken by the persistent Werewolf announcements on the radio. 'Attention, attention, attention! All youth better dead than red, better dead than red!' I just lay there thinking, 'Shut up, please!'

We heard good reports from the Seelowe Heights. We were told our soldiers were winning the battle. Then days later our soldiers began to arrive. They were falling back. I was always told that you only fall back if you are facing an enemy who is considerably stronger than you are. To fall back is merely a retreat and to retreat is the action of a coward, we were always taught. 'What is going on?' I thought to myself. We soon discovered the truth. A few days later, at dawn, Soviet ground attack planes attacked. They fired on and bombed anything that moved. We were forced to move further back. We were forced to retreat over the bodies, arms and legs of our own people. As we retreated we stopped to plant anti-personnel mines. Hitler Youth boys and girls worked together to make traps for the coming enemy. I felt an immense sense of pride in these young people. I just thought, 'With young people like this how can we possibly not win this war we are fighting?'

The reality of the situation was painfully obvious to General Weidling, who was given the unenviable task of defending the gateway into Berlin.

Hitler Youth leader Artur Axman had pledged that he would make more of his youth available for a last defence of the German capital. General Wiedling was of the opinion that Axman's offer would amount to needless sacrifice. The general issued an order forbidding any Hitler Youths from fighting on the battlefront but his order fell upon deaf ears. In a strip of forest in close proximity to General Wiedling's headquarters a whole unit of Hitler Youth soldiers were wiped out.

Thora Weber recalls the end of her war:

> We faced a massive army with endless manpower, aircraft, heavy artillery and tanks. We retreated to the suburbs of Berlin. The enemy came and we resisted them as far as we dared, short of losing our lives. We were among the soldiers and *Volkssturm*. I saw men blown apart before my eyes. I fired at the enemy as they approached us. For every enemy soldier that fell ten more came afterwards. I saw them coming forward, stepping on landmines. As they were blown up others came running over their remains. Soon we were swallowed up by this red storm from the east. They came through us like fire ants. We were surrounded. Those who continued to resist were shot down without mercy or regard to the fact they were male or female, child or adult. It made no difference to them at all. We were disarmed and, while the red storm pushed onwards into the city of Berlin, we sat surrounded by enemy guns, dejected at losing the battle. I felt angry that we had sacrificed so much only to lose. We were raised to understand that pain, struggle and hardship brought success and reward for a people. We had struggled against every conceivable hardship and had suffered pain almost every day of our young lives. I sat with the other girls. We all huddled around each other. Some of us cried, not through fear or pain, but the humiliation that we had given everything we could only to lose our battle.

The defence of Berlin was violent indeed. It was a brutal and desperate fight for survival, almost every yard of ground contested in bitter close-quarters fighting. Those women and young girls who had fought in a vain attempt to preserve an ideology that offered them as a sacrifice to their enemies were to suffer further humiliation. Many would suffer rape, torture and beatings. It all amounted to what was one of history's most shameful episodes. With the surrender of Nazi Germany on 7 May 1945, and with Hitler and the top echelons of the Third Reich either dead or on the run, one would think that finally the horrors of the Second World War were at an end. Sadly, the bodies of babies who had been raped, or choked to death, along with the battered and bruised corpses of old and young women, and girls found raped, stripped, beaten and shot were anything but an omen of peace. The murder of six million Jews under the Third Reich would not be appeased easily. The 'Maidens of Iron' would have to shed the hardened shells that years of National Socialism had grown on them and learn to become women again.

Chapter Sixteen

Say Hello to God

Monica Vanessa Kieler Dorsche, who gave a dramatic account of a late Second World War Luftwaffe ferry flight in my second book *In Hitler's Shadow*, recalled the death throes of the once mighty Luftwaffe near the war's end. She recalled:

I had been flying aircraft for years. Flying was in my blood as my father had been an airman during the First World War. Before the Second World War broke out I had been a mail pilot. I had flown mail runs all over Europe and enjoyed the work. I also took wealthy photographers up on safari flights so they could photograph wildlife in Africa. I had flown stunt aircraft and was as competent a pilot as any man. The Nazis, however, secretly despised women who were equal to men. There were a few exceptions such as Hanna Reitsch. I once met Hanna and she was lovely. It was great talking with her as most women you tried to talk to about aeroplanes hadn't a clue what you were talking about.

I joined the Luftwaffe auxiliary as an operator on the new radar systems. I witnessed the decline of our Luftwaffe. It was not something that happened overnight, but there was a steady deterioration due to lack of resources, fuel and pilots. There were always aircraft, just problems finding pilots to fly them and fuel to get them off the ground. It got to the stage where they were taking worn-out old men, who had been instructors from the training academies, and sending them into the air with the fighter squadrons. That's how bad the situation had become. You would get nineteen- or twenty-year-olds coming in. They would receive the most basic training then were sent into battle against overwhelming odds. You would see them climb up into their aircraft, full of enthusiasm and confidence. You would watch them take off and that was it, you would never see them again.

I begged them to let me fly in combat but there was no way they would ever allow it. Near the end of the war they did allow me to fly short ferry flights with the men. These flights were local and we always had an escort of fighters with us. I had to deliver one of the latest Focke-Wulf models, a Ta 152, and that turned out to be my last ferry flight. During the flight we were bounced by American Mustangs. I was meant to turn back to the departure airfield immediately so as not to endanger myself or risk the loss of the aircraft. I pulled the aircraft up into a corkscrew climb and accelerated. At the top of the climb, around 30,000ft, I rolled out of the climb and levelled up to find an enemy fighter right in the gunsight. Instinctively I depressed the button for the 3-cm cannon but nothing happened. The gun was empty. It was not yet an operational aircraft so the guns had not been loaded. They had not even been test fired at that point. I accelerated away using the emergency boost and returned to the departure aerodrome.

What I'd done hadn't gone unnoticed and I received a reprimand. They revoked my licence and sent me back to work on the radars. Even some of the Luftwaffe pilots came up and said how well I handled that aeroplane. Had the guns been loaded that day there is no way at all that Mustang would have got away. I remember seeing the pilot looking back at me over his shoulder. At that point there was no wingman to help him. I looked back port and starboard to ensure no one was coming up onto my tail. I broke off and returned home. When they stopped me from flying it made me very angry. I have many more recollections from the war years.

Another memorable moment I had was having to bale out of a brand new FW190-D – 'Dora' – while en route to Neustadt-Glewe, in Mecklenburg. The airfield was being used by JG301 at the time. I took off from Marienberg for the short hop over to Neustadt-Glewe. I had no issues at all until

I was off the ground. The idea was to fly fast, stay low and stay close to the treetops. I was not alone. There were sixteen other aircraft all heading for the same destination. I immediately felt something was not right with the motor. On take-off I felt a lot of vibration, which didn't feel natural. A pilot wears his or her aeroplane like a set of clothes and can feel when something isn't right. The vibration continued when I was airborne. I radioed for the aircraft immediately to my port to have a look and see if everything was alright. He couldn't see any smoke or anything out of the ordinary. My instruments all seemed fine but I felt a sense of heightened awareness. I always felt this way before something went wrong. I have always trusted my instincts so I remained on my guard. After a couple of minutes there was a muffled bang from the front of the aircraft. The temperature gauge began to climb into the red. I noticed some smoke in the cockpit then I saw smoke coming from the front-lower starboard side of the engine. I radioed our leader then the other aircraft jostled around in the sky allowing him to come alongside. He said, 'You have an engine fire. Gain height and get out of there.' I put the aircraft into a steady climb, wary of worsening the situation. I watched the other aircraft fly on below me and they soon disappeared. Two escorts broke away and formed up above and several hundred yards behind me. I levelled up and there was now a lot of black smoke coming from the engine. I pushed back the cockpit canopy and unbuckled my seat harness. I rolled the aircraft upside down and fell out of the seat into the air at some 20,000ft. There was the rush of air followed by total silence as I pulled my chord and the parachute deployed. As the other two Focke-Wulfs circled me I watched the 'Dora' fall in an arc all the way to the ground. I watched it crash in a ball of orange flame. I can remember thinking to myself, 'Oh no, that beautiful Dora.' I came down in a ploughed field and thought, 'Great. Now I am going to have a very long walk back home.' I was not alone for long as some boys from a flak artillery unit had been ordered to pick me up. I went back with them to the airfield at Neustadt-Glewe.

When I arrived the others had all got down safely. I had to make a detailed written report of the events leading to the loss of the aircraft to the commander of the unit. He said that there had been a few such incidents recently: 'It's those fucking slave labourers, you know. They leave tools inside the engines deliberately and connect wires so that they catch fire. They fail to rivet airframe parts correctly. I am sick of this shit. I have lost three pilots already to so-called accidents.' He got on the phone and complained to someone on the other end. When he'd finished he turned to me and smiled and said, 'Well, the security forces will be paying a visit to that factory and everyone on the production line for that engine will be dead this time tomorrow.' I felt numb as he spoke those words. I did not want anyone to die for this. He wouldn't listen to my other suggestions, that the aircraft had not been through quality testing so maybe it was no one's fault. He was adamant that sabotage was the cause of the engine fire. He may well have been right, I don't know. The 190 was prone to engine fires so it was nothing out of the ordinary.

We all stayed overnight, enjoying the unit's hospitality. The next morning I was taken to see the wreck of the 'Dora' I had been flying the day before. It came down in a field eight or nine miles away. There was not much left to see as it had all burned out. It was just metal entrails spread over a field. They wanted to remove the engine parts to examine it but it was too smashed and there just was not time to perform a mechanical autopsy. It was the weekend and we headed back to Berlin that evening.

The journey was monotonous and slow due to having to drive without any headlights on. How we arrived in one piece with Gefreiter Krunz driving I will never know. Krunz was a great pilot for such a young man but his driving was terrible. I complained to Krunz about the bruises on my arse. Krunz just laughed at me and made jokes about giving me a massage later. There was always a lot of sexual banter, but I never dated any of the pilots, that was my rule. Sadly, Krunz perished in

March 1945. He took off in a Bf109 and was never seen or heard of again. That was what it was like then.

There were times where there was humour. I recall I was over Neustadt-Glewe in the summer of 1944. There was this cat that lived on the aerodrome and the pilots named him Tommy, after the nickname the Germans had given to the British. The cat had fed himself on the vermin that frequented the aerodrome. Tommy was a large, black-and-white male cat that had little fear, even of dogs. God help any pilot who brought a mascot dog onto the aerodrome with Tommy around. I watched him attack a dog on more than one occasion. You would always find rats with their throats ripped out on the doorways to the huts, or placed on the steps so you could not miss them. Tommy used to sleep on the wings of the aircraft. If there was an alarm he would dive off and run beneath the huts. He was not exactly a pet, but we did give him bits of food. If you had food he would jump up on your lap and be very friendly until he had eaten it all then he would jump off.

I recall one day Tommy was nowhere to be seen. There was an alarm and the boys ran and jumped into their aircraft. There was a commotion around *Unteroffizier* Peter Lescht's Bf109. He had launched himself into the cockpit of his aircraft and found himself sitting on top of a very angry Tommy. The cat clawed his way up Lescht's back to escape. Lescht was shouting 'Fucking cat! Get out of here!' Tommy jumped down onto the wing then onto the ground before running off across the field. There was no time for laughter at that point but when the boys returned from their mission they were in fits of laughter about it. After that the pilots always checked their seats before jumping into their aircraft. *Unteroffizier* Leschts remarked how Tommy had sunk his claws into his arse. The others said, 'Good thing you have a fat one then, is it not, Peter?'

One of the things that became a long-standing joke was whenever I was assigned to deliver an aircraft to a station.

One man once said to me, 'Say hello to God when you get there.' I told him to fuck off, but when I told the others about it the remark kind of stuck. Many men felt that I should not be doing this work and believed I would end up crashing or getting killed. So the boys would always say before I left to take an aircraft, 'Say hello to God for me when you get there.' It was only a joke with the boys, but something I have never forgotten over the years. I never received any of the fancy awards or medals that the other pilots got. I never wanted things like that anyway. Just having the chance to fly aircraft was all the reward I ever needed.

After the war I tried to look up a few of the pilots I had got to know. I discovered all of them, apart from Peter Lescht, had gone. They had all gone in the last few weeks of action while I spent most nights staring at radar screens. It was very sad to go back and ask around for the friends I had made only to be told they went missing during operations.

I felt that our leaders had let the Luftwaffe down. They had been slow in recognising technological innovations. We had a jet-powered aircraft early on in the war yet none of those dimwits in the Air Ministry saw the true potential of such an aircraft. It was absolute madness that they did not push forward and develop jet technology the way they should have. That is why the Luftwaffe lost the initiative in the war in the air. The Luftwaffe was not given the tools or the tactical flexibility in which to fight their war. All of that amazing technology came too late to make any difference. The Me262 was potentially a war-winning aircraft and, had jet technology been given the highest priority, this fighter aircraft would have won the air war.

After the war, in 1946, I met up with Lescht and we walked through a Luftwaffe 'graveyard'. There were aircraft of various types all over the place. Some were wrecked, others not. There were several Me262s and I climbed up into the cockpit of one of them. I sat there and it just felt odd. Here I was, sat in an aircraft that could have delivered victory and I was sitting there as one of the losing side. I felt the control stick and looked at the instruments. I could have flown one of these, I thought to myself. I climbed out of the Me262 and let Lescht have a go in the pilot's seat. He remarked that 'Only the experts got to fly in this beauty.' I walked around the fuselage and admired its lines. I ran my fingers over its sleek, deadly form. Seeing one for the first time close up like this gave me that feeling you get just before you have sex [she laughs]. I stood and stared at the aircraft for some minutes and marvelled at the beauty of its design. It was the perfect fighter aircraft, but it came into service far too late. Had this aircraft come early enough, say in 1942 or 1943, and with improved engines, who knows?

I knew there were many things on the design boards of the Luftwaffe technical branch that were considered revolutionary. At Rechlin they had some of the best minds in the country working on one particular project. We were never told exactly what it was, but I was told that if it were a success no army in the world would be able to stop us. I am not sure what type of weapon they were referring to, whether it was some kind of bomb, missile or aircraft. Everything was top secret and no one said a word then or afterwards about it. I remember that they had a huge cylindrical concrete silo hidden in woods. It had a grey metal lining and you had to climb ladders to get inside the silo. The floor inside had a grey-coloured metal lining, possibly lead or something. Inside it felt as if it was charged with static electricity as all your hair would stand on end, even the fine hairs on your arms. There was some form of electrical field present. It was very strange. Lescht told me that they destroyed it all before the Allies could get hold of it. All the plans and paperwork were also burned. Whether it was some form of launch pad for a new type of weapon or bomb we never found out. It looked like a kind of missile storage silo, but was far too wide for any of the missiles we had in service at that time. It remains a mystery to this day.

Because of my involvement with the radar equipment, I was interrogated by the Americans and then by the British. They wanted to know everything about the equipment; how it worked, how it was calibrated, etc. They asked whether I knew

other things and I told them about the silo I saw at Rechlin. I
know a team was sent there to see what the apparatus was, but all
trace of it had gone. There was no sign that anything had been
there. They cursed me for wasting their time. The place was
swarming with Allied soldiers and some were digging holes in
the ground as if they were searching for something. Whatever
it was had gone or been destroyed. It was very strange and I am
still puzzled by it.

One possible explanation for the strange concrete-and-metal electrified
inner structure that Monica had seen at Rechlin was Nazi experimentation into the principle of anti-gravity as a means of propelling an
aircraft or missile. There has been much conjecture over the years
since 1945 as to whether the Nazis actually carried out any experiments
utilising anti-gravity technology, or whether it was just a myth. With
a lack of any physical evidence to the contrary, there is no doubt the
debate between historians will continue for many years. Monica herself
was quite clear on what she saw and experienced. She sat down with
Lescht later on and he took two magnets out from his pocket and said:

Look, Monica, the principle is really very easy to understand.
Each of these magnets has a north pole and a south pole.
When you put the north pole of one magnet close to the
south pole of another they will attach as if a mating couple.
However, when you take the two magnets and you attempt to
attach them north to north or south to south they repel each
other. There is a strong resisting energy that is created there
that you can see and feel. The two magnets will not float and
remain above one another in this state, they become unstable
to the point where, if you let go, one will be sent flying. There
you have a basic anti-gravity situation that a schoolboy could
understand and create at home.

Monica recalled after their conversation:

I said 'Lescht, what is all this shit? Now you're telling
me you're a fucking physicist?' [she laughs]. He replied,

'Well, Monica, the war is over. We have no jobs now; we can't fly anymore. We could always go back home to Berlin, drink coffee and fuck like everyone else is doing.' I told him, 'No, thank you. Fucking is still nowhere near as good a thrill as flying.' He commented, 'You have led a somewhat sheltered life.' I left it there and kissed him on the cheek, wished him well and asked him to stay in touch by writing to me at my parents' new address.

After the war I went back to the USA and did a little air racing, which was huge in the post-war years. I thrived on the speed and the danger of it all. I had a few letters from Lescht over the years that followed. We met up in Cairo once and toured the place and it was just wonderful. I liked him a lot, but never really in the lovers' sense and not in the same way that he felt about me. I could never have reciprocated at that time. There were so many things I wanted to do after all the shit of the war. I told him I had dabbled in air racing and he wrote, 'Well, say hello to God for me then', in one of his last letters. We arranged to meet up in New York and set a date. I thought it strange that I had not heard from him after several weeks had elapsed. Then I received a telegram from his mother, who I had become quite friendly with, breaking the news that he had died in a motorcycle accident just a few miles from his home. I recall sitting down with the telegram in my hands and thinking, 'Damn you, Lescht. You survived the war only to be killed on one of those two-wheeled death traps'. I felt immense sadness at the news and I felt the pain. As the tears ran down my cheek I said under my breath, 'My dear Lescht, say hello to God for me.'

Monica found the strength to go to New York by herself. It was during this trip that she met the man she would fall in love with and marry. She recalled:

Finally I found a man who turned me on more than aeroplanes [she laughs]. Yes, it was all so weird, but I looked at this man and thought how wonderful he was. I had to have him. Luckily he felt the same way as I did. I know I settled down and had children late in life. But having lived under the Nazis for so many years, experiencing life without them was just so nice. Afterwards I wanted it all, to try and do everything. I did everything I had wanted to. I had an exciting life with many good memories and many not so good memories. That is the cycle of life. I was once a butterfly, though sadly for a while I was a butterfly that carried swastikas upon its wings.

Chapter Seventeen

Victory, War is Over

April 1945 in Berlin saw the red, swastika-adorned curtain of Hitler's Third Reich fall forever. With the war effectively lost in the west and Berlin completely surrounded by the Red Army, an air of melancholy descended over Hitler's staff who had decided to join him at the Reich Chancellery. The details of Hitler and Eva Braun's marriage followed by their suicide are well documented. Traudl Junge has recounted the story many times over the years after 1945, on television and in various publications. Here we will focus on other events which took place around the time of Hitler and Eva Braun's suicide. Traudl Junge recalls the mood leading up to Hitler's suicide on 30 April 1945:

> It was a sad, depressing feeling. Eva Braun was trying her hardest to be cheerful. She even threw a party for everyone. It was a cocktail party to the backdrop of distant artillery that was coming ever closer to us. She tried to lift the mood, telling everyone to 'come on and dance'. It was a very sad spectacle on reflection. It felt like a funeral wake. I felt compelled by loyalty at that time to stay with Hitler. I could have left before, but I didn't. The behaviour of the staff ranged from people sitting deep in thought, people crying and those engaged in activities of drunkenness and low morality. Some of them were acting like they had not a care in the world.
>
> You could not block out the sounds of artillery shells landing nearby or the reality of the situation. The time came for everyone to go down into the Führerbunker, which was located under the Reich Chancellery. It was not the prettiest of places as there was no wallpaper and nothing to make it feel homely or anything. It was all very grey, concrete and official.

It felt like we were all enclosed within a huge, great concrete tomb. For some of us this would become a tomb in some ways. Hitler married Eva and I had already dictated his last will and testament and then that was it. There was nothing else, duty wise, that I could do.

They retired to Hitler's private room to kill themselves. I was sitting with the Goebbels children when the shot rang out. The little Goebbels boy named Helmut shouted 'bullseye' as the shot was heard. He said it in such a comical tone, as if it were all a game. He did not have any real understanding of what was going on. The shot we had heard was that of Hitler killing himself. Heinz Linge, who was Hitler's valet, went into the room first. He was followed by SS adjutant Otto Gunsche. Hitler and Eva were dead on the sofa. There was blood at Hitler's temple but no visible wounds on Eva's body. She had taken cyanide to kill herself. The scene was also witnessed by Rochus Misch. The bodies were rolled up in a carpet and taken out above ground where petrol was poured over them and they were set alight. I was told the task of burning the bodies was somewhat difficult and they had to find more petrol to finish the job off. The amount of petrol eventually used to destroy the bodies left very little clear evidence.

I recall Magda Goebbels discussing her six young children. One of the other secretaries tried to reason with her once her plans to kill them all had been revealed. She had been talking about killing them for months, but she could not be dissuaded from committing the act. Her reasoning in killing the children was quite explicit. For one, what would the Red Army do to her girls if they fell into their hands? Another was that a world without National Socialism and Hitler would not be a world worth living in anymore. For Magda and Joseph Goebbels there could only ever be one outcome and that was death by suicide. They should not have taken the children's lives with their own, but this decision rested with Magda and not one of us could persuade them otherwise. They were beautiful children. I had spent enough time with them to get to know their personalities. They were never spiteful or hateful, just normal, loving children in most respects. Magda was pained by the decision she had made to kill her children, but as much as it pained her to think of it she was never going to change her mind on this.

On 1 May 1945, Magda Goebbels, with the assistance of Helmut Kunz, administered a sleeping drug to each of the six children. It was Magda who would have given the children the drug to make them sleep. They would have been reluctant to take it from anyone other than their mother or father. I am sure of that. I know that the children were drugged to make them fall asleep and then they had cyanide vials crushed in their mouths. The day the children were murdered the eldest of them, Helga, appeared quiet, sad and withdrawn. This was noticed not only by others, myself and Herr Misch [Rochus Misch, the telephone/radio operator in the Führerbunker] but everyone who saw her that day. Helga was a very bright, clever child and she knew things were not right. I sensed the mood between Magda and her eldest daughter had shifted and that they were not getting on as you say. Helga said to me in the days leading up to that horrible event, 'I am not happy with mother.' I did not think too much of it at the time. I just thought it was adolescent anger. I know Magda had cursed her daughter's obstinate mood on what would be their last day of life. There appeared to be little love lost between the two of them. I know it was revealed afterwards that Helga's body bore bruises consistent with being physically restrained. Magda and the doctor probably had to pin the girl down to get the sleeping drug into her body. Before the children were taken to their beds that final time, Helga was seen crying. When the children had been drugged, the cyanide vials were crushed between their teeth. That is what I was told happened. All the children went to their deaths totally oblivious, apart from Helga. Herr Misch told me afterwards, 'Traudl, my one regret is that I did not intervene and stop that woman from killing those babies. I could have, and should have, saved them.' It was something that greatly troubled Herr Misch right up until the end I think.

Traudl Junge left the Führerbunker on 1 May 1945 with a group of others, including SS general Wilhelm Mohnke. She was later arrested by the Soviets and underwent lengthy interrogation prior to her release. Of those last memories of her wartime experience she recalled:

> From the Soviets there were no threats and no abuse. They just wanted to know what had happened in the Führerbunker and how and when Hitler had died and where the others were. I told them the whole story several times over. They then told me their stories of what our soldiers had been doing to their people in the east. They told me pretty hideous things which at the time I thought were just lies. I did not think our people could do the things they were telling me had happened. Sadly, it was all true. Did it change how I had once felt about the man I called my boss: Adolf Hitler? Whenever he was around he seemed to lift everyone in his presence. He had an immense aura about him; a magnetism of sorts. When he was not around the atmosphere was somewhat dejected. It was something I find difficult to describe to you. I feel differently now, of course I do. I was maybe foolish, even naïve, but I was not evil.

The last time I had corresponded with Rochus Misch, the question of the Goebbels children was raised. He explained it was an event which still caused him great sadness and a sense of guilt to the point where he could not discuss it any further. The last vision he had of Helga Goebbels, crying to herself, was one that haunted him virtually for the rest of his life. He somehow felt responsible for her death by not intervening. After murdering her own children, Magda Goebbels joined her husband Joseph in suicide. After the suicide their corpses were doused with petrol and burned, just as Hitler and Braun's had been. The only difference being the Goebbels bodies were still recognisable to those who knew them. As for the absurd question of Adolf Hitler and Eva Braun fleeing the bunker to live out the rest of their days somewhere in South America, Rochus Misch replied:

> It is all rubbish. The dead bodies I saw in Hitler's study, and who Linge and Gunsche also saw, were those of Adolf Hitler

and Eva Braun. There was no doubt about that at all. I had been around Hitler long enough to know what he looked like alive or dead. Anyone who believes otherwise is a fantasist. I believe the root to the escape conspiracy theories were fabricated by the Soviets, for what reason I don't know.

With Hitler dead there were those who prepared their attempts to flee and seek refuge elsewhere. Those who remained in the Führerbunker could do nothing other than wait for the arrival of the Red Army. Juanita Koertzer was the girlfriend of a young SS soldier on Hitler's bodyguard staff. She recalled:

Most of the soldiers began to abandon all of the rules that had been formerly in place within the bunker. As soon as Hitler was declared dead they lit up cigarettes and began to drink very heavily. I wandered along the passages, the air putrid with cigarette smoke, sweat and the smell of piss. There was an atmosphere of paranoia and fear. The lights flickered on and off and the walls were slightly damp, particularly in the soldiers' sleeping areas. I saw pornographic images hanging on the walls and one young man lay drunk in his cot with his trousers around his ankles. I understood the need for this drunkenness as the reality was too dreadful for many to comprehend fully. I walked into an office where there were papers strewn all over the floor and a half empty bottle of champagne on a desk. I walked in and could not remember when I last tasted fine champagne. I wiped the mouth of the bottle and took a mouthful. The champagne was warm, but the taste was magical. A soldier came staggering along the empty corridor with a bottle in his left hand and blood around his mouth. The bottle he was drinking from had a jagged, broken end. He was so drunk he did not notice it had sliced open his lips. He staggered in and slammed the door shut behind him. He started babbling about how we should celebrate one last time. Before I know it he was removing his jacket and trying to push me back onto the desk in the room. With his weight on top of me it was difficult to get him off me. I was shouting, 'Nein! Nein!', but he didn't listen. I scratched at him with my nails as he was tugging at my underwear and pulling up my skirt. I was still shouting at him when another soldier burst into the room and pulled this man from off me just in time. He struck him about the face with several blows and shouted at him, 'What the fucking hell are you doing? You are a disgrace. Look at you.' I ran out of the room and back up the corridor and up the steps. There were people with children there now. They just sat there, expressionless, and some of the children were crying.

On 2 May 1945 the Berlin garrison surrendered unconditionally to the Red Army. The city was in a state of total devastation. It was a less than dignified end to Adolf Hitler's proposed thousand-year Reich. Over the following days the victorious Red Army celebrated their victory with a rampage of looting, rape and drunkenness. In Josef Stalin's view the soldiers of the Russian Red Army had earned their right to the spoils through a passage of blood and fire. The violence and hatred slowly petered out over the weeks and months of occupation. Berlin would have to be rebuilt – and she was after the passing of much time – but would never be the same city again.

Thelma Ortge and Gabbi Becker heard the news of the events in Berlin along with the news of Hitler's suicide. Thelma recalled:

The news was broken by the Americans but the reports of what had actually gone on were not too clear. I was relieved that it was finally over but concerned at what would come next. Would we remain a country under occupation for the rest of our lives? The Americans were celebrating the fact Berlin had surrendered when the news of Hitler's death came through. It was no good trying to ask them questions as they wouldn't really tell us anything more. Some of them appeared very wary of talking to us. I remember my parents whooping with joy at the news of Hitler's death. They no longer had to be afraid of revealing how they really felt. Other Germans were saying 'Thank God that old fascist is finally dead.'

Gabbi's parents had supported the Nazis and they sat quietly eyeing the 'traitors' with scornful looks on their faces. This was difficult for Gabbi and, of course, for us. We had to talk about what we were going to do next, but we were happy the war was now over. It was not a problem between us that Hitler was now dead and the war won by the enemy. The biggest problem facing us at the time was that we had fallen in love with one another. What were we going to do? We decided for the time being to just keep quiet and see what happened.

With the war over, things did not change rapidly. Food was still rationed. Me and Gabbi […] helped out wherever we could. We helped women with their children and helped with cooking and boiling up water. As time passed the Americans were not so sullen towards us. They even gave us some of their food supplies and were good to the little children. There were some that were not very nice to us, but not many that I can recall. Me and Gabbi continued to go everywhere together. Certain people would notice this and make up stories about us. The brief times we could be alone were spent talking about what we were going to do.

In the end, due to the rumours which eventually got back to our parents, we had to explain things to them. We were not really afraid. What we had been through was far worse. So we actually told them that we could not be apart from one another; that we had an unbreakable bond. Gabbi's mother was the first to speak out. She turned to Gabbi and said, 'What is going on here? Don't you dare tell me that you are in love with her because I will never accept it.' There was a brief pause and she continued, 'You are, aren't you? You are in love with this whore.' She then went on about how disgusting we both were and how it was all my fault. My parents sat watching in stunned silence. My father shook his head and buried his face in his hands. My mother just held her hand over her mouth in horror. She said, 'Thea, you can't do this to us. This is not right.' Gabbi's parents basically disowned her while mine refused to speak to me. This caused us both severe unhappiness, but we knew we would be even more unhappy if we broke up.

Of course, amidst all the end-of-war celebrations we had to contend with shouts of 'lesben' [lesbian] and worse. There was more hatred aimed at us by our own people than there was for the occupying Allied soldiers. We didn't feel safe at that farm anymore and we packed what few things we had with us and left. We both left letters for our parents and set off across the fields. We hadn't a clue where we were going. We just wanted to get away from all the hatred and ridicule aimed at us. In the warm dawn of that morning in late May we walked across the fields surrounded in mist. We held hands and smiled at one another then stopped to kiss. We stood there embracing and kissing for some minutes. Gabbi said, 'What I would give for a bed and some clean sheets this instant!'

We came upon an American patrol that stopped us and asked us where we were going. We told them we didn't know. They searched us and let us continue on our way. The Americans were everywhere and we kept bumping into patrols or whole units of them. Every time we were stopped and searched. In fact, one time we saw this patrol coming and Gabbi threw off her coat and held her arms up in the air ready for the inevitable search. She was so funny and this is what so attracted me to her.

We slept the night in a small coppice and next day we came across another farm. We spoke with the owners and they fed us and gave us water to wash in. The farmer's wife had three daughters and she gave us a few of their clothes to change into. We threw our old ones out as they were filthy and stank so badly. We were questioned as to what we were doing and where we were going. The farmer asked us, 'You are not in any trouble are you?' and then, 'You're not wanted by the Allied forces for crimes are you?' We reassured them we were not. We told them things had happened that were difficult to explain. They gave us a room to sleep in and there were two small single beds with blankets and clean, crisp, white sheets on. Me and Gabbi looked at one another and could not believe what we were seeing. There was a small sliding bolt lock on the door and so we slid it across and locked it. We had been so used to sleeping rough that we had to have the windows wide open and found the beds were too comfortable for us. We did not sleep much at all that night.

In the morning we woke for breakfast, which was one of the finest we had eaten in a very long time. Eggs, ham, wild mushrooms, German sausage and rolls that the farmer had baked himself. We gulped down the food to the point they had to tell us to slow down or we would choke on it. We cleaned our plates with the last bits of the rolls and thanked them for giving us such a wonderful meal. Over some coffee they asked where we intended to go next. We couldn't give them an answer. In the end we were asked if we wanted to stay and help the farmer's wife with her work while the farmer went out and made repairs to his buildings. The work was very hard, but at least we would have a roof over our heads, so we agreed to stay for a while. We were at this farm for around a month.

We had spoken with Americans who passed through regularly. They told us that the city of Heidelberg was largely intact. After talking about it the one evening, we decided that if we travelled to Heidelberg we could find work and somewhere to stay. It was not far from where we were and we could walk there if we had to. We decided to go back to the camp first and leave a message for our parents to let them know where we were going. We managed to get a ride some of the way on an American truck. It was all so weird really. When we arrived at the camp there were many new faces there and it was very crowded. We found our parents and, although they refused to speak to us, we left them letters giving instructions that if they needed to speak to us they should send letters to the Burgermeister's offices. We then set off for Heidelberg and yet another adventure.

There were so many American vehicles on the roads that it was easy for two young women to find a lift. We arrived in Heidelberg the next morning and straightaway we began looking for some work. Gabbi was okay as she was the brainbox out of the two of us. She found a job at a chemist in the city. Her job came with accommodation, which was a short distance from the shop. She showed me where to wait, and when the business owner had shown her around and left she sneaked me inside. It was barely two rooms but it was a start. There was just a single bed in the room, but we both squeezed in and slept blissfully. Early next morning I had to leave before the shop opened for business.

We had to do this sneaking around for a few weeks until we could find an apartment we could afford. I had found a job in the hospital there, in the laundry department. It was hot, unpleasant work, but it was a job and I was happy that we finally had somewhere to live together. We mainly kept ourselves to ourselves though we did meet up with some of the friends I made at the hospital. All we did was work and save our money. We had few luxuries, other than going out with the few friends we had made locally. We would go out and have some drinks and sometimes we would go and watch a film at the cinema. Life was steadily improving for us and we were happy. When we went out together we did so arm in arm, but we never dared hold hands as that would have been too obvious. Sometimes we went out into the countryside and, if no one was around, we would hold hands. It felt nice that the war, with all its horrors, had ended.

Although we never went back to live in Cologne, after eight months I received a letter from my parents. It had been delivered to the Rathaus [Burgermeister's residence]. I felt sad for Gabbi as she had nothing from her parents. Eventually, after nearly fourteen months, they sent her a letter asking how she was. We kept in touch via letter but it was a long time before we felt we could finally go and see our parents again. We lived as a couple and, to be honest, we did not care what people felt about that. I mean we did not flaunt the fact we were in love, but if anybody gave us any trouble we were more than capable of dealing with them.

For Thora Weber 'Victory, war is over' was something of misnomer. In her diary she recalled

'Victory, war is over. How wonderful,' they [the Allied soldiers] say. For us it is fucking miserable. We are living like dogs out of basements and there is little food, only what scraps we are given by the soldiers, which is not much. People fight over a few rotten potatoes and I have seen people hacking lumps of flesh off the rotting carcasses of horses. We have been reduced to uncivilised beings that we barely recognise in the mirror. We are dirty, hungry and thirsty, and have lice in our hair. The enemy think this is funny. They say we now know how those we imprisoned felt. I hate them so much and wish I had killed more of them, but these people from the east are never ending. They keep coming into the city. They walk around taking tourist photos, defiling our history with their very presence. They walk into our homes, looking around for things and taking what they feel like taking. This is far from victory, but then we are the losers. I feel we are going to suffer a long time before things get better, if they ever get better. I cannot see beyond the horizon at this time. For me the war is still not over.

Gertrud Soetzer, the twelve-year-old whose sister leapt up onto a burning Soviet tank in a vain attempt to help a wounded crew member escape, recalled:

Berlin was full of Soviet Russian soldiers. Many of them sat in groups, drinking, then they would get up and dance. Some became aggressive and abusive after drinking. They would wander around, looking to pick fights with people. They even fought amongst themselves at times. My parents kept me away from them as they had been told some horrible stories about them. They never told me what the stories were until months after the war had ended. They did not want to frighten me, I guess, with stories of how they had raped girls and women. I know some women who went with them willingly in the hope of getting extra food and other things. The German women who didn't do this despised them and viewed them as traitors long after the war had ended. Such things stuck like shit long after the war. I remember when I was twenty-three years old, my mother talking to her friend about this local woman. She said, 'Oh, you remember her? She was that slut who slept with the Russians for special treatment.' The war ended in 1945 but its stigmas were carried far beyond that terrible year.

Adelen Muller had mixed feelings about the end of the war in 1945:

I was happy that the war was over and that my family had survived it all. Our home was in ruins. The only habitable part was the cellar and even that had to be dug out. We worked through the rubble of our home, pulling out anything that was salvageable. We found a couple of chairs and a table which had to be repaired. These were taken into the cellar, where we lived for some months. By October 1945 we made the ruins of our home partially habitable after much backbreaking work. There was no glass in any of the windows and we had to hang blankets over them to keep the wind out during the following winter. It didn't stop the biting cold or rain from coming in though. We all got sick and were forced to go and stay with friends, which meant we were separated as a family.

I didn't like the fact that we were under occupation and we had these foreigners telling us what we could and couldn't do in our own country. Our occupiers were given these documents telling them they were not allowed to fraternise with us or stay in our houses. I would go out on nice days and these soldiers from America or England would stop me and ask if they could take photographs of me. I let them take their photographs as I felt flattered with the attention. I had nothing at all to smile about, but having my picture taken made me smile. The Americans and the English were very polite and they did offer us things after a while. Talking with them was difficult if they had no one to translate, but there were a lot of them who knew a little German. They talked about going home to their families, wives and children. One told me he hadn't seen his wife or children for four long years. He was worried that his wife would not even recognise him when he finally arrived home. He was also worried his wife might have found someone else for comfort. Their fears were probably much the same as those our soldiers faced. As human beings we all had that capacity to feel some form of empathy for one another now the fighting was at an end. I understood how a soldier felt as I had fought myself, maybe not in quite the same way that they had, but I understood them. I got to know some of them and finally began to smile for their photographs. The Russians too could be kind. Not all of them were monsters. Their rearguard soldiers were the ones you had to be careful of. The professional soldiers were always the first in and the rearguard would follow and take over from them, allowing them to push on. They were not so nice. I knew girls who had been brutally assaulted by them. Those of us who got through that time without being attacked count ourselves very fortunate indeed. Many were not so lucky.

Germany would not be rebuilt quickly and it was us women who had the job of clearing up the rubble in the city. We were what they called 'Rubble Gangs'. All we did was clear mountains of rubble all day long. I recall one day we had cleared a pile of rubble and there was a bomb underneath. Everyone ran like hell away from it. Some soldiers were brought in to make it safe and it was taken away on the back of a truck. Another time we were doing the same when a woman screamed. We all looked to see what she was screaming at and could see several rotting corpses. The building had probably collapsed on top of these poor people. The bodies had to be pulled out of the rubble and removed for burial. One of the women on the gang actually knew who those people were. It must have been horrible for her. It was quite normal to discover human remains during the clearing of rubble. The remains would be placed in buckets, or whatever was available at the time. They would be taken away for burial when the buckets were full. We found the crushed and burnt bodies of old women, men, babies and children. Berlin was the stuff of nightmares and an English soldier once asked me if I felt it was all worth it. I told him, 'These things are only worth it if you win the fight. If you are the loser it is never worth it.'

Elise Pfaff had grown accustomed to taking 'The Führer Drug', the nickname given to the drug Pervitin.

> I took a lot of Pervitin. Once you had taken it you didn't care about anything and you didn't feel tired or anything. It was my way of dealing with my own pain and fear. It caused weird hallucinations and you would see strange things that were not there. People with you would think you were crazy because you were acting like a lunatic. I could not keep still and would pace around and be talking to people who were not there. They fetched a doctor for me and I went berserk on him. It took five of them to hold me down. They searched my pockets and found a few remaining Pervitin tablets. They confiscated them and then tied me up until the effects of the drug had worn off. It was horrible being under the influence of the drug and being tied up as you could not work off the energy that it gave you. They tied my hands and took my shoes off me, and tied my legs up so I couldn't even stand up. My parents were so angry with me when they were told. The doctor who had dealt with me told my parents to make sure I did not use this drug again as he believed it was very dangerous and that I might hurt myself without even knowing it. After that I did not use it again, but I can see how some people, especially German soldiers, had become addicted to it. When you were high on it you felt like Thor. You felt like you could destroy the world single-handed. No wonder Hitler liked it so much.

With the Allied victory, Germany was soon to be divided between east and west. It was the opinion of the Allies that this was the best solution in preventing Germany from threatening world peace again. For a brief time this appeared to work. But the end of hostilities also brought about an end to the mutual co-operation that had existed through the last four years. It seems ironic that Britain, America and France were soon facing a new threat from their former ally in the east. As the Iron Curtain descended with a crash, dividing East Germany from West Germany, a new and more terrible threat emerged. When America lost its exclusivity in the possession of atomic weapons to Soviet Russia, the world would once again edge towards war. It was nothing short of a miracle that a disaster of unrivalled proportions did not materialise from the arms race that followed. The Cold War, as it became known, would last for decades. Luckily for mankind, it remained just a war of words, threats and posturing. The threat of MAD, or Mutually Assured Destruction, ensured the Cold War remained cold. In a few short years West Germany, as part of NATO, would become the bulkhead against Soviet aggression in the new Europe attempting to rise from the ashes of war.

Chapter Eighteen

Erich

The recollections contributed to my two books – *Hitler's Girl's- Doves Amongst Eagles and In Hitler's Shadow-Post war Germany and the Girls of the BDM* – by Berliner Anita Von Schoener reflect the alternating fortunes of war. From a young girl, Anita had been singled out by the Nazis as one of the finest representations of the ideal Aryan German female. As a child she had undergone unpleasant medical examinations and as a young adult she was encouraged to marry an SS soldier, who later went missing on the Eastern Front. When Berlin fell she was the mother of a young son named Anton. She was taken by the Russians and raped while a pistol was held to her child's head. She survived her war only to discover some weeks after the rape that she was pregnant with her rapist's child. In defiance of her parent's wishes at the time to have the child aborted, she went through with the full term of the pregnancy and gave birth to another baby boy. Fearing that she might grow to hate the child, she immediately gave the baby up for adoption […] Anita met and fell in love with an American serviceman. They married and moved to the USA. It was in July of 1964 that Anita received a panicked phone call from her father in Germany. Fearing that there had been a death in the family, Anita was beside herself with worry and rushed to the telephone. Anita recalls the conversation with her father that followed:

> My father said that a young man had called at their home. He told my father that he had been adopted as a baby and was searching for his birth mother. He then went on to explain that there was a record with my father and mother's name and address on. The young man had left a letter for me and my father did not know what to do about the situation. I was in shock for a few minutes and did not know what to

say. My father asked me whether he should burn the letter and forget about it. I told him not to do that and to send it on to me. I would think about what I was going to do about the situation. My father sent the letter to me and it arrived a month later. My husband was very understanding and gave me his full support, whatever I wanted to do. He was such a lovely man like that. He told me to sit down, read the letter and to think about it all. He made me a cup of coffee and I sat out on our little veranda and began to read the letter from this young man back in Germany. The letter read:

To My Dear Mother. Please, I am hoping that you do not show hate towards me for writing you this short letter. I have been trying to find details on my background for a year now. I was adopted by a very nice German family who raised me as their own. They revealed details of my adoption when I was old enough to fully understand it all. They never tried to hide any of the facts from me. I went to the hospital and there was one record remaining regarding my birth. It had an address where you were living at the time and your father had signed the form. This is how I was able to find your parents (my grandparents). I hope that I did not frighten them too much by turning up like that. If you would like to write to me I can send you a photograph of myself. I do not wish to cause you any pain and if you would rather not have any contact with me I will understand and will go on with my life. I feel like there is a piece of me missing, dear mother. I would never blame you for whatever decision made you give me up for adoption. I have read much about the time when I would have been conceived and have a feeling that my conception may not have been consensual on your part. Again, I would never judge you. Whatever your decision will be you will always be forever in my heart, my dear mother. Please write back to me if you are able. With Love from Erich.

By the time I had reached the end of the letter I was crying. I handed the letter to my husband who sat and read through its contents. Even he was almost moved to tears by the words of this young man. I sat for most of that afternoon looking at the letter. During the evening I began to draft a reply. At first I struggled to find the words. I would write, then stop and throw the letter in the bin as I was not happy with what I had written. By late evening I had written a reply that I was happy with. The next day I sealed it in an envelope and took it to the local store where it could be mailed back to Germany. I was curious about this young man and, although I was very scared, I wanted to see what he looked like. Did he look like me? What colour of eyes and hair did he have? I telephoned my father and told him I had sent a letter back to this young man named Erich. I asked my father what he looked like and he told me, 'God, he looks just like you. It was like looking at a ghost.'

Over the weeks that followed I received a letter of reply from Erich and inside was a photograph. When I saw it I had to put my hand over my mouth. I was so shocked at how much like me he really was. I showed the photograph to my husband when he arrived home from work that day. I also showed the photograph to my son, Anton, and my daughter. They expressed curiosity and began asking questions. It was not all easy to answer them truthfully. Erich was conceived through rape in Berlin and that is not a happy memory for me at all. I felt I could not reveal the circumstances to him at this time. I would need more time to tell him all of the details, and with time I was able to do this. I had no choice. It was then up to him if he wished to continue writing to me. He did say, in his heart of hearts, that he had the feeling he had been conceived through rape. He was not stupid. He had done some research and knew the things that had happened in Berlin around that time.

After some months we agreed to talk on the telephone to one another. I was extremely nervous speaking to Erich this first time. He told me about himself, where he had lived and so on. I told him as much of my story as I could. I had grown fond of his letters and when we discussed it as a family I felt the next step would have to be to meet the young man. It was decided I would fly out to Germany on my own. I would stay with my parents and arrange a meeting at their home. My parents were very good about it all and supported my decision. This was unusual at the time. Many families would not have agreed to do this as it was considered a shameful act. To be honest, living in the USA had made me so much wiser to everything in the world. I no longer cared what people would think of me; it was my life.

In February 1965 I flew out to Germany. When I arrived I was surprised by how little things had changed. I expected to see many new buildings where the ruined ones had stood, but very little had changed. I recalled all the old roads leading to my parents' house. When I arrived outside I took a deep breath and walked up the path to the front door. Before I could even knock on the door my father and mother were there to greet me. We hugged and they were so happy to see me that they were crying with joy. We went inside and I looked around the old house. It brought back so many good memories and some not so good ones of the days when our relationship deteriorated. I sat down and my mother brought in hot drinks. I was very tired as it had been a long journey to get here. I had stopped in Ireland and England before finally arriving in Germany. My father put my bags away and I felt myself falling asleep. Mother made my old bed up and I was so tired that I was fast asleep in my old room by 8pm.

We arranged for Erich to come and visit three days after my arrival so I could have a bit of a rest and go and see some old friends who I hadn't seen in many years. The night before Erich was due to come to visit I could not sleep. All kinds of thoughts went through my head. I had relived the rape many times over the years but was waking up in hot sweats and having nightmares again. My mother came in during the night when she heard me shouting in my sleep. She was worried that the meeting with Erich might make me ill. I assured her I would be alright, but I lay in bed staring at the ceiling just thinking for most of the time.

It was a relief when dawn came and the birds began to sing outside. I got up and helped mother with some of her washing. We did a little housework so all was tidy for our visitor arriving. At 11am we heard a car pull up in the lane outside the house. I took several very deep breaths and went and opened the door. I watched a young man get out of his car and as he turned to walk up the garden path our eyes met for the first time. He froze and stood by the gate for a minute until I told him, 'Please, come on in.' As he reached the front door I held both my hands out to him. I could not believe how much he looked like me. He began to cry and his emotion affected me greatly. I held him in my arms as he sobbed like a child. We both cried very hard for some minutes. My parents helped us both in to the small living room where we sat down and my father brought some coffee in for us all.

It was hard to know what to talk about at first but we soon became relaxed and I began to ask Erich about his life and the people who had adopted him. I was happy that he had had an upbringing that was happy and filled with love. It was not easy to talk with my parents around so I suggested we go for a walk. We left the house and walked down the lane to the fields and meadows. We sat down by the small stream and were able to talk about everything. I told Erich the reason why I had to let him go as a baby. I explained that I did not want to risk him growing up and being resented by his own mother. He understood and told me he had a feeling that he had come about through rape. We talked openly about how many women were raped after Berlin fell in 1945. I told him the whole story and I told him that, now having met him, I could never resent him. We walked some more and ended up walking arm in arm through the countryside. We talked about the future and agreed that we would both like to stay in touch. Erich asked me if I minded if he called me mother and I asked him if he minded if I call him son. It was very emotionally charged, especially when I told him he had an older brother and younger sister living in the USA. When he left to go back home it was like we had known one another for years.

When I returned home everyone was eager to know how everything went. I told them about it all and I wrote a letter and enclosed some photos for Erich from us all. Six months after that first meeting Erich came out to the USA and he stayed with us for a couple of weeks. His adopted parents had raised a fine young man who they could be proud of. I was very proud of him too and, as the years went by, we became almost like any other mother and son. It was like the closing of an unfinished chapter. I had never guessed that this would ever happen. It was not easy. Not many women would have gone to the lengths that I had gone to reconcile with my past. I could be happy in myself as there were no more demons hiding in my life.

My mother and father soon warmed to the young man. They would tell me in their letters and weekly phone calls how Erich had taken them out for a drive in his car and had tea with them every weekend. It was heart-warming for them. I recall one of the last conversations I had with my father before he died. He told me that it was wonderful having Erich in their lives and he had never felt it would have worked out the way it had. Mother too was very happy although it was not easy for her at first. They had once tried to persuade me to terminate the pregnancy from which he resulted. I know they felt guilt, but then we all did. The main lesson of it all was that we had learned a lot from each other. We reciprocated the love we had for one another. I made sure that there were certain things left in my will to Erich. There wasn't much, just a few things that I wanted him to have when I died that he might pass on to his children.

Over the years that followed, Erich featured in Anita's life as much as her other two children. The distance between them was never an obstacle to their relationship. When Anita passed away in February of 2017 she was laid to rest in a quiet cemetery near to where she lived in the USA. Her husband and all three children were there. Each one of the children read a eulogy, describing their mother thus: 'The strongest most loving and most wonderful mother any child could have. Despite a troubled past, she helped build a future filled with happiness and hope. She had time for those of her society that others wouldn't bother with. She always put those she loved and cared about before herself. She was a remarkable yet humble woman, emotional yet strong. She will be sadly missed yet her rest is well deserved.'

Each one of her children placed a red rose on Anita's coffin as it was lowered into the ground. And so the curtain was drawn on yet another life associated with *Hitler's Girls: Doves Amongst Eagles*. The time I myself had spent talking and writing to her had also been painfully brief, but so much had been documented that Anita Von Schoener's memory will live on through the pages of my books and in the memories of all those who knew and loved her.

Chapter Nineteen

In the Absence of Men

The reconstruction of Germany in the wake of the Second World War did not happen overnight. On the contrary, it would be a very lengthy process. Four million out of the sixteen million German homes had been destroyed as a result of the Allied bombing campaign and, in some cases, subsequent ground fighting. A further four million homes were assessed as being damaged. Those homes that did remain were barely fit for habitation. Many of Germany's men had either been killed, incapacitated through their wounds or taken as prisoners of war. As a result of the sheer absence of men, the initial task of rebuilding Germany would fall to Germany's women.

From the years 1945–1946 the Allied powers in both West and East Germany ordered all young girls and women between the ages of fifteen and fifty to enrol in the post-war clear up initiative. These females became known as the *Trummerfrau*, or 'Ruin Woman/Rubble Woman'. The *Trummerfrau* were made up of volunteers and regular workers and they worked together in large chain gangs in all weathers. The women at the head of the chain would put rubble into the buckets and the full buckets would be passed down the chain before being tipped into carts or vehicles to be taken away. The work of the *Trummerfrau* was thoroughly unpleasant and backbreaking work. Bertha Wuremfjeld recalls:

> They told us we had to sign up for work duty clearing rubble in the city. I can remember being in the western sector of Berlin. I stood and gazed about and I just thought 'where do we even start to clear all this mess up?' The Allied soldiers would say, 'This won't clear up on its own. Get to work and clear it. You created this mess yourselves.' This remark made me so angry that I couldn't help myself and I shouted back at this man, 'No, you fucking men caused all of this so why don't

you clear it up?' I was told not to be so insolent and just get on with it.

It was very depressing early on. Whole communities and families became involved in the rubble gangs. We formed lines and passed full buckets to one another all day long, from early morning till dusk. The work left you dirty and feeling like death. We did not have an awful lot to eat either. We did have supplies of food that were distributed amongst us, but it was not much. The worst days were when it poured with rain all day long. The monotony of the work itself, the aching back and sore hands, made it very miserable. Sometimes on a bad day we all suffered in silence. We just worked quietly on the mounds of rubble, wishing it would just vanish away like magic. Other days we would be happier and we would sometimes sing songs.

We took it in turns at the front of the gang to pick up rubble and fill the buckets. Under some of the rubble piles you just knew there were dead bodies or other human remains. You could smell them as the rubble was removed. We covered our mouths and noses with pieces of rag. Often when bodies were found they were so badly crushed they were hardly recognisable. They looked like meat that you would buy from a butcher's shop. The worst thing was finding the bodies of children. We did find many dead children under the rubble. Some of the houses had burned down so the bodies were charred black by fire. Bodies and body parts were put into caskets or empty bath tubs and taken away for burial. We all knew this was the best deal we were going to get in Germany at the time. Clearing up the mess was as much a punishment as anything else, including the rape of our girls and women.

Sofia Weiss, who turned twenty-two in the aftermath of the Second World War, was another young woman who joined in with the *Trummerfrau*.

We had nothing to do anymore. Surviving was one thing and keeping yourself occupied was another. I was told I would have to help clear up the city. They were not very nice to you back then just after the end of the fighting. I joined one of the gangs in what had been my old neighbourhood where I had grown up. My hands soon became sore and blistered through the work. The thing was there were barely any German men left to do this work so we had no choice. There were boys and they were made to do all sorts of things like help bury corpses and collect up bits of dead bodies. The Allied soldiers were very suspicious of the boys as many had been in the Hitler Youth. The Allied soldiers didn't trust them at all.

I recall we were working on clearing rubble one morning. I was taking my turn at the front, pulling what rubble away I could and placing it in the buckets. It had been raining steadily throughout the night and morning. It made the work even more miserable for us. My mother was helping on the same rubble gang. As I cleared one bit of rubble away I saw something metal sticking up out of the ground. It was dark green in colour and I continued to remove rubble from around it. Then another woman spotted what I was doing. She called out, 'Stop! Get away from that thing!' She dropped her bucket and gestured for the line of women to move back, away from the rubble. A soldier came over to see what was going on. He was shown the object in the rubble and his face turned pale. He ordered everyone off the pile and to move away. It was not a bomb but an artillery shell. It was still very dangerous and had to be removed. Had it gone off it might have killed all the women in that line, including myself. Some more soldiers arrived and they carefully examined the shell. It was a Russian 17.5-cm explosive and they could not risk removing it so they blew it up where it was. The shrapnel from bombs was also a hazard amongst the rubble. You had to be careful as some shrapnel had edges that were as sharp as a razor blade.

As it got dark, the work stopped and we returned to the cellars we were using as shelters. We were tired, sore and hungry. We had some bread, soup and, sometimes, some German salami. We would share it out between the family. Sometimes we had a lot, other times not enough. Food was being brought in by the Allied soldiers and if you were lucky they felt sorry for you and gave you some more food. The Russians once gave me one of their ration packages and I took it home and shared it with my family. It was lovely, even though the food was slightly different from our own. When you're hungry you will eat anything. There was a small bottle of vodka in there too. Before my mother and father could do anything I had broken off the top and taken a huge gulp. My father said, 'That is pure rocket fuel. You can't go drinking this stuff like that, my girl.' With the food and that big mouthful of vodka I slumped back, burped loudly, and slept better than I had done in weeks.

Helen Giehl, who had worked at the Krupp factory in Essen, recalls a similar regime of work at the end of the war.

The destruction wrought by the fighting had been extensive. It could not be just left so we women had to do it as there were not enough men now. Many of the Allied occupation forces wouldn't speak to you at first. They were told they were not allowed to talk to us by their commanders. This was, however, impossible as we had to talk with one another to accomplish certain goals. When one of the Americans began to talk to me I told him I had been employed by the Krupp works and that I had worked on machines. I also told him about the slave labourers who had been used at the factory. They showed quite a lot of interest in me after that. I was asked questions on operations at the Krupp works and if I knew my way to the offices; things like that. Most of the Krupp works was in ruins but I took them there and showed them what I could remember. I am not sure what it was they were looking for, but once I had showed them where certain offices had been they told me I could go back to the rubble gang.

Later on, the soldiers who had questioned me about Krupp works brought me some chocolate and some other food. These were the kinds of things we could never have normally obtained, not unless we had the money to buy from the black market. I was grateful for these extra items of food, especially the chocolate. You have no idea just how good that chocolate tasted. That first piece I placed in my mouth was sheer ecstasy. I sat with it in my mouth with my eyes closed, not wanting to swallow it. Oh, it was just heaven. I also had this tin of condensed milk. Then there were tins of peaches. But I bolted it down so quickly it all gave me tummy ache. All this rich food after the small rations soon took its toll [...] I thought back to the slave labourers at the factory and hoped they were all safe and well now all this was over. I thought about those poor people a lot over the years. I did try to help them, if only in a small way, and I can be happy with myself for that.

Kathi Emler, who had assisted the SRD, experienced different fortunes at the end of the war.

Somebody had told the Allies I had been a German spy and that I had been working with the security division and Gestapo. I was arrested and detained for three days, after which they began to question me on my activities. It seemed someone had already told them everything about me. The Russians who interrogated me threatened me with violence if I refused to talk or if they felt I was lying to them. They forced me to strip on one occasion and I was sure I was going to be raped by them. They just made me stand before them, naked, while they asked me questions. It was in a sense a thinly veiled threat of what they could do if they wanted. I told them everything; what I had done and how it all worked. After several days they brought me some ill-fitting replacement clothes and said I could leave. They told me not to try and go away anywhere as they might have an interesting proposition for me. They told me they would be in touch and to go and make myself useful with the other women. I did as I was told and joined the *Trummerfrau* clearing up rubbish. Some of the women I knew and used to call friends, but they refused to talk to me now. They were unpleasant. Two or three of them called me a whore.

After some weeks the Russians asked me if I would work for them and gather information on what the British and

Americans were up to in the western sector of Berlin. They told me the best thing I could do was to answer 'yes'. If I refused, the outcome might not be favourable for me. I agreed to their requests and they told me to go and see what I could find out. They told me not to try and disappear. If I did they would issue an arrest order saying that I was a criminal who had worked for the Nazis. It was no different in the western sector of the city. I was told to help the women. The Allied soldiers there never really spoke to me and when they did it was only to give me work detail instructions. If you asked them anything else they just ignored you. I guess they were not stupid and kept things to themselves. I reported back to the eastern sector to my Russian friends. I think they had sent someone to watch me as they appeared satisfied with what I had told them. They told me, 'Get out of here and go back to your work.' I went back to the rubble gangs and my future was as uncertain as everyone else's at that time.

Wiener Katte, the fifteen-year-old BDM girl from Aachen, also joined the *Trummerfrau* gangs in Aachen.

Hard work was nothing new to the girls of the BDM. We never had the attitude that the youth of today have: 'Oh sorry, I can't do this,' or 'Oh no, I can't do that.' If we were set a task that we did not know how to do then we learned how to do it. There were no excuses, no whining about not wanting to do it. We just got on with it. We had no choice but to join the women on clearing duty. We joined them and we worked very hard. We wrapped our hands in bandages to protect them from cuts and blisters and we got stuck into the work. We wanted our beautiful city to be rebuilt. It wouldn't happen on its own or by magic, it would only get done if the women of Germany helped to make it happen. The future began in that rubble. Amongst the stones, dust, body parts and bomb shrapnel. There were some young men who had been in the Hitler Youth who complained about having to work with girls and women. I said to my mother once, as we worked away, 'With World

War Two won and Germany beaten they are going to have to find something else to fight about now.' I think the boys were frightened that we were at last being given a degree of equality in our country. German women would have a long fight for equality and certain rights, but that fight began in the ruins of 1945. It was like wiping the slate clean and starting all over again. In the absence of men we had to do it.

Many remarkable stories came out of Germany during the immediate post-war years. Perhaps one of the strangest is the following, which occurred around 2 October 1947 at Rhein-Main air base in Germany. Baggage handlers were busy with their work when they noticed the lid of a wooden crate lift up. The baggage handlers were shocked to discover a young girl momentarily peer out from the crate to survey her surroundings. Having been noticed, the girl quickly slammed shut the lid, locking it from the inside. The startled baggage handlers summoned William Waring, the operations representative for American Overseas Airlines, to investigate. The crate was prised open and the men found themselves gazing into the sad eyes of a scantily clad young German girl. The girl climbed out of the crate and said in fluent English, 'Imagine the horror of being inside there for so long and then being caught.' She had drunk most of a 5-oz bottle of tea while inside the crate. There were also three slices of bread left inside, along with a red heart cut out of a piece of felt material. It was soon revealed that the wooden crate had been bound for the home of the young girl's sweetheart, a Mr Rolph Berndt of 539 West 49th Street, New York City, USA. After being given some food and drink she was questioned by army investigators and taken for a thorough medical check up to ensure she was alright. She exclaimed in less fluent English 'much hurt'.

Thankfully this incident was reported in the *Stars and Stripes* military newspaper and remains in their archives today. The girl's name was Doris von Knoblock; her age at the time was twenty. Doris had worked as a dental technician from the previous April in Darmstadt. Her fiancé was a German refugee, Rolph Berndt, who told the press: 'I am mystified by this incident. I thank God that she is alive but I don't think that this could have been her idea.' During her questioning by the military authorities it transpired that Doris had been brought to the airport in the crate by Private 1st Class Robert Seidentopf, a colleague of Doris's at the Darmstadt dispensary. Doris explained to the Darmstadt court martial that Seidentopf had helped her 'as a personal favour'. Seidentopf had collected the crate from the girl's home, as arranged, and had assumed it had been packed with a tapestry or some other heavy household goods. He recalled being puzzled that the girl was not at home when he collected the crate, which a German driver helped him transport. Seidentopf explained there had been no romantic interest in the girl on his part and that he had delivered the crate simply as a favour.

It was lucky for Doris that she had been found. Had the crate been shipped it would have been loaded in the unheated forward section of an aircraft. Flying over the North Atlantic at 9,000ft, the temperature would have dropped to –15°C. Doris would have almost certainly died in those conditions. She gave no explanation as to why she was so scantily clad for her journey. Although a sweater and other warm clothing was found inside the crate there would have been no room for her to put it on. The crate may also have been stacked with others and left for some days before being shipped from the airport and she could have been trapped inside. It transpired that at the end of the war Doris was working at a Berlin hospital. She had met the half-Jewish Rolph Berndt shortly after he had been released from the Sachsenhausen concentration camp. The pair soon fell in love. Rolph, being a political refugee, was offered a visa to the United States and left Germany and Doris behind in the spring of 1946. The pair had planned to meet up at a later date and get married in New York. Doris described life in the Russian-occupied sector of Berlin as dismal; there was nothing to keep her there. She travelled the roads at night in order to reach the American zone. When she arrived in Darmstadt she was able to find a place to stay, but the schools where she had hoped to study medicine, pharmacy or nursing were full and turned her away. She found work at the army dispensary at Darmstadt where she was described as a very efficient worker. It was here that she devised her plan to join Rolph in the USA.

Whether Doris eventually joined Rolph in the USA and married, as she had dreamed, remains unknown. Doris's story is quite a remarkable one and clearly reflects much of the hopelessness many young German women felt about their lives back in those early post-war years.

The Future

The problems of rebuilding Germany were greatly compounded by steadily deteriorating relations between east and west. Life for Germany's women in the aftermath of the Second World War was harsh, if not almost intolerable. Had it not been for the threat posed by the spread of communism in Europe and around the world after 1945, Germany may well have been left a ruin, reliant upon the charity of those who had destroyed her. The fear, paranoia and distrust of the Soviet Union that emerged from 1947 onwards led to the beginning of the Cold War.

The formation of NATO on 4 April 1949 forced the Soviets into retaliating with the creation of the Warsaw Pact in 1955. The erection of the Berlin Wall, dividing east from west from 1961 until 1989, ensured that West Germany would emerge from the ashes of the Second World War as the first point of defence against any Soviet aggression in Europe. Germany's position as an economic power essential to European stability was also a guarantor. It was a priority that German industry in particular be reactivated as soon as possible. As Western-Soviet relations continued to deteriorate, it soon became obvious to the powers in control of West Germany that, in the event of Soviet aggression, West Germany would form the bulkhead preserving western democracy.

From the moment Russia detonated the RDS-1 on 29 August 1949, the first test of a Soviet-built atomic bomb, the race was on to either match the Russians or maintain nuclear superiority over them. The Soviet bomb was an implosion bomb, modelled on the US-designed 'Fat Man', which was used over Nagasaki. The bomb's explosion yielded twenty-two kilotons. Construction and testing of the Soviet atomic bombs continued throughout the 1950s. On October 30 1961, two months after construction on the Berlin Wall began, the Russians tested the most powerful nuclear weapon to date with the 'Tsar Bomb'. This was a three-stage hydrogen bomb producing a blast yield of fifty megatons. To place the power of this weapon in its correct perspective one has to imagine all of the explosives used throughout the Second World War being detonated as a single mass. The heat generated by the bomb on detonation was capable of delivering third-degree burns at a distance of 100km [62 miles]. The Tsar Bomb never entered operational service, but it demonstrated, particularly to the USA, the extent of Soviet nuclear capability. Against the backdrop of Soviet aggression in Europe, West Germany faced a painfully slow journey from the ruins of war. The last thing many Germans wanted was to be effectively living over the fence from an angry dog, one that would most certainly bite if provoked.

Elise Pfaff recalls the post-war paranoia that permeated every aspect of West German society at the time:

> It felt like they [the Russians] could come steaming across the border at any time. There was a feeling for a while that we should forget everything of the past years and concentrate on the present. Western Germany will need to be rebuilt and its people prepared to repel a possible threat of invasion from the east. Although few of us would ever have admitted it at the time, we were quite terrified the Russians would attack and take West Germany. The thought of being enslaved under that tyranny was too much for some. There were some Germans I knew who were so convinced Russia would eventually invade West Germany that they took their own lives. These were German people who were down on their luck; they had lost homes, families and loved ones. They could not see a legitimate future beyond the destruction of the Third Reich. We all felt that way at times, but knew we could not just sit on our hands. At the same time I did not relish the prospect of having to go through another war again. The fact that they had atomic bombs made things even scarier. What would there have been to live for had those things been used.

'Denazification', the Allied initiative aimed at disposing of any residual National Socialist influences in Germany, proved very successful during its very brief implementation. The denazification process in West Germany was officially abolished in 1951 but had been more or less abandoned at the onset of the Cold War. Elise Pfaff continues:

> Denazification they called it. Yet I was already convinced of the fact that I had been lied to and did not need telling that or re-educated. The sheer cowardice displayed by the leading figures of Hitler's government during the last months, weeks and days of the Second World War told me they were not worth any of the bloodshed or the murder that they had caused, or asked us to try and defend. Where was Bormann, Himmler, Axmann, Von Schirach, Von Ribbentrop and all the other bastards while women and girls were doing their fighting and dying for them? The contempt I have for those bastards is far more than what I had for any of our enemies. Our soldiers were some of the finest in the world but that amounted to nothing as their leadership was weak and cowardly.
>
> Hitler was stupid. He would never have listened to rational argument on tactical matters. Even a child could have grasped the situation better than he did. Most children understood the theory that sometimes you have to lose battles to win wars. Hitler was deluded and under the impression that he was God, some divine figure that would win through eventually despite all of the problems. I knew some people, what you would call 'convinced Nazis'. These were people who you could not re-educate or convince that Nazism was a terrible thing. These people often kept it to themselves for fear of getting into trouble. I went to have tea at a friend's grandparents once. In the kitchen there hung a small painting of Hitler on the wall. I sat drinking their coffee and eating their cakes thinking to myself, 'Have you people not learned? Are you really this stupid?'

The mid- to late-1960s saw many social changes that were initially perceived as decadent. While East Germany continued to languish under the grey blanket of communism, West Germany embraced, and enjoyed, its freedoms. Although the youth culture of West Germany reflected much of that of the free world, rights for women were still far from satisfactory. Gabbi Becker recalled:

The 1960s were sort of funny. There was this 'Flower Power' Hippy movement and all these colourful musicians who were spawned by the scene. The Beatles and bands like them helped create an air of musical freedom that spread into young people's lives. I knew girls who wore the flowery dresses and smoked the marijuana. One of them loved the Beatles even though she could not understand what they were singing about [she laughs]. She just liked the actual sound and what they looked like. It didn't matter that they were British boys either.

It was a kind of time where you felt a little liberated and free. Me and Thelma didn't smoke marijuana, though we did both try it once. We didn't like it so we never tried it again. It may have been 'Flower Power' and 'Free Love' slogans daubed on walls, but me and Thelma had been more open than many other gay women about our relationship. It almost cost us our parents so we were damned if we were going to sneak around everywhere denying we were in love with one another. No, I said to Thelma, or Thea as I often called her, 'Fuck them. If they don't like it, that is their problem. We are doing no one any harm so to hell with the world.' We were very strong-minded girls who had experienced so much during our youth and the war years. I said bollocks to them, we have earned our right to be free, equal and to love who we want, even if it's another girl. We went on holiday to Spain once in the early 1970s. We held hands in this one bar and even kissed and no one gave a shit what we were doing. The barman thought it was exciting I think as he just carried on cleaning his glasses with a big smile on his face. Those people were great, they didn't give a shit. It was like heaven there, walking along the beach in the surf, hand in hand and being able to kiss. It would have been great if we could have moved there, but back then we were making just enough money to pay our way and buy clothes, food and pay our rent.

Back in West Germany if you went into a bar and kissed or held hands the men would make crude remarks. They would offer to pay for our drinks in exchange for a sex show. Can you believe it? One dirty old sod once asked if me and Thea would make love while he watched us. He offered to pay us but I told him, 'Go and fuck yourself. Go and buy a prostitute and leave us alone.' The women would stare and hiss at you like angry cats and say, 'Look at those two queers over there, aren't they disgusting.' If I heard them I would go up to them and tell them 'shut up'. I was not afraid of them at all. If you stood up to them they were often scared of you. I would have hit them without any hesitation if I'd had to. Thea was definitely the quieter one out of the two of us.

In my view women's rights in Germany after 1945 were slow in coming. The issue of abortion in particular was very controversial. In my view it should have always been up to the woman to make her own decision on this. There are men who have no idea of just how tough life is for some women. All those girls who were raped in 1945 by the so-called victors did not even have the right to terminate their pregnancies. Our country supported the anti-abortion law at that time. These decisions should be for the woman to make, not the men, not the church and not the government. Thea and me were certainly not feminists. I actually despise feminists. Many of them are among the most misinformed of women on this earth. They make a mockery of what real women are all about. If they had seen some of the things we had seen and done some of the things we had to do they would think differently. They remind me of the CND movement that would see all our defences removed to the point where anyone could just roll in and claim our country or anywhere else as its own. Thea and me have lived through a lot and we can see through people's bullshit. A lot of people don't like us for that but we don't care.

Throughout the 1960s, West German female students and older women campaigned for equality. There were many demonstrations that forced the West German government to review certain laws, such as those that made abortion illegal. It took Germany's women many decades to earn rights that many today take for granted. Many of the Hitler Youth generation were, by this time, married with children of their own. They were eager that their children should not make the mistakes of their parents or grandparents. Nor should they have to carry the stigma of Nazism to their graves, as their parents and grandparents undoubtedly would. Ruth Goetz, who had worked as a female camp guard at Ravensbrück, had mixed feelings about what the future would bring.

> At the end of it all I had to sit down and examine my own conscience. I did not need anyone to tell me that what I had done had been wrong or that Nazism was wrong. I knew that. I was not stupid. Our nation had failed to win the war and had failed to rid the world of its ideological enemies. I knew that I would drift back into menial jobs in factories or shops as that was the only route I could take. I had never been academic as a child and it was people like me who were, I suppose, the easiest to indoctrinate. Having been at Ravensbrück, and having done the things I had to do there, will always be a regret to me. I wish it had never happened. If I could go back in time and change it all, I would. Like many others, I did the right thing and married and had children, and I have had a happy time overall. My life has had its ups and downs over the years, but isn't everyone the same in that respect? Am I sorry for being involved in the Nazi camp system? Yes, I am sorry, but no matter how many times I say 'sorry' it never makes a difference. It never goes away.

Giselle Junghman, another former female camp guard, recalled:

> The years after the war were very tough. It seemed no matter what job you applied for or worked at, someone would find out about your past. I understood I was guilty in part for the murder of six million people. I could not reverse that, so, in the end, I stopped trying. People respect you more when you are forthright about something, so I soon learned that lying about it was a waste of time. Finding work was a real problem.

To become independent you needed to be able to work. I hated the thought of being twenty- something years old and married with screaming kids to some selfish pig who just wants his dinner and newspaper. I guess I had a pessimistic view for some time. I did eventually find work in a cinema, where I worked for some years. I met and married my husband and we had three girls. In the end I led a domestic life, but there are those who will curse me for that. They will call me names, say I was evil because I served as a Nazi camp overseer. I don't listen to these people anymore.

Adellen Muller's reflections mirror those of many in the post war years:

It took a long time for Germany to recover from its immediate past. You'd see cities of rubble and think 'how the hell are they going to rebuild all of that?' The amazing thing was that it was all rebuilt over time. We had lost many of the old buildings, but the new ones replicated many of the old ones in some ways. We all lived in fear of nuclear war. The threat was ever present because we were right next to people we regarded for a long time as enemies. Rebuilding Germany began and we grew older and got married and had children, or chose career paths. Being able to pursue a career was a luxury we never had under the Nazis. I loved art and I loved music too. I had learned to play piano, violin and saxophone. Many of us could never have conceived that life could be as good as it was without the Nazis ruling the country. We all had to learn that we had been wrong. The death of Hitler and Nazism brought about changes we could never have imagined.

The years after the war were very hard indeed and I think we, as German women, did not really feel that we were fully appreciated until well into the 1970s. There was so much being done against women in Germany, even after Hitler had gone. It was as much prejudice as anything else. Looking back, though, I feel things have changed for the worse today. The fifties, sixties, seventies, eighties and nineties were our glory years, but now things are different here in Germany [...].

Anna Dann also expresses grave concern for the country that she loves:

> We, the Third Reich generation of Germans, understand
> fully our past. We could not be ignorant of it. Some of us put
> our hands up and admitted what we did was totally wrong.
> Yet today my children, grandchildren and great grandchildren
> are being made to pay for our mistakes still. The stigma still
> exits and the shit sticks as they say. We have this government
> that has consistently failed the German people.

Gabbi Becker also fears for the future of Germany:

> I thank God that it was never possible for me and Thea to have
> children. I couldn't bear the thought of bringing any child into
> this world today. We are living in a world of great instability
> where wars and conflict are breaking out everywhere. Things
> are not good at all in Germany today. You worry about going
> out on the street these days. We are old and vulnerable now.
> We are not the strong young women we once were. Do we feel
> safe here in Germany today? The answer is no, we do not feel
> safe or secure here anymore. We feel let down by the current
> breed of political leaders here in Germany. I have nieces and
> nephews and it is them I am anxious about. What will things
> be like in Germany in another fifty years from now? Sorry
> if I am appearing to put forward a pessimistic picture of the
> future, but it has to be said. Silence and censorship achieve
> nothing. I have learned that much over the years since the
> Second World War.

Ellie Kaufmann's view on the current situation in Germany was, I felt,
the best point to close:

> The future is here, isn't it? It is happening now. The future is
> what we created from the ruins of the Second World War. I feel
> today we are a powerful yet troubled country for many varying
> reasons. Yet war, aggression and violence are not the answer.
> It is, of course, a government's duty to nurture and look after

its people. It's like a child who gets sick. If the parents ignore the sick child it will get worse and maybe even die through neglect. Societies the world over are just the same. I am no politician and I had no desire to ever be one. We Germans have placed our trust in the people who are supposed to make things right for us all. Many of us feel greatly let down by our politicians. If the youth of our country begin to feel the same way, which I know they do, then this is a very dangerous time indeed. It's very sad, isn't it, don't you think? What did we go through all that hell, destruction and hardship for? Have those in charge of us learned nothing or are they just stupid?

It is a sad fact that almost every contributor to this book still alive today is critical of the current German government. It would appear that, all these decades on from the Second World War, Germany is now facing cultural reparations primarily for its conduct of the past. It is now politically incorrect to speak the truth. It would appear that Germany is not the only country that is currently witnessing the death of its own democracy. The moment freedom of speech, culture and tradition are suppressed in any society then it is no longer a free society or democracy. It is somewhat troubling to have to admit that Germany today, although a unified nation, is more a victim of her past than she has ever been since 1945.

Afterword

Traditionally an Afterword is intended to reflect upon the end of a literary journey, but I feel that this particular journey needs little overall reflection on my part. There are few of us who will depart this earth with a completely clear conscience on how we have lived our lives. Our unhappy chapters are often conveniently suppressed, becoming mercifully blurred by time and overtaken by the happier events of our lives.

The question as to whether mankind has learned from its turbulent history should now be painfully obvious to all. We can only keep reminding ourselves of our own ignorance for so long. History is often viewed as possessing little relevance to the high-tech present. Today, we live in a twenty-four hour society where basic values, principles and respect have fallen victim to the necessities of the modern world, one dominated by celebrity culture and the pursuit of wealth and fame. The German women that I have spoken with during the gathering of research material for my books over the years are, to me, a physical connection to the history I have sought to record. I never tired of being in their presence. With each meeting something new was revealed.

As for the question 'was Nazism eradicated from the world following the years of war?' In my opinion it was not. It had merely been removed from its position of power as opposed to being destroyed. It retreated, a wounded beast, into the dark underworld of humanity from where it came. Yet it has remained alive and active in the shadows of society, away from mainstream politics.

For the women of Third Reich Germany I can only recite this simple piece:

Cruelty had no clear definition within the Third Reich's ultimate thought processes. Had its society not been raised with an unbending cruelty, if it had failed to issue pain as recompense for every individual success, then it deserved to perish among the weaker races – the 'sub-humans' – as its doctrine warned. The Deutscher *fräuen*, as all women of the world, understood this philosophy more so than the males of their society. Upon insemination, the *fräuen* were receiving a gift, a miracle of pain unlike no other. As the foetus slowly formed within her womb, she nurtured, nourished and psychologically prepared for its entry into her world. Her waters break, the pain begins, the infant breaches, draws her blood and tears her skin, yet she defies her agony. At its end there is a smile followed by a gentle kiss on the infant's head. It leaves blood on her lips, much like a lioness at a kill. This is the hardness, strength and triumph that no man could possibly understand, even less obtain.

Further Reading

The majority of information used during the production of this work was obtained largely via the contributors themselves. Diaries, memoirs, letters and photographs were all made freely available for my perusal. However, the following works and historical institutions were consulted during the course of the writing of this book in an effort to assist with the corroboration of facts:

Goetz, R., *In the Company of Murder* (unpublished manuscript)

Russell, E., 2nd Baron Russell of Liverpool, *The Scourge of the Swastika: A Short History of Nazi War Crimes* (Cassell & Company Ltd, UK, 1954)

Theodore, A., *Why Hitler Came to Power* (Cambridge Harvard University Press, 1986)

Toland, J., *Adolf Hitler* (Doubleday & Company, Inc, Garden City, New York, 1976)

The Bundesarchiv, Aachen, Germany

The German History Museum [DHM], Berlin, Germany

The Imperial War Museum, Department of Documents and Printed Books, London, England

The National Archives, Kew, Richmond, Surrey, England

Yad Vashem, The World Holocaust Remembrance Center [online resource]

Acknowledgements

I would like to acknowledge the following contributors without whom this work would not have been possible:

Traudl Junge, Rochus Misch, Ursula Betmann, Trudi Lehrer, Thelma Ortge, Gabbi Becker, Bertha Wuremfjeld, Sofia Weiss, Hilde Ahrens, Helen Giehl, Danielle Heimer, Kathi Emler, Ruth Gellert, Dagna Baier, Dana Hahn, Krin Metzl, Ursula Krause-Schreiber, Vaida Raab, Martin Schneider, Jochen Maier, Wiener Katte, Ruth Goertz, Giselle Junghman, Dela Bachoulz, Diana Hollberg, Elizabeth Hunsche, Bernadette Metschuldt, Matilda Weyergang, Celina Mayer, Diana Urbacher, Emma Klein, Kathi Frier, Klara Wyborny, Elise Maschmann, Inge Gursche, Klara Binz, Bella Schonn, Kirsten Eckermann, Hanna Burowitz, Anna Dann, Theresa Moelle, Olga Kirschener, Katherine Rumfeld, Maria Kottinger, Barbie Densk, Magda Heppel, Heidi Koch, Sophia Kortge, Melissa Schroeder, Hilde Hartmann, Ursula Schiemer, Celina Earhart, Elise Pfaff, Adelen Müller, Gertrud Soetzer, Monica Vanessa Kieler Dorsche, Juanita Koertzer, Thora Weber, Wiener Katte, Kyla Pacchianoa, Hilde Ahrens, Ellie Kaufmann and Emmi Dorr.

The time spent with you all was both informative and memorable. Although time was on my side it was not on yours. Thank you all so much for giving up your time for me.

Chris Warren photography, Evesham, for taking care of all my photographic requirements. Claire Hopkins, History Editor, Pen & Sword Books Ltd, for her faith and valued assistance and all of the staff at Pen & Sword Books Ltd. Duncan Evans, Editor, The Armourer Militaria Magazine, Ian Tustin and Jenny Powell of the Vale Magazine, Evesham, Lenny Warren and the MCN [Militaria Collectors Network], Stars and Stripes archives, USA.

My partner, Paula, who has had to contend with my endless hours on the computer, sharing in the occasional stresses and frustrations along the route to completion of this volume. My family, for their encouragement and support with all aspects of my work.

Thank you all.